What Really Happens in Bed

QUANTITY SALES

Most Dell books are available at special quantity discounts when purchased in bulk by corporations, organizations, and special-interest groups. Custom imprinting or excerpting can also be done to fit special needs. For details write: Dell Publishing, 666 Fifth Avenue, New York, NY 10103. Attn.: Special Sales Department.

INDIVIDUAL SALES

Are there any Dell books you want but cannot find in your local stores? If so, you can order them directly from us. You can get any Dell book in print. Simply include the book's title, author, and ISBN number if you have it, along with a check or money order (no cash can be accepted) for the full retail price plus $2.00 to cover shipping and handling. Mail to: Dell Readers Service, P.O. Box 5057, Des Plaines, IL 60017.

What Really Happens in Bed

A Demystification of Sex

Steven Carter and

Julia Sokol

A DELL TRADE PAPERBACK

A DELL TRADE PAPERBACK
Published by
Dell Publishing
a division of
Bantam Doubleday Dell Publishing Group, Inc.
666 Fifth Avenue
New York, New York 10103

ISBN: 0-440-50330-2

Reprinted by arrangement with M. Evans and Company, Inc. in the United States of America

Printed simultaneously in Canada

October 1990

10   9   8   7   6   5   4   3   2   1

RRH

Contents

For Pad

Acknowledgments

As is always the case in a project such as this, there are a great many people to thank. First and foremost, to all the men and women who agreed to talk to us and so generously shared their very personal thoughts, feelings, and experiences, our most sincere thank you.

We would like to thank the following individuals for their vital professional contributions to this book: Ken Starr, Sheila Starr, Michael Frankfurt, Kathy Saypol, Karin Lippert, Dr. Bernie Zilbergeld, Dr. Irwin Goldstein, Bruce MacKenzie, Dr. Harvey Kramer, Dr. Harold Levinson, Betty Dodson, Patty Moynihan, Don Ahn, Gio, Freddie Wellman, Peter DeMarco, and, most important, Evan Stone, Susannah Greenberg, and the entire staff at M. Evans.

We would also like to thank several organizations who were kind enough to give us information about their viewpoints and services: F.U.N. Products, Inc., The Eulenspiegel Society, The Hung Jury, Sexaholics Anonymous, and Impotents Anonymous.

A personal thank you to Peter Coopersmith, Marilyn Whitney, the staff at Starr & Co., Helen Sokol, Tulip, Alfred and Sydelle Carter, Mary Jane Nolan Kelly, Elizabeth and Michael Foster, Suzanne Kramer, Shirley Jonas, and Norman Haggie.

Our deepest thanks must go to our publisher, George de Kay, for his unfailing support, encouragement, guidance, and friendship.

A very special thank you to Dr. Marilyn Griffin for her professional and personal support and advice.

Finally, our most sincere thank you to Don Schimelfenig for patience and understanding above and beyond the requirements of the marital contract.

Authors' Note

We wrote this book because we believed that many men and women have sexual expectations of both themselves and their partners that are based on performance myths and romantic fantasies. From the people we interviewed, it was our perception that most had been affected to some degree by these unrealistic expectations, as well as by an inability to communicate about them honestly and constructively. We started this project with the goal of providing the reader with a realistic picture of what is happening and not happening in bedrooms across the country—a snapshot, so to speak, of contemporary sexual behavior and attitudes. We wanted to give as comprehensive a representation as possible of what people are doing and saying about what really happens in their beds.

It is our hope that from this portrait, readers will be able to develop a clear and more realistic sense of what can be expected from themselves and their partners in a sexually intimate relationship.

What Really Happens in Bed

Part I

Talking About Sex

1

What Really Happens in Bed; and Why Do We Care?

THE REALITY OF SEX

In the fantasy world of sex, nothing ever hurts, nothing rubs or chafes, nobody is anxious, no one is tired, there are no menstrual cramps, strange viruses, or pregnancy fears, nothing bad ever happens and everything fits perfectly; in the fantasy world of sex, erections function, orgasms are easy, desire surges, birth-control methods don't interfere with spontaneity, and bodies melt. In the real world, it doesn't always happen this way.

This book is about the real world of sex, what is really happening in bed, and how much or how little that has to do with sex manuals, statistical studies, erotic literature, and steamy Hollywood love stories. This is a book about sexual expectations, realistic and unrealistic, and how the two often conflict when they are played out in bed.

The idea for this project was triggered by a conversation that we had with a man who was being interviewed on another subject. Thirty-five, sexually experienced and newly married, Alex confided that he was becoming very anxious about his sexual performance. He had recently married, expecting—for the first time in his life—to be able to have sex every day. To his consternation, he found that making love two or three times a week felt like his physical limit. Despite his new wife's assurances that she was satisfied, he worried that his level of performance was somehow sub-standard. He loved his wife, he found her very attractive, but many nights he wanted nothing more erotic than to fall asleep. What was wrong with him? Was something wrong with her? Was something wrong with the marriage? He thought that the "problem" might have a physical component. He said he thought his hormone levels had taken a nose dive, and he should consider seeing a doctor. No matter what we said to reassure him that he was well within the norm, he was convinced that other men were infinitely more sexually active than he was. His attitude immediately made us wonder where he formed his expectations of appropriate marital sexual behavior.

Alex was not the only person we spoke to who articulated confusion about how he or she fit in sexually with the rest of the world. For our last book, we interviewed several hundred men and women, the majority of whom were single, about their relationships. The common denominator that struck us most: Whether they were talking about their own patterns and behavior, or those of their partners, they were all unsure about what was realistic in terms of sexual expectations.

To some degree we have all been influenced by the media, both in terms of the judgments it makes or the reporting it does. Take the so-called *Playboy* mentality, for example. Although few of us know anyone who lives out the *Playboy* fantasy, our typical male interviewee (including the most blatantly promiscuous) expressed disdain for the *Playboy* mode of relating to women. However, the same men also expressed a nagging insecurity that they would never be able to measure up to the expectations of either contemporary women or the mythical *Playboy* Advisor. These men had never discussed—either with friends or professionals—what constitutes normal male sexual performance, and they were legitimately confused. On the one hand, they had read or heard about Masters and Johnson or other sex therapists, who were talking about the vast numbers of men who were dysfunctional either in terms of erection or orgasm; on the other, they were seeing magazines in which men were talking about erections that appeared to be permanently in place, as well as orgasms described in terms that seemed better suited to a natural-wonder state park. And all of this is described as having been accomplished with a variety of willing women in the sort of positions that would make an Olympic gymnast reach for his heating pad. Which view of sex is the realistic one?

And our average female subject was no less confused. Many of them had been sexually programmed by a particular lover who had by suggestion or innuendo made them feel either too passive or too aggressive, or too demanding and voracious, or unresponsive and frigid. Typically she was also convinced that she was the only woman in the country who was still faking orgasms.

Then, when we began to discuss with each other the ways in which these people expressed their insecurity over sexual expectations, we realized that we were confused also. Despite the plethora of statistical data about frequency, ejaculation, and orgasm, it was blatantly apparent that most of us didn't really have a clue about what was normal and what was expected of us sexually.

The fact is that few people share their sexual experiences, even with their closest friends. Consequently we have no real way to evaluate our own behavior and patterns. Of course there are some exhibitionist types who like to regale us with their exploits. We all know people like this, who talk endlessly about sex, who have tales to tell and stories to weave. But how do we know whether or not these folks are exaggerating? How about the rest of us? When it comes to sex, are we all speaking the same language? Sure, we are all using the same words, but do we mean the same thing?

When we started doing research, it quickly became apparent how much general information and how little specific information is available about sex. Because as much as has been written about the mechanics of sex, about our genitals and how they function, there is almost no information about the specifics of sex, what kind of sex life the average person is really having, or not having, on a day-to-day basis, and how he or she feels about it. Most of us don't share these details easily with anyone. Many of us, if not all, are not even open with our mates, and instead rely upon sign language and body language to convey what we are feeling.

The confusion that was expressed to us, combined with the lack of communication in most relationships, made us realize that we wanted to do a book about the reality of sex. Specifically, we wanted to give people a realistic perspective from which they could form equally realistic sexual expectations.

THE PROBLEM: HOW TO FIND OUT WHAT REALLY HAPPENS IN BED

Let's face it, this is not the kind of information you're going to get in a library. There you'll find stacks of periodicals that contain articles that talk *around* sex, popular articles about flirtation and dating, as well as statistical studies that spew out numbers that have little real meaning. There are several manuals that tell us what we *should* be doing in bed, and even more manuals for couples who feel they aren't doing what they should be doing in bed. We have all heard about Krafft-Ebing and the Marquis de Sade, and, indeed, a great deal has been written about deviant or pathological behavior.

For the more visually oriented, there are, lest we forget, the local video stores where one can find soft and not so soft pornographic videocassettes. If you can last through the ludicrous story lines, you will witness a rather amazing range of sexual acting out, and we do mean acting out. But nobody who has had any sexual experience believes that these films have very much to do with real life.

And then, of course, there are the articles and books about the mating patterns of primates, which are fascinating and wonderful. But when it comes to this very special member of the animal kingdom, the fragile human being, precious little nonfiction has been written to describe normal sexual behavior.

THE STORIES BEHIND THE STATISTICS

It turns out that there is only one way to find out what people are really doing in bed. You have to ask them. So that's what we decided we would do: interview several hundred men and women, all ages, married and single, about their sexual experiences, their affairs, their marriages; the good sex, the bad sex, the nonexistent sex. We wanted to know not only what they were doing but also what they weren't doing, and what they were thinking and feeling about it all.

We decided early on that we were not going to try to accumulate any statistical information. We had several reasons for feeling this way: (1) It's practically impossible for two writers working independently of a large research organization to accumulate the data and get a scientifically acceptable cross sample of the public. To get research like this is cripplingly expensive; (2) Even if we could get a questionnaire out to a large enough cross sample of the populace, would it be meaningful? We had already learned that people equivocate when they answer questionnaires about sex. We spoke to the heads of several large market-research organizations and were discouraged from attempting this sort of questionnaire. It was pointed out to us that, using standard sampling techniques, there were enormous problems in obtaining answers for these kinds of highly personal questions. And if we could devise a questionnaire that would be answered, we were also concerned whether or not the respondents, by definition, would be more uninhibited than the average person; (3) National women's magazines and large organizations, such as Kinsey, have already published statistical information about sex practices, frequency, etc. We had read much of the statistical information, and while acknowledging the effort in compiling this informative data, we found that these statistics often provide only part of the story. They tell us what people are doing, but they don't tell us why. We wanted to get the stories behind the statistics.

WHAT WE WANTED TO FIND OUT

We are not sexologists and don't wish to have our perspective confused with the perspective of Masters and Johnson or Dr. Ruth. We are primarily interested in relationships. But sex, by definition, is an important part of what goes on between men and women in relationships. In our last book we tended to tiptoe around sex, and many, if not all, of the other books on relationships per se have done the same thing. In the past, books on relationships either disregarded the sexual connection or failed to go into any detailed exploration about the specifics of what was happening in bed. We thought it was time that some attempt was made to integrate sex and relationships, as they are integrated in real life.

From the statistical information available, we knew that the frequency of marital sex drops off depending upon the length of the marriage. But we wanted to know whether or not the individuals in these marriages were still as sexually satisfied, and satisfied with each other, having sex once or twice a week as they were when they were first together and having sex five or six times a week. And what did less sex actually mean? Did less sex mean less intimacy, or had these couples found other ways to reaffirm their intimacy? Are marital commitment, love, and the bonding process dependent upon ongoing sex? How about affection? Did that change in quality? In a happy marriage, how much communication is there about sex? Does anyone ever totally get rid of their inhibitions, or do they essentially stay the same, no matter how long one is married or how close the emotional connection?

We were also curious about the differences between the young marrieds and the older marrieds. The people who came of age during or after the sexual revolution are infinitely more experienced than their older counterparts, many of whom married their first real lovers. Has this made a significant difference in what happens in bed, and the ways in which these couples communicate about sex? Because they are less inhibited, have younger couples found a better way to deal with some of the mechanical and technical problems associated with sex?

How about the outcome of the torrid relationships and affairs? What happens to the relationship in which one has the "best sex"? Why do so many of these affairs fall apart? And when they don't and the couple marries, what happens to sexual intensity? Does it diminish at the same rate as those couples who are less "turned on" at the beginning?

We wanted to explore some of the different ways in which men and women think and talk about their sexual relationships, and we wanted to know the ways in which men and women make each other sexually insecure, and why.

Basically we wanted more details. We wanted to know what really happens in bed. What people said to each other, what people did to each other. We wanted to know what is motivating sexually promiscuous men and women, and we wanted to know more about long-term marriages. We wanted to know about the good sex, the bad sex, the weird sex, and everything in between.

ASKING PEOPLE TO "KISS AND TELL"

It wasn't easy asking people to "kiss and tell." The Catch-22 of sex: People love sex, people are obsessed by sex, people are fascinated by sex, but the average person is reticent when it comes to talking about sex, at least about his/her sex life. It's a rare person who gives Technicolor detail about sex without a lot of encouragement. When we started out doing these interviews, we both felt terrifically uncomfortable. We had no experience in getting people to give an accurate reporting of sexual behavior. Neither one of us is particularly prurient or voyeuristic, and at first we had a difficult time talking to each other about what we were discovering in our interviews.

For obvious reasons it was decided that Carter would interview the men and Sokol the women. We put our emphasis on the long in-depth interview, and we did

more than 250 of these—half women, half men. The youngest person we interviewed was 19; the oldest was 74.
Our sample gave equal representation to those who were
single and those who were married. A fair number had
been married more than once, and a good number of our
singles had been divorced. Socioeconomically, they were
middle class and working class with a variety of educa-
tional, ethnic, and religious backgrounds. We interviewed
people from most sections of the United States, rural, suburban, and urban. Because we are no longer a one-rela-
tionship society, most of the people we interviewed had
a number of sexual partners before they settled down, or
after they settled down. Consequently we ended up collecting details on more than a thousand relationships. We
tried as much as possible to restrict ourselves to men and
women who did not outwardly appear to be too "far-out."
We wanted people who in the normal course of events
would not discuss their sex lives. We wanted to talk to
the typical man and woman next door, whether next door
is an urban high rise, a suburban split-level, or a mobile
home.

We contacted most of our interviewees through personal
or professional acquaintances, through word of mouth,
as well as by tapping into lists of people who attended
various relationship-oriented seminars. Although we started
out with a specific set of questions, early on it became
apparent that the interviews themselves were shaping the
book. People often told us about things that were totally
foreign to us, or volunteered information that we didn't
ask for. An example: Our initial interviews were all with
young men and women who were: (a) married less than
three years; and (b) self-described as very happy sexually. Naïvely, it didn't occur to us to include enough
questions about masturbation until we realized that all
of these early interviewees were masturbating at least
several times a week, if not more. We worked up another set of questions for the rest of our interviews and
also went back to the original group. From this we think
we got a much clearer picture of the role that mastur-

bation can and often does play even in a sexually content union.

TALKING ABOUT SEX/TALKING AROUND SEX

When we began interviewing people, we were not totally convinced that we wanted to do this book. Besides the obvious embarrassment that we felt at appearing to be voyeuristic, we weren't altogether certain there was that much new to be said. But as we continued with the interview process we realized that the most important thing we were finding out was how little had been said and how inadequately most of us communicate about sexual issues. Few of us are able to be direct about sex, and most of us tend to talk around it. Some people communicate poorly all the time; others only become bashful or tongue-tied when it counts or when their egos are at stake.

Perhaps the major lesson we learned from doing all these interviews is that we are not all alike sexually. We don't all like the same things, we don't all dislike the same things, we don't all want the same things, and we don't all fantasize about the same things. We don't all have the same level of sexual energy or need. However, individuals tend to feel quite intensely about the way they are sexually, and although someone may recognize that differences exist between himself and others, there is still a tendency to be harshly opinionated about these differences and to place values on them. If it is something you like, it's good; if it's something you don't like it's bad. If you don't have the urge to do it personally, it's difficult to understand it. However, although we all have different preferences, we are all using the same language, and there is a limited choice of words. Two people viewing the same situation can use the same language, but the words can have totally different meanings depending upon individual values and desires.

When we began interviewing people about sex, we realized almost immediately that for the most part we use sexual terms, and describe sexual events, without clearly defining what we mean. Fans of Woody Allen all remember the scene in the movie *Annie Hall* in which Woody Allen and Diane Keaton, on a split screen, are visiting their respective "shrinks," each talking about sex. Woody's male analyst asks him how often they have sex, and he replies, "Hardly ever . . . maybe three times a week." When Diane Keaton's female analyst asks her the same question, she replies, "Constantly . . . I'd say three times a week."

We had forgotten that scene until early on in our interviews when we spoke with a 32-year-old tennis pro, who was describing the four women he was having affairs with for the past six months, and all the sex he had been having. Almost as an afterthought, we asked him how many times he had slept with each of these women. It turned out that he had only had sex with each of them a few times, and since his total sexual encounters with these four women added up to about twenty, it averaged out that he was having sex once every ten days, which is less than many overworked 50-year-old males in 25-year-old marriages; it is also less than the 2.1 figure Kinsey published as the mean average for married males ages 31–35 back in 1948. (*Sexual Behavior in the Human Male* by Alfred C. Kinsey, Wardell B. Pomeroy, and Clyde E. Martin, W. B. Saunders Company, 1948.)

That made us realize that we had to be very specific in our questioning. One person's "all the time" clearly was another's "hardly ever," and the only logical conclusion is that whether they are having sex once a day or once a month, when people are having more sex than they want, they feel as though they are having it all the time, and if people are having less sex than they want, they feel deprived.

What we tried to find out as we interviewed these people is probably what you are trying to find out as you read this: Is everybody doing the same thing you are doing, are they doing it with the same frequency, and are they thinking about it in the same way? Do we all have the same sexual insecurities? There is, after all, reassurance in knowing that everybody is more or less the same. Well, the answer is that everybody is—and everybody isn't. One of the things we hope that this book may illuminate is how extraordinarily similar we all are, and yet how amazingly different.

2

What Really Happens in Bed; and Why We Don't Want to Talk About It

THE MAJOR SEXUAL PROBLEM—HIDING WHAT WE FEEL/HIDING WHAT WE DO

"TRYING TO BE AN EFFECTIVE LOVER FOR ONESELF AND ONE'S PARTNER WITHOUT COMMUNICATING IS LIKE TRYING TO LEARN TARGET SHOOTING BLINDFOLDED."
—*Helen Singer Kaplan*, The New Sex Therapy

Every single person we spoke to told us that he or she was not satisfied with his/her ability to communicate honestly and openly about sexual matters. We know that sex experts tell us that good communication is the key to a satisfying sexual relationship, and that as far as sexual problems are concerned, the failure to communicate is a major contributing factor. Certainly all the people we interviewed agreed that communication is incredibly important. But they weren't doing it. In their own lives they readily acknowledged that communication around sexual issues was often frighteningly difficult, if not impossible. We found that the vast majority of our interviewees were concealing sexual feelings, sexual desires, and sexual behavior from just about everyone, including mates, lovers, family, and friends. Many were painfully aware that within their relationships, sexual patterns and sexual futures were being shaped not so much by what *was* being said as by what was *not* being said.

Although there were obviously different levels of reticence, all the men and women we spoke to said that to some degree they clammed up when it came to talking about sex. Some said that talking about sex made them feel tense and uncomfortable, and that this feeling often manifested itself physically. Shoulders would tighten up or stomachs would knot. By and large, our interviewees were not disturbed by this inability to have sexual conversations with strangers, or even friends. They were, however, genuinely distressed at all the ways in which they were unable to communicate with their mates.

Everyone we spoke to wanted to be more capable of opening up to their partners and talking honestly and openly about sex, but they didn't know how to go about doing it. Those who were in ongoing relationships kept hoping that their partners would be able to let go of inhibitions and initiate better communication. However, these same men and women realized that there were certain kinds of conversations that were taboo and that there were "secrets" that they would prefer not to disclose, or share, unless someone could guarantee a partner's response.

Basically both men and women said they were concealing from their partners not only current dissatisfactions, but also much about his or her individual sexual history and the experiences that might have helped shape their sexual response.

This attitude of secrecy was often operative, no matter how inexperienced or experienced the person. Someone with a colorful sexual history might be concerned, for example, about appearing sexually cynical or too experienced—this was particularly true of women. But someone with little experience typically didn't want to appear as though he or she was a sexual wallflower.

When David, a 27-year-old M.B.A., remembers his first sexual experience, he describes it as "having a large element of fraud attached to it." He says it was a "classic example of embarrassment overcoming all my naturally honest tendencies.

"I was a virgin. So was she. I was 20, and it was the end of my sophomore year. In the meantime, all of my friends had been sleeping with girlfriends for years—some of them

started at 15 and 16. I didn't know how to go about it, and
I was totally embarrassed by my inexperience. So what I did
was lie. I went away summers, and when I came home, I
would conjure up these fantasy sexual experiences, and I'd
talk about them. I did the same thing with my summer
friends, only this time it was my winter girlfriend they would
hear about.

"By the time I met BettyAnn, I felt like I was going to
die without ever having sex. She was also a virgin, but she
was a virgin with *experience*—she had had *oral* sex. At the
time this boggled my mind. But before I found this out, we
went through all the stages—necking, petting, heavy petting,
etc. At first she acted like everything we were doing together
was weird and new, but I could tell that wasn't the case.
For one thing, she was unusually proficient in having orgasms. She knew exactly what to do and how to position
herself, and she would sort of indicate what she wanted me
to do. Finally it came out that she had had oral sex with
her last boyfriend. I was a little put off by this, but she told
me that he really didn't count because he had an 'ugly penis,'
whatever that meant, and that I was the first person she
really wanted to have oral sex with, so I was really the first.
I was sufficiently naïve and egomaniacal to *really* believe her.
Also I was having problems with my own little deceptions.
I had indicated to her that I was vastly experienced sexually,
but in truth I didn't know *anything*. I had put my hands
down a woman's pants before, but that's it . . . I didn't know
what to do with my hands once they got there. I didn't know
how hard to press, how fast, how slow, or what she expected.
I mean, how do you get experience in something like this?
They don't teach it in health class, that's for sure. The first
time we had oral sex, I wasn't even sure where to put my
mouth. I think she realized that I was confused because she
even asked me, 'Are you sure you've done this before?' I
remember I said, 'Don't be an idiot.' The next morning I
cut class and went to a bookstore on the other side of town
where I wouldn't run into anyone I knew and bought a couple
of sex manuals. I hid out and read them, cover to cover.

I even hid those books from my roommate. Finally I threw them in a garbage pail on the other side of campus when nobody was looking. I didn't want to keep them in my room because I didn't want anybody to know that I had to look anything up."

SEXUAL SECRETS:
WHAT WE REVEAL/WHAT WE CONCEAL

"IN THE POPULAR VIEW, WHICH IS SUFFICIENT FOR ALL PRACTICAL PURPOSES IN ORDINARY LIFE, SEXUAL IS SOMETHING WHICH COMBINES REFERENCES TO THE DIF-FERENCE BETWEEN THE SEXES, TO PLEASURABLE EX-CITEMENT AND GRATIFICATION, TO THE REPRODUCTIVE FUNCTION, AND TO THE IDEA OF IMPROPRIETY AND THE NECESSITY FOR CONCEALMENT."
            —*Sigmund Freud*, The Sexual Life of Man

All sexual secrets are different; the common denominator seems to be that everyone has one. Some people hide feelings and desires; others conceal behavior; still others are secretive about their sexual history. A 45-year-old machinist in Chicago doesn't want his wife to know that he isn't always ejaculating; a 24-year-old lawyer in New York doesn't want *anyone* to know that he is still a virgin; a 38-year-old suburban matron is always worried that her husband will discover that she had an affair with her son's math teacher; a 23-year-old married mother doesn't know how to tell her husband that she is faking orgasms during intercourse, secretly masturbating twice a day and guiltily concealing her vibrator in the laundry hamper.

Individuals don't have exclusivity on sexual secrets. Couples sometimes form an often *unspoken* truce to keep secret some of the things they do together. Some couples, for instance, think that others might not understand a less tra-ditional way of relating sexually such as cross dressing, mild bondage, a preference for anal sex, swinging, etc. Men and women in these relationships are typically reluctant to discuss or disclose their behavior to the rest of the world.

Other couples are silent about those things that they *don't*

do together sexually. Men and women in marriages with little
or no sex are often unable to talk to each other, much less
to anyone else, even a therapist or counselor, about how
little sex they are having. We talked to one 35-year old man,
for example, who said that for the first four years of his marriage he was unable to penetrate his wife because of her fear
of pain. It took her that long before they were able to discuss
it and she was able to seek treatment. He said that both of
them "didn't want anyone else to know" about the sexual
problems they were having. This misplaced sense of embarrassment is often a major reason why couples resist getting
treatment for sexual problems.

"The idea of impropriety and the necessity for concealment"

Freud wrote these words back in 1916. Since then, reams
have been written about all the ways in which we humans
prefer to keep sexual matters and feelings hidden, repressed,
and/or private. Then and now, most of us conceal thoughts
and feelings that are associated with sexual behavior, and it
would appear that the average person still thinks it is improper
to discuss one's personal sex life. Sure, there is a lot of sexual
joking and sexual innuendo, but when we talk to our friends,
and even to our mates, the vast majority of us limit ourselves
to nuance and allusion.

Traditional psychoanalysis tells us that there are complicated reasons for this, and that many of our sexual feelings
are always left unconscious, trapped, by repression and guilt,
in a netherworld of fantasy peopled by "ghost" figures from
our childhood.

Think about it. Do any of us talk about our sex lives with
the same kind of detail we use when we discuss choosing a
restaurant, renovating a kitchen, finding a school for the children or a kennel for the dog? Everyone we spoke to agreed
that talking about sex carries with it a certain level of exposure.
No one is comfortable sharing his or her fears, disappointments, or sexual secrets. Total openness leaves one feeling
too vulnerable. To protect from this sense of overexposure,

the average person tends to limit what he or she tells, whether it is to a mate, a best friend, or even to a therapist. What we discovered in the course of interviewing people about "what really happens in bed" is that unless one continues to ask questions, a part of the story is often vague or left unfinished.

SEXUAL HISTORIES RELATED IN WHISPERS AND FRAGMENTS

June, 40, twice married, currently divorced

From June's interview it's very easy to see that she remembers and is willing to share all the details except those surrounding actual sexual contact. Here, she is talking about her first orgasm, which she says was the . . .

". . . turning point of my life. Until then I never had any sexual feelings, really. After that, sometimes I think that's all I had. We went down to the swim club—it was a very big, fancy club, and I guess I was impressed by the fact that his father had money—I don't know. Either that or his shoulders did me in . . . he was on the football team. I still remember the way his back looked, and his number, 21. Anyway, on this night, nobody was at the pool. They were having a big dance in the club itself. We could hear the music, but none of the members were using the pool. It never ceases to amaze me how the rich don't always use their facilities.

"Anyway, I guess I wanted to impress him with my domestic skills, because I had packed some food. I even made brownies, which we never ate. But we started, uh . . ." At this point she drops her voice to a whisper and continues. ". . . fooling around . . . you know . . . in the pool. That's when it, uh, happened."

"Did you have sex in the pool?" (interviewer)

"I don't think so. I don't really remember. We must have done something, but we weren't really having sex. However, I had my first orgasm, and I remember thinking, 'So that's what this is all about.' "

"But you don't remember how you had it? Did he touch you with his hand . . . was it just the pressure of his body . . . how about his knee?" (interviewer)

"He must have done something, but I don't remember what. I think we finally started to have sex in his father's car the night of the senior assembly. His father had this insanely large maroon Buick. We climbed into the backseat, but I don't remember whether we actually did it or not. . . ."

Bryan, 33, single

In Bryan's case, the reluctance to discuss a sexual event cannot be blamed on poor memory. He is talking about his current relationship with a 28-year-old woman he says he cares about. He says he wants a deeper, more committed relationship.

"But there's a problem."

"What is it?" (interviewer)

"I'm used to different kinds of sex."

"What do you mean by 'different?' " (interviewer)

"Well, usually sex is a really big part of my relationships."

"Well, what is it now?" (interviewer)

"Well, sometimes she is in a rush in the morning."

"So you're not having sex in the morning, and that's bothering you?" (interviewer)

"Yeah, but it's not that. Usually for me in the beginning, that's when you're spending hours in bed."

"And you're not doing that now?" (interviewer)

"Well, not really."

"And you're thinking to yourself that if you're not doing it now, what will you be doing in a year?" (interviewer)

"Yeah, but that's not it."

"All right . . . what is it?" (interviewer)

"Well, there's certain things she doesn't like to do."

"What? Your laundry?" (interviewer)

At this point Bryan laughs, but he still doesn't volunteer further details.

"Is there a problem with a specific aspect of sex?" (interviewer)

"Yeah, maybe . . . well, I'm not sure."

"All right, is there a problem with oral sex?" (interviewer)

"Well, she hasn't done it yet, and most of the women I've

been with like that, and I like that . . . but it's not happening here yet."

"Are you talking about it with her?" (interviewer)

"Well, I don't want to talk about it, because I don't want to create a problem."

Both June and Bryan illustrate a natural reluctance to discuss sex. In June's case, when she tries to describe an event that took place twenty years before, she remembers everything except the sexual happenings that made the event memorable.

Bryan clearly doesn't want to talk about a situation that is bothering him. His attitude has several components. He doesn't want to share his sexual concerns with the interviewer, which is understandable, but he also hesitates at communicating his concerns to his sexual partner. It's almost as though he feels that talking about sexual details will somehow jinx his sexual relationship.

SOME REASONS WHY WE DON'T TALK ABOUT THE DETAILS

The Fear of Telling More and the Corresponding Fear of Asking More

"People feel vulnerable when they talk about sex. . . . They don't want to appear as if they are having too much, and they don't want to appear as if they are having too little."

—60-year-old man

"I think every woman would like more specific details about her husband's sexual history, but I know that I'm afraid to ask. I don't want him to think I'm more experienced than he is, or that I expect more than he can give."

—28-year-old married woman

"If you start asking people about sex, they think you have a dirty mind. I never asked my daughters enough because I didn't want them to think I knew that much."

—50-year-old married woman

Most of us would like to be able to talk more openly about our sexual history, and our average interviewee agreed that if a trusted friend or mate asks for more specific details, the inclination is to reveal more, if—and this is a big if—one feels very confident that the person to whom one is talking is not going to make one feel foolish and ashamed for exposing one's sexual secrets.

However—and this is a big however—trusted friends and confidants typically don't ask for more details because they worry about appearing to have an embarrassing sexual curiosity, and they think that in the asking, they will somehow "give away" or reveal something about their own sexual experiences.

It appears that both concerns are justified. When it comes to sex, whether you are the teller or the asker, you run the risk of being judged by others, and from the people we talked to, it seems clear that most of us are quite judgmental when it comes to sex. While the sexually cautious view the sexually adventuresome as being "promiscuous" or lacking in moral values, the man or woman who has had many partners and a variety of sexual experiences tends to regard those who are less experimental as being "uptight," repressed, or just plain boring. Whether you are "doing it" a lot or a little, with one person or many, in traditional positions or upside down on freezing balconies, it seems to be human nature to think that everyone who is "doing it" differently is slightly askew and may be doing it wrong.

Maintaining an Image, Fear of Partner Rejection, and Other Reasons Why People Don't Talk Openly About Sex

From our interviews it would appear that the sexual double standard has not disappeared, although it has been updated. While men no longer insist upon virginity or total inexperience, the vast majority of the younger men we spoke to said that they would feel uncomfortable marrying a woman who was the more experienced partner. In short, these men seemed to want their wives somehow to convey an ingenuous and almost "virginal" attitude.

What does this mean in real life? A man who thinks he appears more manly if he is experienced sometimes keeps silent rather than reveal that he is not as knowledgeable as he would like to be; a woman often resists initiating conversations about sexual matters because she is concerned about appearing more knowledgeable or experienced than her partner. Sometimes she is doing this to protect her image; other times she may think that she is protecting the man's ego or self-image.

The only notable exceptions we found were several women who said that when they were young, they were so naïve and inexperienced that they lied, making up stories about sexual adventures simply to conceal their innocence; at the time they were embarrassed by the extent of their naïveté. And, of course, there have always been sexually cynical men who feign an innocence that doesn't exist, for the sole purpose of getting a woman into bed.

A Woman's Fear of Appearing *Too* Sexually Knowledgeable, and Consequently Less Romantic

Most of us have heard Joan Rivers do jokes about her friend Heidi Abromowitz, the "tramp." But every woman knows that tramp jokes did not originate with Rivers, and unfortunately they will not end there, either. Whether you grew up in the thirties, forties, fifties, sixties, seventies, or even the eighties, the image of the tramp is still with us. We're not exactly sure what it is that the tramp does or does not do, but about one thing we are certain: The lady knows a lot about sex.

Many women worry that if they act as if they know "too much" about sex, they will appear "trampy," and consequently be too far removed from the romantic image or ideal. This has been said so many times that it seems foolish to say it again, but it is still true. The average man, even a modern, contemporary man, has a difficult time dealing with

the fact that his wife is sexually experienced. He accepts the
fact that she has had some experience, but he would prefer
to think that it is less than his, and basically he still doesn't
want to deal with the idea of his wife as a sexual person
outside of their life together. This is a reality that most women
are aware of.

Chris, a 32-year-old nurse, is one such woman.

"My husband's attitude toward me is really weird sometimes. He is very experienced and talks about sex all the
time, but he gets annoyed if I swear, and he gets embarrassed
if I talk about any man I knew before him. For example,
I am still friends with the man I dated before I met my
husband. I have to be careful to talk about him as though
we were *always* more friends than lovers.

"Anyway, I thought this attitude was limited only to sexual
experiences with other men, not to sex itself. But a few years
ago, one of my friends called me up to say that her cousin,
Jan, was going to be staying at her house for a few days,
so why didn't I come over to meet her. I've always been
curious about Jan, because she used to be a hooker in
New York. She was a very fancy hooker, sort of like the
debutante madam who got arrested, but she was a hooker
nonetheless. She worked at it for five years and saved her
money and bought real estate and settled down and married
a therapist, would you believe. In any event, two other
women came over, and we ordered in a pizza and it was
like being in a dorm again. We had a wonderful time. All
of the other women were single and were talking about
their experiences with men, and Jan, who evidently likes
to talk about how she was a hooker, was regaling us with
stories about some of her clients. We all drank too much
wine, and by the end of the evening, Jan was giving us
lessons on how to perform oral sex on a man. She was using
a soupspoon to demonstrate. We all had our own soupspoons
and she was grading us. One of the women was laughing
so hard, I thought she was going to die right there. She just
couldn't stop.

"When I got home, I tried to tell this story to my husband. I thought he would think it as funny as I did. Just think about the image of four women with soupspoons in their mouths practicing oral sex! It's hilarious. Well, not only did he not think it was funny, he started to get annoyed, and I quickly had to change the story around and pretend that it was only Jan with the soupspoon, and lie and say that she really hadn't been a hooker—she had known a hooker.

"It was ridiculous, but it just confirmed what I really knew all along—that my husband cannot handle explicit conversations about sex, unless he's telling jokes with the boys and it's all very unreal and not threatening."

Chris said that she was upset that she had to alter the facts in order to maintain the image her husband had of her.

Many women confided that they engage in this sort of mild subterfuge when talking to the men they are involved with. And, from the following anecdote, which expresses the point of view of a young, theoretically sophisticated man, this sense that women have about the need to conceal certain sexual experiences is not misplaced.

Don, a 33-year-old photographer, relates a memory that is similar to Chris's story, but from a man's point of view.

"I try very hard not to feel upset when a woman I'm involved with shows an interest in raw sex, as opposed to romantic sex. I know it's stupid and chauvinistic and all that, but I still have the same reactions. I've changed over the years, and I'm not as bad on this score as I used to be when I was younger. I remember once, when I was married to my first wife, she and her sister went off on their own to see the movie *Deep Throat*. When they came home and wanted to talk about the details, I was really disgusted. My wife told me that they got disgusted, too, and left the movie in the middle. At the time I believed her. Now I realize that she probably took a look at the expression on my face and lied about leaving the movie. In fact, if a couple of male friends had dropped by to tell the movie's details, I would have laughed with them, and we would have had a fine old time. But my wife . . .

"With the woman I'm with now, I would probably go out and rent the movie and watch it on the VCR with her. But I would still prefer to be the one who initiated it, and if she went to see a dirty movie by herself or with a friend, I would probably get a little weirded out."

Both of these stories reflect masculine attitudes that seem old-fashioned and unrealistic. Yet both of the men involved think of themselves as nontraditional men who are sensitive to women's issues and feelings. But Chris reads a sense of disapproval on her husband's face when she appears too interested in sex, and Don admits to a somewhat chauvinistic attitude.

So how, then, is the average woman going to feel free to describe her needs, even in an accepting and nonthreatening marital situation? Hope, 36, now married for the second time, verbalizes something that many women expressed.

"I've been married to my second husband for almost two years, and we lived together for a year before that, and dated for another year before that. I'm very much in love with him and he's a good lover, but I don't have good orgasms with him. It's really not his fault. I know what position I need to be in and how I need to be touched, but I don't know how to express that need. I'm afraid that if I show him what to do or, heaven forbid, do it myself, he'll know that this was something I did with somebody else, and he'll feel threatened. At first I didn't show him because I didn't want him to think I was that experienced or that sexually greedy; I sort of figured that with time it would happen naturally. But it didn't. Now I think if I say something, he'll think I've recently had an affair and learned some new technique with another man. Or else he'll think that I never enjoyed sex with him before, and he'll always be suspicious that I'm just pretending to be satisfied."

Protecting the Male Ego—Another Reason Women Give for Curtailing Conversations About Sex

"I'm very sensitive around my clitoris, and many men have caused me intense pain by touching me the wrong way. I realized in therapy that I never said anything to any of them, not to my ex-husband or any one of a half dozen lovers. Instead I would just lie there and hope that it would soon be over. I think I believed that if I said anything that implied he was not a good lover, he would immediately become impotent. I don't know who told me this, or if I read it, or if it's something I just feel—but I believed then, and I still believe to some degree, that most men can't handle any sexual criticism. It's just too intense for them."

—*42-year-old woman*

A large majority of the women we spoke to indicated that they think that most men interpret any semblance of sexual dissatisfaction, no matter how kindly or sensitively phrased, as sexual rejection.

This need to protect the male ego was not limited to "old-fashioned women." We spoke to quite a few women who prided themselves on being sexually open, as well as experimental. Some of them, feminists who had been in consciousness-raising groups, felt that they were capable of openly discussing sex. A couple of these women have even written about sex. However, even these women acknowledged that when a sexual problem occurred within the context of an intimate man-woman relationship, they found themselves tongue-tied and unable to deal with it in an honest, direct fashion. The following interview with Elizabeth, 32, illustrates the level of repression that even the least inhibited woman can feel. Elizabeth, who lives in Colorado, is an active feminist and considers herself extremely liberated. She is a dance therapist in an alternative therapy group. Her current lover, who is also an instructor with the same group, leads workshops in relating to others. In the course of their work, they have both counseled couples about sexual matters. Elizabeth is generally dissatisfied with the level of intimacy and passion that her lover exhibits, but she doesn't know what to say to him.

"Sometimes I feel like saying, 'Okay, sure, you know how to fuck, but that's all you know how to do. There's no warmth, no tenderness.' Sometimes when we're finished, I go into the bathroom and cry."

"What happens when you try to talk to him?" (interviewer)

"The other night, when we were finished, he started this whole dissertation about how he was a terrific lover. . . . I wanted to say, 'No, you're not, you don't slow down, you're always directing, you're always controlling. . . . It doesn't feel good.' "

"Why didn't you say something?" (interviewer)

"He says he thinks he's a great lover, but I know his story. I know he didn't go to bed with anyone until he was 25. I know that he's just insecure. I don't want to make him feel bad by pointing out his deficiencies. It always occurs to me that I'm going to say the wrong thing to a guy, and then he'll have problems getting it up. It's never happened to me, but everyone's heard stories like that. Besides, if I did say something, he would say that I was trying to control him, or give him instructions. He says I'm always trying to tell him what to do, and he would use this as another example."

Several of the men we spoke to validated what many women said: They simply didn't understand the ways in which women expressed sexual dissatisfaction or made sexual requests. Many of them definitely agreed that when a woman tried to change or alter the way they made love, they interpreted it as an overall criticism of their performance. This makes some men feel like failures; it makes other men annoyed. One 45-year-old single man expressed this point of view, saying, "I hate it when a woman starts moving my hands around or acting like I'm doing something wrong. I believe in pleasing a woman, and I think I know how to do it. When someone starts telling me what to do, it makes me angry. It's easier being with women who appreciate you as a lover."

Protecting a Woman's Sensitivities—Why Men Often Prefer Not to Talk to a Partner

On the other side of the coin, several men told us that they felt that women just can't handle any requests or suggestions from a sexual partner. Tom, 37, tells the following story.

"I gotta tell you, if I even try to get my wife to do anything different, she starts crying. 'What's the matter?' she says, 'You don't like me the way I am? You'd rather be with somebody else. The way I do it isn't good enough for you.' Then she cries some more. I've learned to just shut up and be grateful for what I got, which isn't bad."

Several women we spoke to agreed that their husbands had tried to change an ongoing sexual pattern, and that their first reaction was a sense of rejection. Sandy, a 34-year-old married woman, admitted, "I think it was the fact that we had been sleeping together for close to two years before he said anything to me. Then he told me that when I went down on him, I wasn't doing it right. It seems he wanted me to use more saliva, or lick everything . . . I don't even know . . . but what it came down to was that he felt that I wasn't being passionate enough, and didn't love doing it enough. It just ruined that part of sex for me. Now I feel totally self-conscious about it, and I just don't want to have oral sex anymore."

Another Masculine Reason for Not Talking About Sex—Hiding Feelings of Inadequacy

"I think men are afraid to ask each other about sex. I think they are worried that they will find out that they are not doing it good enough and that they are physically incapable of doing it any better."

—*Cliff, 31*

In these complex sexual times, it shouldn't come as any surprise that many men periodically feel inadequate, but what concerned the men we spoke to was not so much feeling inadequate as *looking* inadequate. Carl, a young single man, defined his attitude as follows.

"On some level I'm always worried about appearing sexually inadequate. You know: What will she think of me? What will they think of me? Am I doing it right? Am I doing it enough? Can anyone tell that I'm not confident enough?"

Although many men spoke about their fears of appearing inadequate, they also admitted their reluctance to share these fears with either close friends or sexual partners. A large number of the men, particularly the younger ones, said that they felt women were hypocritical when they said that they wanted "sensitive" men, because these same women always fell in love with the opposite type. Bob, a 30-year-old photographer, said it best.

"Listen, women say they hate 'macho' men, but when you act different and try to be sensitive, they treat you as though you are a jerk."

Bob related the following story, which illustrates many of the feelings that men described, including the way in which some men berate themselves for what they perceive as sexual failure or rejection. Bob says that this incident made him feel like a total washout with women, and that as ridiculous as it may appear, it makes him feel embarrassed whenever he thinks of it.

"About five years ago, I was spending my summer vacation at a beach house I was sharing with friends on Fire Island.

It was the middle of the week, and Stan, another guy in the house, and I were walking along the beach, late in the afternoon. It was maybe four-thirty, and the beach was pretty empty. Near the dunes, sitting on a boulder, were two women playing Scrabble. They were both topless. We waved; they waved back.

"It was pretty funny. Both Stan and I simultaneously did a one-eighty, ambled over to the women, and one of us said something fairly stupid about the Scrabble game. They said something back, and we started talking. We talked about the weather, their vacations, the ferry schedule . . . everything, except their breasts, which was the only thing I wanted to talk about.

"Anyway, one of them was planning to leave on the last ferry. The other wanted to stay, but she looked at me, I thought invitingly, and said she had no place to stay. 'You can stay at our place,' I said.

"That night I took her to dinner. She was sort of half covered, wearing this really low-cut top. Obviously she had no tan line. We went dancing and for a walk along the beach, but every time I tried to get physically friendly, she sort of drew back. When we got to my room, there were two beds, catty-corner. She got undressed in the bathroom and crawled into her bed in the dark. I didn't know what to do . . . what was expected of me. Finally I reached out to touch her. She retracted. I tried two more times, and each time I could almost feel her recoiling.

"As you can imagine, I had a terrible time sleeping. And the dreams! Well, when I woke up the next morning, there she was on my deck without a top. Can you imagine? Stan was making coffee and two guys from the house next door were visiting—all three were walking around the house trying to look casual.

"Well, you can imagine what happened. Everyone assumed I was having this hot, torrid affair. I actually have a picture of the two of us together on the porch, with my arm around her. She looked gorgeous. Everything looked perfect, except we weren't sleeping together. Well, that was one of the worst weeks of my life. Next night same thing.

I didn't want people to know we weren't sleeping together because I didn't want them to think that this totally sexual woman didn't find me attractive. I didn't want to say anything to her because I didn't want to say, 'Hey, you're not sleeping with me, you gotta go.' It was just awful, and I felt like a total jerk.

"Well, it gets worse, because two days later this other guy next door comes out for the weekend, spots Ms. Bared Breasts on the beach, and he practically attacks her. The next thing you know, she has moved into his room and they are lovers.

"I have never felt like such a jerk in my life. I felt as if everyone was laughing at me and knew that I didn't make it with this woman. I thought, 'Maybe if I had just grabbed her the first night.' I blamed myself for not being more aggressive. Not only did I feel like a jerk, everyone else knew I was a jerk."

On a much more serious level, we heard the following story from a 43-year-old college professor who recently suffered a serious back injury.

"Since I hurt my back, I don't enjoy sex as much. It sounds like it's not related, but it is. I don't have the stamina; I can't do anything really athletic, but I don't know how to tell the woman that I live with that I'm just not that interested in sex. So what I do is grit my teeth and pretend not to be in pain. I can't blame her because she asks me things like, 'Are you sure that you should be doing this,' and I pretend that I'm Mr. Super Stud who is so interested in sex that nothing can turn me off. We always made love several times a week, and I guess to some extent I worry that if I'm not satisfying her, she'll find someone else who will. I know that she is loyal to me, and I don't think this will really happen, but it's what I feel."

Or this anecdote from Herb, a 68-year-old retired dentist, married for three years to a woman who is now 45.

"I've always thought of myself as being oversexed, you know. It sometimes seemed as though I thought of nothing else. I was like a character in a Phillip Roth novel. Now, however, I'm slowing down, and my wife, who is a very loving and understanding woman, is still young and she likes sex.

"I find myself in a constant state of apprehension. Can I skip tonight? How about if we don't make love two or three nights in a row? At this stage in my life I would prefer making love in the morning, but I think that if that's the only time I initiate sex, will she think, 'This old goat isn't good for anything else'?"

We asked Herb why he didn't talk to his wife about some of these anxieties, and he said that he didn't want to do that, just yet.

"I feel that if I say anything to her, it will confirm her worst fears about me. She had some hesitation about marrying someone who was so much older. What I'm doing instead is trying to get her to be less interested in penetration and more interested in oral sex. I figure I can keep going down on her till the day I die."

Waiting and Hoping for Your Partner to Initiate Better Sexual Communication

Although everyone wants better communication with his or her partner, we found that the vast majority of men and women, no matter how new or well established their relationships, were playing a waiting game.

Those who were newly committed said things such as:

"I'm sure once my wife and I get more accustomed to each other, we'll be able to talk about these things. Right now I don't want to appear demanding. Once she's more comfortable with me, I think she'll be less inhibited about expressing herself."

—*26-year-old new husband*

"Andrew always asks me if I want him to do anything else. I guess I want him to guess or figure it out. I don't know how to ask. I assume with time we'll work it out."

—*24-year-old wife*

Those who were in more established relationships were often extremely saddened by the fact that the better communication never happened. One 37-year-old wife, married ten years, told us: "I think I wanted him to be the one to start talking. I would have liked it, for example, if he talked more during sex. Sometimes I feel left out, and I need to feel closer. But he never did, and now we have such an established pattern, it's too late. I think he would like it if I started . . . but I can't."

Several men and women were very clear in realizing that they wanted their partners to give them permission to be more open about what was happening in bed. But in most cases, the permission was not forthcoming. One woman had this to say about the man she lives with: "I think what I want is for Daniel to ask me specific questions, like, 'How long do you want oral sex to last, what do you want me to say during sex, what really turns you on?' Then I want him to figure out the answers and tell me without my having to say a word. The problem is that I don't want to worry about his laughing at anything I say. I want to know that it's okay to say it, before I say it."

Protecting Your Partner—The Primary Reason for Not Having Explicit Conversations About Sex with Friends

"While Ned was still alive, I never told anyone how much he rejected me sexually. I guess I didn't want anyone else to know how mean he could be."

—*65-year-old widow*

"Ask me anything you want about me, but I don't think it's fair if I talk about my wife. . . . You know what I mean."
—26-year-old husband

"Look, I'll tell you the truth, but I've never told anybody else. Dick pretends to be a very macho man. In reality, he's a sensitive pussycat who can't sustain an erection for more than twenty seconds. But he is totally oral, and I am completely satisfied."
—43-year-old wife

"I don't think my wife can have orgasms, but I don't think she'd be happy if she knew I was telling you this."
—38-year-old husband

The people we talked to were most reluctant to discuss their sexual relationship with a current partner. Whether the sexual relationship was satisfactory or disappointing, a sense of loyalty keeps both men and women from sharing the details with an outsider. However, once a relationship begins to fall apart, these feelings often fall by the wayside.

Heidi was very clear about what went on with her ex-husband.

"When I was 36, I started a relationship with a 38-year-old man. On the fourth date, it became apparent that although there seemed to be a great deal of sexual attraction, he wasn't going to do anything. I was trembling with excitement if he so much as brushed my hand, but he didn't do much else. On about the sixth or seventh date, he sat me down and told me that he was impotent, and had been impotent with his wife as well. He was extremely upset when he told me this; his hands were shaking and he was perspiring. Well, I guess I thought time would change it because we began going to bed regularly and trying. Sometimes it would get a little harder; sometimes nothing would happen. He wasn't a totally selfish lover, and he always made sure I had an orgasm, either orally or with his hands, but he never got it up. After about six months of this, he proposed. I said yes.

"In the meantime, I had, of course, fallen deeply in love with him. I didn't want to embarrass him in front of the world, so I told no one about his sexual problem, which of course had become my problem. God, at the time I loved him so, so much. It seemed that telling someone, even my best friend, would be a major act of disloyalty. She asked me what he was like in bed, and I said wonderful. When we were around people, I would say little things that indicated what a fabulous lover I thought he was. I wanted to build his confidence.

"Almost as soon as we were married, he changed. He became cruel and unkind, and although sexually things improved somewhat because together we had learned how to make his limp penis ejaculate, he was still totally nonerect. To make a long story short, within months he started to have affairs, if you can call them that, because as nearly as I can tell, he was impotent in all of them. But the fact is that he was a good-looking, intelligent, successful man, and he had no difficulty in finding women who were prepared to try to help him cope with his problem. Of course, I was devastated.

"The idea of him exposing himself and his problem to strange women wiped me out. I thought it was a total betrayal of the kind of trust and intimacy that I thought we had. It was worse than if a sexually untroubled man had affairs, because every woman he went to bed with had to know not only how he was, but also what I was like, and what I put up with.

"I moved out. And my fury was so incredible that I started telling everyone about him. I did a total turnaround. I changed; instead of wanting to protect him, I wanted to expose him. I would have told strangers on the street, but I didn't think they would listen. My friends were shocked that I had never said anything to them about it before we got married. But he was too important to me, and I thought it would be disloyal."

It is worth noting that Heidi was so determined to convince everyone she knew that her husband was a "good lover," she was careful to not reveal the specifics of their sex life, even to her closest friend.

Good Sex/Bad Sex/Good Lover/Bad Lover
—Sex and the Language Barrier

"My ex-husband always used to accuse me of being frigid, and I would say to him, 'I don't know what that means.' Finally I told him right out that my problem was that he was a 'bad lover.' Then he asked me what I meant. If he didn't know, then I sure wasn't going to tell him."
—*42-year-old divorcee*

Another problem we became conscious of when we began to talk with others about sex is that most of the language we use is extraordinarily judgmental. It seems nothing has as many judgments attached to it as the language of love. Almost all the phrases used to describe what happens in bed convey an attitude or issue a verdict, while carefully omitting all the information that might help the listener understand or form an opinion. We say someone is "good in bed" or "bad in bed." We say it was "good sex" or "bad sex." We say someone is a "good lover" or a "bad lover." Rarely do we say what that means.

Most of us know that when we say someone is a good lover, we are talking about something ephemeral, a passionate quality to which we are personally responding passionately, and that this does not necessarily have anything to do with the lover's technical expertise. However, it's easy to see how the phrases *good sex* or *bad sex* stress perfomance rather than loving.

The words used to describe various sexual practices sometimes also come with labels attached to them. When we read that someone is masturbating, for example, it implies that he or she is either not in a relationship or dissatisfied with a sexual partner, which is not necessarily the case in real life. We assume that the couple who engages in a great deal of oral sex is more adventuresome than the couple who does not. Oral sex, anal sex, clitoral stimulation—all have implications, and sometimes judgments, attached to them that far exceed the actual physical activity involved.

There are also a whole series of sexual shibboleths that are by definition judgmental. Language, which is equally tough and demanding on both men and women, creates an atmosphere in which both sexes feel a pressure to perform.

Let's take the phrase "There are no frigid women, only bad lovers."

To many men the term *frigid* means, incorrectly, that a woman can't have orgasms from intercourse. We spoke to many men who were involved with women like this, and all of them were concerned that this might be a reflection on their "performance." On the other side of the coin, several women told us that they didn't have orgasms during sex, but because they didn't want to bear the label *frigid* or cause partners to feel like "bad lovers," they often resolved the issue by "faking it."

And how about: "A real man is always ready."

And what does that mean? The man whose erection is not always in place and cooperative feels that he's not a real man; the woman who is with the man without the erection feels as though it is her fault. A real woman should be able to give a real man an erection.

A great many men over the age of 26 or 27 said that they were a little concerned because they could no longer have erections simply by thinking about sex—as they did when they were in their teens. They wanted assurance that this normal pattern of behavior was indeed happening to other men their age.

The next problem we noticed is the way we use sexual terminology that we don't fully understand. If the people we spoke to are representative of the rest of the population, and we obviously think they are, then men and women are also confused about the terms that the sex experts use to define sexual behavior. Since for the most part these terms fall into the category of labels, they are also judgmental, and nobody is happy being placed in categories such as retarded ejaculation, premature ejaculation, impotent, frigid, non-orgasmic, etc., all of which fall under an umbrella termed dysfunctional. Even more relevant, the vast majority of the people we spoke to didn't know exactly what these terms meant, except that they aren't ideal and that they indicate bad sex.

We found, for example, that both men and women were confused about female sexual response and didn't understand the difference between frigidity and orgasmic dysfunction; also nobody seemed to understand what retarded ejaculation meant, except, of course, the men who suffered from it.

At first we were surprised that most of the men were unclear about premature ejaculation. But then we realized that since men rarely speak to other men, and since heterosexual men are not apt to be intimately acquainted with any other man's sexual behavior, the only way they could judge their own sexual behavior was by the reactions of the women they were with. The men we spoke to were not totally certain of what the term *premature ejaculation* specifically meant. How long does a guy have to sustain an erection to get out of that class? Several of the men we spoke to said that they were only able to maintain an erection for a minute or two, but since none of the women they were with were complaining, they assumed they were not ejaculating prematurely. Others talked about sexual encounters that lasted five minutes or more and said that they had problems with premature ejaculation, and it disturbed their partners. This indicates not only that the language is confusing, but also that it would appear that a problem is only a problem when it's a problem.

Throughout all of our interviews, the single most striking element was the sexual language barrier. Because we have all become accustomed to speaking about sex by rendering judgments while at the same time leaving out all the relevant details, it is nearly impossible to develop an easy conversational style that allows for authentic description. The average man doesn't know what other men are doing; the average woman doesn't know what other women are doing. And even within the most intimate relationships, partners are likely to withhold a great deal of specific sexual information from each other, often for the lifetime of the relationship. In a peculiar way each hopes the other will initiate such conversations and be able to extract the intimate particulars that will lead to a more complete and fulfilling relationship. We have no role models for such conversations, and consequently most of us don't know how to begin.

3

What Really Happens in Bed: Talking About Real Men and Women, Real Erections, Real Orgasms, and Other Assorted Facts of Real Life

UNDERSTANDING THE DREAM WORLD OF SEX/UNDERSTANDING THE REAL WORLD OF SEX

"Sometimes I have these fantasies of what I want to do with my girlfriend, but when we get together, they just don't work. In my fantasies, my body position can change instantly; so can hers. One minute she's on top, the next second we're on the floor; suddenly we're in the shower. Asking her to enter into my fantasies is like asking her to walk into my dreams. Who can do that?"

—*28-year-old man*

"Listen to me. I'm going to say something important. The reality of sex can never be the same as the fantasy. In the fantasy, the woman is responding the way you perceive her. In reality, you can't do exactly what you fantasize because somebody else is involved. The minute you have two people, you have two bodies with two sets of legs, two sets of arms, and two sets of ideas about where everything should go."

—*56-year-old man*

Fantasies are make-believe, and everyone we talked to indulged in some form of sexual fantasy. But as one of our interviewees said, "Fantasy is what takes place in your head; reality is what takes place in your bedroom."

The sex therapist Helen Singer Kaplan once wrote: "It may be said that sex is composed of fantasy and friction." (*The New Sex Therapy* by Helen Singer Kaplan, M.D., Ph.D., Brunner/Mazel, 1974.) Our fantasies can include just about anything—romance, intensity, passion, illusions, more than a few delusions—not only about our lovers but also about ourselves. We can dream up anything that makes us happy, from total romantic tenderness with an adoring mate to out-of-sight sadomasochistic rough sex with an agreeable, or not so agreeable, partner. Our fantasies are like sexy novels in which erections, sometimes referred to as "ramrods of steel," never falter, and the heroine, of course, is unresponsive until she meets the hero and immediately becomes multiorgasmic. It goes without saying that in novels and fantasies nobody ever takes time out to insert a diaphragm or fumble with a condom. Well, everyone knows that it is not like that in the real world, where real men sometimes have problems with erections and real women often fake orgasms while worrying about birth control and pregnancies that really *do* occur.

The fact is that all of us can control the fantasy parts of our sex lives with far greater ease than we can control the real or "friction" parts. When we asked people to tell us about their sex lives, we were particularly interested in some of these real issues. Everyone accepts the fact that emotions affect one's physical responses. Well, we wanted to know how physical realities and physical responses affect the emotions. How do men and women feel about fragile erections and frigidity? How about other physical facts, such as differences in size and precarious birth-control methods?

We were also curious about the different types of sexual patterns and levels of sexual response and urgency; and we wanted to get a better sense of the different levels of sexual drive. Are we all more or less the same, or do some people really need more sex? We have all heard the myths about the "man who is always ready" or the "man who can go all night." How about the woman who is capable of having so many orgasms that she faints from the sheer joy of it all?

We wanted to know if these men and women really exist, and how their responses and attitudes affect their partners' needs.

TALKING ABOUT SEXUAL PATTERNS

Emotional Needs/Physical Realities—You Are Who You Are, And Everybody Is Different

Everybody is different, and no two people have the same level of sexual interest or sexual drive. Several men mentioned that they were shocked when they first discovered that all men were not identical in terms of sex drive. One man who considers himself an extraordinarily sexual person says that he first learned that there was a difference in men . . .

". . . at the beach. I must have been about eighteen, and these beautiful women kept walking by. My friend Fred and I would sit on the sand, and I would get so turned on, I would excuse myself, go to the men's room, and whack off. I assumed that he was doing the same thing but that we were both being polite.

"One day I made several trips to the men's room within an hour, and he asked me if I was sick. I said, 'I was just whacking off.' He looked at me in alarm. So I asked him what he did. That's when I realized, no, he doesn't do this. He doesn't whack off every couple of hours. And I thought, 'That's amazing.' I was totally blown away by the difference in the urgency. He just implied that he found the whole thing totally ridiculous that I could go and beat off just because I saw a woman walking out of the ocean with water dripping off her breasts."

From a woman's point of view, Marge, a 33-year-old married woman, remembers an exactly opposite kind of feeling.

"Sexually I was the least precocious kid on the block. When I grew up, the sexual revolution was flourishing, and every-

body was talking about what they were doing, what they
were going to do, etc. I remember my friends giggling and
talking about guys and feelings and orgasms and masturbation. I didn't know what they were talking about. I never
had those feelings, and they seemed ridiculous to me. Eventually I got married, got sexual, had orgasms and all that.
I even masturbate. But if my husband and I have sex and
I don't have an orgasm, I don't feel that terrible. I enjoy
sex, but I can't imagine myself being overpowered by sexual
emotions. Some of my friends have had affairs, and they say
it is purely for sex. I can't understand it."

Nobody seems to know precisely why some people have
stronger sex drives than others. All we know is that some
people do. And it doesn't seem to have anything to do with
gender. We spoke to men and women who said the only
time they felt alive is when they were having sex, and we
also spoke to men and women who said that sex was not all
it's cracked up to be. From the people we spoke to it would
clearly appear that each of us has his or her own sexual pattern
and sexual drive, and that although it changes as we age,
it can really only be gauged or evaluated in relation to itself.

MEN—TALKING ABOUT SEX DRIVE AND PATTERNS

The Body/Mind or Mind/Body Connection

There was a marked difference in the way in which some
men described their sexual drive, and their patterns pointed
up two extremes. At one extreme were the men who described sexual desire as something totally driven by hormones
and physical need. They said, for example, that their sexual
desire was controlled by a bodily response, and that their
emotions sort of tagged along. Some said that they could go
for a certain specified time without thinking about sex. Once
that time period had passed, they would begin to find themselves easily aroused, and that their erections were almost
spontaneous. Satisfied, they put their sexuality on a back

burner until the physical desire surfaced yet again. The time period between these arousals varied from man to man and was, at least in part, partially dependent upon age. Some very young men said they felt that way every day; other men in their fifties said that they felt sexual once or twice a week.

On the other extreme were men who said that they thought about sex constantly, even though they felt no actual physical desire. They said that they constantly fanned their desire with fantasies or other forms of erotic stimulation, then waited for their bodies to catch up.

Following are examples of both attitudes.

Luke, 44, married

"I've always had a very functional approach toward sex. Even when I was younger. Basically I respond because my body desires sex, sometimes even when my head is in a different place. That doesn't mean that I don't enjoy it. I do. And I enjoy being with my wife. But there are times when I almost resent the fact that I have to take time to have sex. It doesn't always seem to be the best use of time. As far as being with my wife, we can be together in dozens of different ways, and we are.

"Even when I was younger, I felt this way. Of course I had fantasies and thought about sex more then, but even then I was never that driven sexually. It's just that physical need would reassert itself that much more often."

Roger, 58, had a totally different attitude.

"When I was in my twenties and thirties, sex had an urgency for me that you can't believe. I was totally obsessed. Hell, I would have gone down on a mailbox if I thought a woman was inside it. I would have sex with my current partner once or twice a day, and then masturbate once or twice a day, all the while fantasizing. I was driven by my fantasies. I would masturbate or have sex until I was so exhausted, there would be no way for me to have another erection, and yet I would keep trying. I would chase strange women down the street to try to fulfill my Henry Miller–type thoughts.

Now the woman I live with and I have sex most days, and I masturbate a couple of times a week. It isn't as easy getting excited as it once was, and I have to resort to some fairly fancy fantasies sometimes before I can get an erection, but it doesn't feel right to me to let a day go by, so I do whatever is necessary."

Although the vast majority of the men we spoke to assumed a more middle-of-the-road attitude, one can still see a tendency toward one attitude or the other.

Jeffrey, 32, single

"My sexual pattern is that I don't have a pattern, and I don't understand it. There can be months when there are no women in my life and very little masturbation; then there have been times when there are lots of women and no masturbation; and times when there are lots of women and lots of masturbation. I think I use sex for a variety of outlets, and one is frustration. During periods when things aren't going well for me, sometimes there's this sexual fantasy world I can go into, and a bomb could go off near me and it would be like, 'Excuse me, did somebody say something?' "

Matt, 28, single

"If I'm seeing a woman, once the relationship is established, we usually fall into a pattern of sex twice a week. When that happens, I usually don't masturbate. But if I'm not seeing anybody, or if I haven't had sex in a two-week period, then I'll probably masturbate three or four times in the second week. It seems that my body only goes so long before it demands sex."

One of the things that became apparent to us is that each man knows his own sexual pattern. Although he may not discuss it with his friends, or even his mate, by the time he is past adolescence, the average man is keenly aware of his attitude toward sex, his preferred sexual pattern, and how much or how little sexual activity he requires. Typically a man's sexual desire slows down as he ages, and his pattern is altered accordingly. Obviously other outside factors—such as illness, medication, fatigue, or depression—will often affect desire and behavior.

ERECTIONS AND ORGASMS— HOW MANY/HOW OFTEN

When we started working on this book, our heads were full of stupid mythologies, such as, "A man may not be able to make love to one woman six times a night, but he can make love to six different women in the same night."

We discovered that the man who is capable of making love six times in one night is almost as unusual as the dodo. But if this rare bird did exist, from what we've heard, he would be able to make love to one woman six times, or six women, once each. Men made it very clear that one has to differentiate between desire and performance. Although a man's desire and enthusiasm may be affected by different partners or new and more exciting situations, his maximum sexual capability is pretty much a constant and does not change drastically from partner to partner.

Young men, as one would expect, do tend to be "turned on" more often than older men. But that does not mean that every older man is by definition less sexual than every young man. We spoke to one man of 70 who said that he can still, on occasion, have as many as three erections and three orgasms, in one twenty-four-hour period. On the other hand, we spoke to at least a dozen men in their mid- to late twenties who said, no matter what they did, they were unable to manage more than one orgasm in that same time frame.

Mark, 32, single
"I used to be able to make love a couple of times in a night, but now that's really exceptional. For the most part I need a full twenty-four hours between erections to recycle."

Paul, 28, single
"Personally I'm not satisfied unless I have two orgasms. I usually find that oral foreplay will bring me to orgasm fairly

quickly. Then I like to perform oral sex on the woman until I'm erect again—normally this takes about fifteen minutes. Then it's straight sex until I have the second orgasm. I really need two erections and two orgasms to feel satisfied. But then I probably won't feel like sex for two or three days."

Gordon, 48, married

"Twice a week is it for me at this point, and sometimes not even that often. It definitely takes me longer to get stimulated, and there's no way I'm going to have an erection for at least another couple of days. Whether or not that would be different if I were in a new relationship, I don't know. But I'm not, and that's the way it is."

Ian, 26, married

"I have about two orgasms a day. Usually one is with my wife, and one by masturbating."

Many men told us that they often have a second erection in response to direct sexual stimulation, but they just can't have another orgasm.

Kenneth, 29, single

"In college I think I was just too excited. I remember times when it seemed as though I had barely entered the woman and I would come—maybe fifteen seconds. Now that never happens. I don't know if it is training or age. But then—and now—if I try to have sex again too soon, I just can't have an orgasm."

Mason, 50, married

"I need about three or four days between orgasms. I can get erect before that, but no way I'm going to have another orgasm."

Bill, 68, married

"I can't have as many orgasms as I once did, that's for sure. But with me, I was never one of those men who could come several times. I've always been able to have an erection within a short period of time, even if I can't come again. Now sometimes it goes down, sometimes it stays up. My wife and I have sex every couple of nights, but I don't even try to have an orgasm every time. I do make sure she has an orgasm even if I don't. Myself, I pace, and I average about two a week . . . maybe."

Jerry, 38, single

"I can get another erection within an hour or so of orgasm, but I rarely have the second orgasm. I remember one weekend, the woman I was with must have tried everything. We had sex on Saturday night about seven-thirty, and then made love off and on for more than twenty-four hours. I didn't have the second orgasm until the following night, Sunday, at about ten o'clock. I would have given up, but she seemed determined."

Many men said that although they couldn't always manage a second or third orgasm by having sex with a woman, it was usually possible when they masturbated. One 28-year-old said: "You can bring yourself off by masturbating within sixty seconds, so of course it's easier to do it again and again. Sometimes I've been with a woman and had sex twice, and then gone home and masturbated to orgasm a third time, remembering what happened between us. I know that having sex a third time, I would not have been able to reach a climax— it's just not that easy."

SEX AROUND THE CLOCK

Although we spoke to many men who could climax through masturbation more than once a day on a regular basis, we talked to few men who could regularly have several orgasms every day through sex with a partner. Men typically point out that sex with a partner is simply more physically demanding than masturbation. However, we talked to many men and women who remembered the long weekends of sex that accompanied the start of an important relationship. Quite a few men under the age of 35 said that they have within

the last few years spent three-day weekends in which they
made love ten or twelve times. In almost all instances, these
highly charged sexual weekends marked the beginning of a
highly charged relationship or affair.

Jim, 25 and single, vividly recalls the beginning of one
such relationship. The sexual behavior and attitude on this
weekend seems to typify the way in which many men and
women establish a sexual relationship.

"Peg and I met on vacation, and the first time we slept
together was there, at the hotel, but it was like a lot of first
times—a little bit awkward and not terrific, although there
was still a lot of attraction. She returned a week earlier than
I did, and by the time I got back and we made another date
two weeks had gone by. I asked her out for the following
Saturday night—it was Labor Day weekend. She sounded
real easy, and she offered to make dinner. I guess that told
me something, and I figured we would be having sex, but
I didn't want to take it for granted because anything could
have happened in those two weeks. Old boyfriend returned,
new boyfriend . . . these things happen. Nonetheless, I took
my briefcase and packed my toothbrush, my razor, and a
change of underwear. To be honest, I always bring a change
of underwear, but I hide it. Sometimes at the beginning of
a relationship, when I don't know what's going to happen,
I actually carry a pair of shorts stuffed into a pants pocket
because I don't want the woman to notice it.

"Anyway, during dinner with Peg, I was real nervous because I'm always insecure until the relationship is established.
After dinner we did the dishes and started playing around
near the sink, lots of nudging and physical-type fooling
around with the sponge. Finally we kissed there in the
kitchen, and when we moved out to the couch with coffee,
I pulled her down on the floor with me. That's where we
started. I started to undress her, took off her top and bra,
and then she unzipped my pants and started to play with
my penis. I'm never fully erect, even at this point. To me
it feels like it is, but it's not. Sometimes the first little bit
of physical contact at this point will make me erect. In this
case, she went down on me and that's what happened. I'm

still so insecure that lots of times I wind up having sex on the floor because I'm afraid that she might change the action and we won't make it to bed. I asked her if I should use anything, and she said no, so I assumed that she was on the pill.

"It's interesting because when I first start having sex, I always think I'm going to be able to go on for twenty-four hours. But I can't. Usually after the first orgasm, I've had enough and that's what happened this time. We moved up to the bed for comfort, and I couldn't tell whether or not she was satisfied.

"Some women will do everything they can to get you started again, which is fine if you're interested and terrible if you're not. How the woman responds makes a big difference in whether or not I bother again. Once I've had an orgasm, something has to happen to get me erect again. I'm not going to get excited sitting around staring at my penis. In this case, she seemed to want a little more, so I went down on her and that got her excited, and then she went down on me and we started again. The second time is always more difficult for me. I tend to get hard, get soft, get hard, etc. We made love like that for about an hour before I came again. In the meantime Peg said that she also had two orgasms, one orally and another from intercourse—the second time—with her on top. Finally we raided her refrigerator, ate a quart of Häagen-Dazs, and went to sleep.

"I woke up at about six, definitely erect, so we made love then, but we didn't kiss—I mean, I didn't kiss her mouth. The only thing that's wrong with sex that early in the morning is that you're very conscious that your breath probably smells. I'm always aiming my breath over the woman's shoulder. Otherwise, when you're half asleep like that, it's nice and easy. We cuddled up, fell asleep again, and didn't wake up until ten. Then we went out for breakfast, came back with the paper, and went back to bed. I guess I was trying to drive her crazy. I haven't changed that much since college. Something about me always makes me want to chase a woman's private parts until she's totally tapped out and can't bear to have sex anymore.

"The only problem is that by the time we've had sex a

couple of times, I'm usually not totally together sexually, so
a lot of the pleasure I was getting on Sunday morning was
strictly from the physical contact with Peg. I would get it
up, and we would have sex for twenty minutes or so, and
then I would lose it. We fooled around, joked, had a little
more oral sex. You know, just when I was about to give up,
I'd find myself erect and then I'd start again. . . . Finally
I came again. I thought I would die first, but it happened.
About four o'clock in the afternoon. It was a pretty weak
orgasm. Then we went out and did some survival errands
together, came back, showered again, and went out for dinner. That night it was a little more normal. We came back
after dinner and watched television. I don't think I could
have done anything if I tried. Also, I had discovered by now
that she wasn't on the pill; she was using a diaphragm, and
it was irritating my penis. I kept hitting it when I was in
her, and I was so sore . . . you can't imagine.

"We went to sleep about midnight. That night I certainly
didn't wake up. The following morning I expected to leave
without sex. But when I was at the door, she grabbed my
crotch, and so we wound up back in bed again. This time
it was like a little good-bye present, a real quickie . . . a
five-minute thing but sweet."

Jim said that as their relationship progressed, he imagined
that the sex would find a pattern in which they would have
less sex. That's what happened in his other relationships.

"At the beginning, you spend more time in bed. If you
are starting to care for a woman and you want a relationship,
I think you want to be so intimate with her that you know
for sure that she cares too. You want to figure out all her
buttons and clear her memory banks of all other partners.
You want her to do things with you that she never did with
anybody else. Let's face it, you want some kind of control
or power over this woman sexually. The only way to establish
that is in bed. Later on you expect to have less sex, or at
least to spend less time on sex."

Jim's attitude toward sexual frequency and intensity was

articulated by almost all of the men we spoke to. The only exceptions were those men, who by their own definiton were sexually driven and felt compelled to bring a high level of fantasy and sexual variety into their lovemaking. Even these men, however, said that they "pooped out."

Charlie, who told us that he uses "amazing" fantasies to stay sexually aroused with his wife, said, "Of course there's a limited number of erections and orgasms. My top with a woman? Probably three. My head is still spinning long after my prick has called it quits for the night. I'm always willing, however, to use whatever left that's working, i.e., mouth and hands. However, to be truthful, my hands have been known to cramp, and my tongue has become numb. It's interesting, however; sometimes, even though I can't get another erection or have an orgasm with a woman, my fantasies are so intense and I get so excited that I go into the bathroom and masturbate until I have an erection and reach orgasm."

Real Erections Work Most of the Time and Don't Work at Least Some of the Time

"Listen, when a guy is young, he's hot all the time. He spends so much time worrying about getting his erection down that it doesn't occur to him that he will ever worry about getting it up."

—45-year-old man

The typical man we spoke to said that if he wanted an erection, he could count on its being there—most of the time. Our typical male interviewee, whether he was single or married, at the present was enjoying anxiety-free erections and relaxed sexual activity.

However, several of the men told us that they were going through a period of sexual adjustment that sometimes included temporary impotence, and just about all of the men told us that every now and then they find that their erections don't always behave the way they are supposed to.

Many said that when they were young, and consequently high on enthusiasm and short on experience, they would become anxious during their often infrequent sexual encounters. The end result was sometimes an erection that failed to stay erect. Many of the men said that their "first time" was the first time they discovered, usually to their amazement and embarrassment, that an erect penis cannot always be counted on, no matter how intense the desire.

You will remember David, the virginal young man in the last chapter who lied about his past experience. When last seen, he was reading sex manuals to try to learn how to orally stimulate his girlfriend, BettyAnn, to orgasm. Well, he and BettyAnn eventually decided that they were ready to go to bed together.

"I finally got the oral business right, and BettyAnn and I were two hot kids manipulating and licking each other and generally having a terrific time. I never would have pushed for intercourse, but she decided that she wanted to have it because of the way she felt about me. So we sent her poor roommate to the library, and we locked ourselves up in her room. I was nervous as hell for starters. I didn't know quite what the deal was. I didn't know what to do, and since she had no experience in penetration, either, she certainly couldn't guide me. In short, I couldn't really find where I was supposed to go. And once I found it, I couldn't penetrate. She was too tight, and I was too nervous. She kept asking me if this was unusual, if this kind of thing had ever happened before. Remember, I had presented myself as some kind of superstud who had been sleeping with young virgins since junior high.

"She kept asking, 'Are you sure you're doing it right?' and I kept saying, 'Listen, this kind of thing has never happened to me before.'

"In the meantime I guess that the stress of it all got to me because that's when I discovered for the first time how easy it is to lose an erection. I would have done anything just to get it up and keep it up. But no such luck. I would try to penetrate and push it in, and just as I thought I was about to make some progress, I would lose my erection. I got it up again, tried to penetrate, and lost it again. That kept repeating itself. I thought I would die from the humiliation, and I kept thinking that this was always going to happen to me. It was going to be my future, and I would never penetrate a woman. Don't forget I had also read all those sex manuals, and I remember reading about impotence and all that shit. Well, I thought that was going to be me.

"Finally we both had to admit it was a disaster, a total failure. It just didn't work. She was devastated. She blamed herself and thought that she was so tight, she would never be able to have sex. She didn't know what to do. So she called her mother. Her mother said lubrication. That's when I really wanted to die, or at least run the other way. I figured that as far as her parents were concerned, at least we hadn't really done it yet. I figured, better to be the guy who failed rather than the guy who succeeded.

"What happened? Well, we waited a couple of days and then we tried again, after we made a trip to the drugstore for some K-Y jelly. This time we succeeded. But I don't really think it was just the absence of lubrication; I was just too nervous."

The Absence of an Erection Does Not Always Mean the Absence of Desire

Anxiety and nervousness, the most frequently cited reasons for erection failure, are not necessarily associated with an absence of desire. Many men typically said they became nervous when they were with new partners or in new circumstances. These were often instances in which they were particularly anxious to please the woman. Several men said that ironically they were apt to have this problem when they were experiencing the strongest levels of desire.

Richard, 29, told us a story that reflects the problems he sometimes has when he is with a new woman. According to the men we spoke to, "first-time jitters" are a common phenomenon.

"Erection problems—yeah—every now and then. It usually happens the first time I'm with a particular woman. I couldn't get it up with my current girlfriend the first time, and I'm very attracted to this woman. It was our first real date, and after dinner she asked me if I wanted to take a look at her sister's new apartment. I said sure, and we drove over to the complex. She let us in with a key. When she said new, she should have also said empty; the apartment was like an empty warehouse. She went into a closet, took out a blanket and pillows, put them on the floor, and I know I'm in trouble. We sit down on this little thin blanket on this bare wood floor. And we start kissing. The next thing you know, I'm buck naked in this buck naked apartment, and I don't have to look down to know that my erection isn't going anywhere. Man! The situation was new, the woman was new, and for me it was like trying to make love on a street corner. I was frozen, totally frozen, and no matter what I did, I couldn't get hard enough to penetrate. She kept telling me not to worry about it, but I did. I felt like shit. The next time it was in my apartment, on my turf and on my terms, and everything was fine. But that first time was awful. I never before felt that totally incapacitated."

ERECTIONS AND SHORT TERM FAILURES

A fair number of men reported that they had gone through periods of temporary impotence that appeared to be directly related to complex psychological circumstances or health-related problems.

Edward, 36, told us:
"When my last girlfriend and I split up, I was shocked and upset. After a few weeks I met this new woman—attractive, nice. We went out a couple of times, and finally I took her home and we started necking. I was totally embarrassed. Nothing happened. I just couldn't get it up. It happened with two more women—all these women were really attractive. Any guy in his right mind would have wanted to be with them, but I couldn't do anything. This condition lasted for several months. Finally I met another woman I really liked. This time I took it real slow. We must

have dated for for a full six weeks before I tried to have sex, and when I did, I did it in stages. So I wouldn't find myself lying there with a limp dick again. It's okay now, but it really made me aware of how much power a specific woman can have over me."

Marshall, 52 and married, remembers that after his father died, he was unable to have an erection for over a month.

"My parents and I were very close, but I had no idea of the kind of emotional turmoil and depression I would experience as a result of my father's death, particularly since he had been ill for a long time. My wife said that she was surprised that *I* would be surprised. We normally have sex a couple of times a week, and it has gotten into a routine, which, to tell you the truth, I enjoy. But when I initiated sex, as I usually do, no amount of stimulation worked. I kept trying and trying. My wife was more sensible. She said, 'Let's just cuddle for a few weeks.' "

Stuart, 34 and single, remembers that he once went through a brief period when he couldn't get an erection.

"It was a combination of fear and some kind of conflict that caused it. For one thing, I was guilty because I wasn't sure whether or not I should be faithful to my girlfriend. The other, which was upsetting, was that I had developed a very close relationship with a male friend. I had never felt that close to another man before, and it scared me. I became very concerned. It was like, uh-oh, could I have some kind of hidden homosexual tendency or something? It didn't last very long, and I realized that you can feel that way about a man without being a homosexual. But in the meantime I was away at a resort in the kind of atmosphere where there were tons of beautiful women and sexual opportunities knock every ten minutes. Well, every time these opportunities knocked for me, nothing happened. I didn't know what to do when a woman approached me."

Ray, 38, remembers that he became temporarily impotent when he was recovering from an appendectomy.

"I was just too weak to have an erection. No way. In the meantime I had just started a relationship with the woman I later married, so I was very turned on to her. Even so I was too weak to be interested in sex. It lasted until I fully recovered from the surgery, which was about a month. It sure surprised me."

"Sometimes my penis seems to have a mind of its own."

When one talks to men who have had problems with their erections, one can see that these problems tend to occur when normal desire is overwhelmed by other emotions. These men seem shocked when they discover that an erection is not a permanent appendage, and that desire is a necessary ingredient in sexuality. These men usually express surprise that pure willpower cannot overcome all emotional or health-related problems, and a recurring theme is the sense of frustration they get from realizing they cannot will an unwilling penis to become erect.

A lack of desire can be caused by many factors, including sexual disinterest. A man can simply be turned off to a particular partner. This sometimes happens in destructive marriages. Several men who told us that they grew to hate wives, whom they later divorced, reported that they could not force their bodies to overcome their intensely negative emotional feelings.

One 49-year-old man explained: "My wife was the most difficult woman imaginable. She criticized and complained and whined all the time. I'm not really a fighter, and I'm afraid I took my anger out by refusing to perform sexually. I just had no interest. She said I was hostile. At the time I disagreed. I even went to see a doctor to see if I had anything wrong with me. Now from the perspective of many years, I realize she was right. I didn't want to sleep with her! The miracle was not that I didn't get it up, but that I didn't kill her."

Fatigue is another desire-killer. Ask a career driven man

just how much he is thinking about sex at the end of a twelve-hour day and you will learn, as we did, that sexual thoughts are sometimes fleeting at best.

Just about any strong emotion such as guilt or conflict can interfere with desire, and often does. A married man who is having an affair, for example, may discover that he is so guilty or experiencing so much conflict that he can no longer have sex with one or both of the women involved. There are also a wide variety of physical problems that can interfere with physical performance, which is why the possibility of a medical problem should always be ruled out.

Some prescription medications are also implicated in cases of temporary impotence. Several men to whom this happened told us that they had not been forewarned by their physicians. Consequently they experienced a great deal of unnecessary anxiety and, in some cases, marital stress.

And, of course, the experts tell us that depression can trigger any variety of sexual problems, including an absence of desire or erection failure.

AGING AND ERECTIONS

Men told us that the intense sexual response they experienced in adolescence diminishes gradually over the years. Some men felt very strongly that aging has drastically reduced not only desire, but also ability. One 60-year-old man who said, "A penis, unlike a loaf of bread, does not get harder as it gets older," complained that he frequently failed to get fully erect. Most men report that their erections lose a certain amount of oomph as they age, and one man who was only 26 complained that he was not as firm as he'd been at 19. Men in their thirties said they were beginning to notice that they don't want sex as often, and even when they do, that it may take longer to achieve an erection; several of them also felt that the erection itself may not be quite as firm as the ones they remember.

However, several other men were equally convinced that they hadn't changed that much, or if they had, the trade-off was worth it.

Burt, 58, married

"Let's put it this way. I know more than I did when I was 25. Although I enjoy sex in a different way than I did then, I think I perform every bit as well, and I have it a lot easier now because I'm more sure of myself. Frankly I don't feel a day older. As a matter of fact, I had more trouble with erections at 30 than I do now."

Other older men disagreed, however. These men felt that their erections were definitely weaker and less frequent. However, they made a clear distinction between desire and performance. Even though erections wane and orgasms are less frequent, these men stated very clearly that they had not experienced an eroding of desire and still wanted the intimacy and sensual experience of lovemaking, often with the same regularity that they preferred when they were in their thirties.

ERECTIONS AND LONG-TERM PROBLEMS AND SEMI-PROBLEMS

Lots of men fail to get fully erect much of the time if not always. This can be associated with several chronic physical ailments, as well as with some of the physical changes that occur naturally as a result of the aging process. Interestingly, some medical experts now feel that effective medical treatment is available for many physiologically as well as emotionally determined problems.

The men we spoke to pointed out that there is a difference between no erection and a weak erection. They also stressed that in these instances the absence of an erection does not mean a lack of desire or disinterest in sex. They also reiterated that a man can ejaculate and reach orgasm even though his penis is not erect. As a matter of fact, one man was careful to remind us that the quality of his orgasms had not changed, even though he could no longer become erect. This is something that the average woman doesn't understand. Conditioned to believe that an erection is the symbol of male desire, when they are with a man who fails to become erect, or whose erection falters, they immediately assume that there isn't enough desire, enthusiasm, or passion. The typical woman interprets this as meaning that he isn't really interested in her and that she is not desirable. This is a devastating feeling for the woman and can be deeply distressing to the man as well if he senses her unhappiness.

How Do Women Respond to Erection Difficulties?

Some women say that they handle the situation well. Others admit that they respond badly and get annoyed or upset. Many women question their desirability and are made very insecure. A great deal depends upon the circumstances, the way the man handles the situation, and the nature of the relationship.

Penny, 46, told us that she has slept with at least a hundred men and that she remembers a fair number who failed to get an erection. She says her reaction depends entirely upon how the man handles it.

"The one thing I really hate is when a man can't get an erection. It puts too much burden on the woman. I'm never sure what to do when that happens, but it makes me feel as though it is somehow my responsibility to do something to make it better. I remember being with one man, and it just couldn't get erect. We tried oral sex, manipulation, everything. It was apparent to me that it wasn't working, but he kept trying to stuff his limp penis into me. All it did was make me feel totally undesirable. It seemed like he was doing this for hours, and it was boring and it was awful, and I hated him for it. I wondered if he thought what was happening was sensual. I couldn't believe that was the case, but you never know. Afterward he was all sour-faced, and he did nothing to make it better emotionally, even though I tried.

"Another man I was with had the same problem, but he acted like a human being. After a couple of failed attempts, he said, 'Hey, this isn't working. Want to order in a pizza and watch a movie?' That's what we did. He spent the night even though the sex hadn't worked and didn't make me feel rejected. We shared some wine, ate the pizza, watched television, and had a nice time. The next morning it was a different story, and he had no problems with his erection, but he also had no problems with his personality."

Judy, 38, has been married for three years, and remembers that her husband failed to get an erection the first time they slept together.

"It was really odd because he had been pursuing me for ages, but when he finally got me to take my clothes off, he didn't seem to know what to do. I kept looking down, and he had no erection whatsoever. I felt badly for him, because I thought he felt foolish under the circumstances. I finally stopped the action because there was none. I suggested we just lie there and talk. Eventually I put my clothes on and we went out to dinner. When we came back to his apartment, we started kissing. I was nervous because I thought, 'Oh, no, here we go again.' But this time it was fine. I went down on him the minute we got into bed, and he got erect within minutes.

"Sometimes he still has problems—like if he's tired. Or if I'm not really interested, he seems to be able to sense it, and he never really becomes erect. When that happens, we usually just forget about sex. Sometimes, though, he will try to make me come . . . sometimes, I do, sometimes I don't. He says he thinks it's a function of being forty, and that he was not like this when he was younger."

Mary, 34, said that the first time her husband failed to get an erection, she blamed herself.

"When my husband started having problems with his erections, I assumed it was me. You know, it's pretty awful lying next to a man who isn't responding. When they start giving instructions—like push here or there, or use more lubrication—it ceases to be fun. Everyone gets anxious and it becomes upsetting. Also, I thought he was no longer in-

terested in me. I think he really got scared because he thought he was losing something. For a while we didn't talk about it. Finally he brought it up and said he was sorry for all the trouble he'd been having in bed. I told him the way it made me feel, like he wasn't interested. That upset him so much that I realized that he still loved me. Talking about it made us both feel better. Anyway, we decided that he was just tired, and now we have sex less often. We had been having sex about three times a week. I think it was just too much. Now we have sex every five days or so, and it seems to be fine."

Denise, 62 and married, remembers that her husband started having problems getting an erection after his first heart attack.

"I think he was scared of becoming too excited. But he had never had any problem sexually before. Until then, we had made love almost every night of our marriage so I should have realized that his illness was affecting him sexually, but it still made me feel insecure. Eventually we worked it out. The strange thing is that we never discussed his potency problems. We both pretended that it wasn't happening, even when it was."

The female consensus seems to be that if a new lover who normally doesn't have problems is failing to get an erection, he should just say so, stop pushing on with something that is making everyone feel uncomfortable, and do it without making the woman feel that it is her fault. Several women said that men told them, "I like you too much and it's making me nervous." The women who heard this were of course flattered and touched. In all these cases the problem dissolved the second or third time the couple tried to have sex.

If a man always has difficulties achieving an erection, he should tell the woman about it before trying to have sex. Most women agree that if he explains his problem, assures her that he still feels desire, and proves that he is a tender

and enthusiastic lover in bed, if the woman has any feelings for him whatsoever, she will be prepared to make whatever adjustments are necessary. One woman said, "It's amazing how quickly a warm tongue will make me forget about an erection."

Some women we spoke to said that their husbands or long-term lovers developed erection problems. Typically a woman in this situation would tell us that her primary difficulties stemmed from the man's reluctance to talk about his erection failures and a fear that she was being rejected. A couple of divorced women did tell us that their husbands *had* been having affairs, and that in these cases the failed erections seemed to be directly related to conflict and guilt.

But several other women said that they had been totally wrong when they assumed, erroneously, that a failed erection meant that their husbands were having affairs or had lost interest in the marriage. This put additional stress on the relationship.

These women often told us that when their husbands began having sexual difficulties, they also began avoiding all physical contact, including affection. The women complained that they could live without the erections. What they couldn't bear was the absence of affection.

A factor that many men don't take into account is that a fair number of women prefer oral sex to penetration, and they are not always as distressed by the absence of penetration as one might think. The following is a story of one woman's sexual relationship with an impotent man.

"He told me he was impotent and that he had been for years, even though he was not that old—he wasn't even fifty. In his case it is a medical problem.

"The first time we went to bed, I knew he wouldn't get an erection. But I had no idea what else to expect. I didn't know what he could or could not do. At the time I was accustomed to men who knew how to use their penises but didn't know how to do anything else. I actually thought I would seriously miss penetration. Nonetheless, I had grown to care for this man, and therefore I was prepared to try this new way of making love.

"You have to understand that I was very turned on to him. The first time we made love, it was in my bed, and I think he was really anxious because he quickly removed all his clothes and jumped into bed. When he started to kiss me, I knew it would be okay and I wouldn't feel foolish or stupid because he was so obviously passionate, even though he really didn't have an erection. I think at first I didn't believe it because I kept looking down, expecting to see something. But there was nothing, nothing. Absolutely limp!

"We basically did a lot of very erotic kissing and fondling. He was extremely oral and seemed to get off on watching me get excited. I also got excited from watching him get excited. Also, he talked. He talked about what we were doing and how it made him feel. That first time he didn't have an orgasm; we just curled up and went to sleep. The second time, however, he explained to me that he could have an orgasm and ejaculate with a nonerect penis. So from then on I used my mouth and my hand, and he sort of instructed me. He becomes a little harder sometimes but not much—and it is definitely more difficult for him to come than for most men. He doesn't do it every time, but he does most of the time."

Amy, another woman in her early thirties, said that she had a four-month relationship with a man who had serious problems with an erection, and again she found him to be a very satisfying lover as long as he was impotent.

"The irony is that we started having problems once he stopped being impotent. As long as he couldn't get erections, he was kind and considerate and thoughtful, in bed and out. He said he had been depressed for a couple of years and had had sex problems for that whole period. Well, after we started to go out, things got better for him. He got a great new job; I was very attentive and loving; he got some money from an insurance settlement. Eventually he began to get an erection again. Then there were real problems. First of all, with an erection, he was a terrible lover—inconsiderate, thoughtless. Also, as things began to get better for him, he became inconsiderate out of bed also.

Eventually the relationship ended because he was just too difficult."

Obviously what every woman we spoke to hated most is when a man fails to get an erection and makes her feel as though it is her fault.

One of the more entertaining stories we heard was told by Janet, a 35-year-old housewife from St. Paul, Minnesota.

"This happened right after college. Ross and I went out for several months before we tried to have sex, and when we did, nothing happened. He just couldn't get an erection. We tried again and again. Nothing worked. Every time he blamed me. He said I was too demanding and too needy, and somehow made him feel bad. In short, it was my fault that he couldn't get an erection. In the meantime we belonged to the same club, and we had all the same friends. He knew everyone I knew; I knew everyone he knew. So when we broke up, which of course we did, it was awful. I met my husband about eight months later, and although I would sometimes see this guy at the club, I forgot about it. About two years later I was at a dance at the club, and I was in the ladies' room with a friend. My friend recognized another woman named Eileen and introduced her to me, saying, 'You two have a lot in common, you both used to go out with Ross.' Eileen looked at me and said, 'Do you really believe it was your fault?' and we both started laughing. Can you believe—he did the same thing with her. Of course, we talked about how crummy he made us both feel. He was a real jerk about it."

ORGASMS AND THE CONTROL ISSUE

Some men are so controlled that it is a problem. These men cannot "let go" and reach orgasm inside a woman. Other men ejaculate so quickly that they don't always manage to penetrate before they reach orgasm. Most men are someplace in the middle. According to the men we spoke to, this middle range is wide. Some men find that after five minutes of intercourse they are prepared to climax; others typically sustain an erection for up to thirty minutes or more. A few men

seem to be able to go either way without difficulty, depending upon their partner's response and preference.

Many men, of all ages, said that five to ten minutes was pretty much their limit. These men usually indulged in extended foreplay or afterplay if they felt that their partners were not totally satisfied.

Other men we spoke to were concerned about ejaculatory control and consequently tried to learn how to last longer. The methods they use, which range from the mystical to the humorous, often include the old "think about baseball" technique.

Scott, 27 and single, gave us his solution, which he said he, in turn, got from a friend.

"My friend always had this problem, and he said he took bee pollen—it comes in little capsules like vitamin C—which he thought worked. I never did this, so I don't know. But I do a variation of his other method. He said that whenever he was about to reach orgasm and he didn't want to, he would think about Mets baseball games when they would lose, and he would get so upset that he could last forever just thinking about why they blew a double play in the bottom of the seventh.

"It's bizarre, and I guess only guys could think of this, but I think about stuff the Orioles did that bug me. If I really want to last, I think of game seven of the '79 World Series. Now remember, I'm not a psychologist and I'm not a urologist—I can only tell you about Orioles games."

At least five other men told us that they practiced mind control. One woman told us that her husband had unusual control, so we interviewed him as well. Here's what he said.

"I never had any real problems with control. However, years ago I took a course in self-hypnosis. The first night I was ready to say, 'This is ridiculous,' but the instructor stood up. It was a woman, and she raised her arm and said that through self-hypnosis and mind control you can do anything with your body. You can keep your arm as stiff as you want and keep it that way all night. So it registered in my

mind that if I could keep my arm stiff, I could keep something else stiff all night. That was more than twenty-five years ago. After that course I was able to do it longer—that's all. Now I go a half hour to an hour typically, but I could last longer. I can stop and ejaculate pretty much whenever I'm ready."

Insufficient Control

"The more a man cares about pleasing a partner, the more he has to think about maintaining an erection and not coming too soon."

—Bob, 30, single

Bob's ideas on male sexuality and orgasms are very female-centered, and what he says is at least partially true. However, the fact is that some men can't always maintain an erection until the woman has an orgasm. Some of these men care a great deal about pleasing their partners; as a matter of fact, some of them may care too much. We know from the women we've spoken to that some of these men are married to women who are basically satisfied with all aspects of the relationship, including sexual; other men are involved with women who are bitterly unhappy over the man's failure to sustain an erection.

Often poor orgasm control is directly related to age. Young men without an ongoing sexual relationship frequently are so readily stimulated that they reach orgasm very quickly. Some of these young men realize fairly early that if they can get a second erection, it typically lasts longer. Sometimes a lot longer, even longer than they may want.

Some men ejaculate quickly but have found ways to compensate. One 25-year-old single man said: "Control. Let's face it, I'm still a boy in that department, at least the first time. The second time I can really last."

Several older men, remembering how quickly they ejaculated in their younger days and how much it concerned them at the time, said that it was a shame that they had not fully realized that it was a function of age and a spotty

sex life. They didn't understand that for many men age alone resolves the lack of control. As these men get older, they are quite simply less excited by the mere presence of an attractive woman.

"In college I would come within seconds. It really bothered me at first. But it changed when I got into a long-term relationship. At first we had sex so often that I thought I would wear it out. Eventually I gained more control. Through practice and exhaustion. The less nervous I became about sex —by having it a lot and not worrying about not having it —the easier it seemed to be to control it."

Other men simply cannot seem to control their ejaculations, even as they become older. Some of these men rarely have a second erection that lasts, and growing older does not automatically give them orgasmic control. Are they bothered by it? Probably. Do they talk about it? Rarely.

From the men and women we have spoken to, it would appear that the only reliable way to determine the degree to which a particular man is distressed over his poor orgasmic control is to look at how it is affecting his relationships. Obviously if his partner is not distressed—and some women are not distressed by it—then the control issue is moot. However, if the woman is feeling unsatisfied and her partner is aware of it, poor orgasmic control becomes a major issue. With these couples we were told that it is often the woman who presses for sexual counseling. Failing that, she may become annoyed and withdrawn or begin having affairs. The way in which the woman views her partner's performance and the way in which she expresses her satisfaction or dissatisfaction would appear to have a great deal of influence on how the man feels about himself and his sexuality.

Walter, 61, said that he has always had poor orgasm control.

"I think my first wife made it worse. On the one hand, she would complain that I didn't sustain an erection; on the other, she would turn down sex. She said she was tired, or it was too much bother. I started using condoms because

I read somewhere that I would be less sensitive and possibly last longer; so she started complaining that she hated the way they felt. It became a vicious cycle because the less frequently we had sex, the more difficult it was for me to not come. I just got too excited. Finally, when we were in our late thirties, we went to a sex therapist. Did this make it better? No, not really. But it ultimately did a wonderful thing because it contributed to the end of the marriage. It brought so many things out in the open—there was a lot of anger between us. We got divorced, and a year later I met my current wife. At first I was nervous about going to bed with her, but it's different. I'm still no great shakes in the control department, but we have sex more often, which helps. And then I'm older, and I think I have more control now."

Several women told us that they had suffered agony as a result of being married to men who couldn't sustain erections. But several other women also stressed that a good lover is a good lover, and that control is not always an essential requirement.

Jodi, who is now 42, remembers that her favorite sexual experience was with a lover who couldn't maintain an erection for more than a few minutes.

"He really had a problem with ejaculation. I don't know if he got so excited or what. What I do know is that he was a fabulous, fabulous lover.

"First of all, he was a terrific person—very mature, very giving, very understanding. And he seemed very secure and sure of himself and his masculinity. What that meant was that even though he had problems, he never made me feel as though I was anything but the most desirable woman on this planet.

"I still remember the first time we made love. He had offered to drive to another state to help me pick up a table at my parents' house, and when we got back, we dropped off the table and went to his apartment.

"We stopped on the way and bought this fabulous dinner

for the two of us—an Italian feast. It was wonderful. We went to his apartment and had dinner and drank wine. He asked me if I wanted a massage, and he gave me this really incredible massage, without taking my clothes off. Just a massage, nothing else. Then he said he thought we should take a shower. He had a Jacuzzi, and he got me this great big towel and the two of us hopped into the Jacuzzi. He started to kiss me, but he told me that he was a premature ejaculator. 'Listen,' he said, 'the minute I enter you, I'm going to come. So let's both of us make sure that I don't enter you for a long time.' He played with all parts of me, and he made love to me with his mouth. I have to say that I loved his level of excitement. It really thrilled me. We went out for several months, and he eventually ended the relationship because he and his wife (from whom he had been separated) decided to try a reconciliation. I believe the marriage lasted."

EJACULATE TOO SOON? YOU'VE GOT TO BE KIDDING!

Some men wish that their erections were not quite so permanently in place. Joe is a man who has never been able to have an orgasm inside a woman. He simply can't relax enough, although every now and then he has been able to reach climax through a combination of masturbation and oral sex.

Joe was married when he was in his early twenties, but the marriage lasted only a few years. He recalled:

"My sexual problems definitely had something to do with the breakup. It drove my wife crazy that I couldn't have an orgasm with her, and she also worried about how she would get pregnant—whether we'd have to artificially inseminate her with my sperm; she said the idea bothered her. I think my problems with orgasms bothered her a lot more than they bothered me, and she said that she felt rejected by my inability to come inside her.

"As a teenager, I masturbated a great deal and had no

problems having an orgasm when I was alone. My first sexual experience was with my high-school girlfriend, right after graduation. I was really shocked. I couldn't come. I didn't know what to do. On one hand, I guess it was sort of built-in birth control. On the other, it was terrifying. I would get wildly excited, but nothing happened. I learned to wait until I was exhausted, or I would decide the girl was exhausted. Then I would fake orgasm. When I got home, I would masturbate. It takes me less than a minute to have an orgasm through masturbation. But I really can't even masturbate and reach orgasm with the woman in the room. That has also upset a few women—the fact that I need privacy.

"Other than that, I think I'm a good lover. I can last for a very long time—hours, sometimes. I will do just about anything to please a woman, and I think I'm unusually sexual. My current girlfriend and I have a fairly good sexual relationship, but sometimes she complains that she gets sore and that I last too long. I remind her that there are men who wish they were me, and women who wish that they were her. I'm seeing a therapist now. I don't know if anything can be done about this, but I'm hoping. It's a real problem."

Because Joe was able to reach orgasm through masturbation, he was fairly certain that his problem was not medical. But there are sometimes medical problems that will make it difficult or impossible to ejaculate. Some prescription medications can also create ejaculatory problems.

Women—The Way They Respond

Nearly every man we spoke to stressed how important it is for him to feel that the woman is responding. Several men said that they had no way of evaluating what was happening or if the woman was enjoying herself unless she spoke up. Typically men hated it when women gave no indication whatsoever as to what they were feeling. One man complained: "I could never tell if she was close or not, so I would keep going. It was a lot of work, let me tell you. . . . I like sex that moves around, in different positions, but with her, it was all pretty much missionary . . . me on top. I would go about half an hour or forty minutes. I would be about to have a cardiac arrest, and I couldn't tell what was happening with her. Finally I had to orgasm from fatigue—I couldn't keep moving."

Men say that women often don't understand how important it is for them to feel that they are satisfying lovers and how fatiguing sex can be for them. Some typical comments: "Sometimes I get so tired, I can't finish. I just knock myself out. Basically it's what I was taught, to concentrate on giving the woman pleasure and not ending quickly. It can work against you. There have been times that when it was my turn for my own orgasm, I just couldn't make it. I was too exhausted."

The message that men kept repeating was that the only way in which they could judge their competence as lovers was by the ways in which their partners responded. As one 33-year-old man said: "Sex for me, and for most of my friends, does not exist in a vacuum. My partner's input totally affects my experience. If she's into it, I'm into it; if she's not, I'm not."

What Really Happens in Bed: Talking About Women and Sex

Ask enough women about their individual sex lives and you soon begin to realize that their responses and personal histories are totally different. But if you break the women down into different age groups, the disparities begin to make a bit more sense.

Consider all that has happened in the ways that the average American woman has been told to view her sexuality in the years since World War II. In 1940, the average unmarried young woman had few sexual expectations and fewer sexual experiences; chances are that even her masturbatory explorations were accidental. For whatever it's worth, the *Kinsey Report on Sexual Behavior in the Human Female*, published in 1953, determined that by age 20, only 33% of women had masturbated to orgasm, compared to 92% of the men. The sexually inexperienced woman was a fact as well as an ideal.

Typically a woman of that generation was prepared to marry and follow her husband's lead, and her idea of an appropriate orgasm, if she thought about it at all, was probably totally based on the Freudian concept of vaginal orgasm. One of the reasons why masturbation was particularly discouraged in women was based on the notion that a woman who had become accustomed to clitoral orgasms would be less likely to have "true" or vaginal orgasms. When married, such a woman and her husband may have been bold enough to purchase the best-selling sex manual, *Ideal Marriage* by Th. H. Van de Velde, which addressed itself primarily to married men as the natural "educators" of women in matters sexual. Van de Velde did acknowledge the importance of a woman deriving pleasure from sex, but he offered little in the way of useful advice. *Ideal Marriage*, which had more than forty printings between 1941 and 1966, had a clear male bias; in offering advice on sexual positions, for example, it allows that the female on top position is useful under certain circumstances, such as male fatigue, but says: "The main disadvantage in complete and frequent practice of the astride attitude lies in the complete passivity of the man and the exclusive activity of his partner. This is directly contrary to the natural relationship of the sexes and must bring unfavorable consequences if it becomes habitual. Therefore, on these (profoundly psychological) grounds alone, we cannot recommend the choice of this attitude in connection."

By the mid 1950s, when *Ideal Marriage* was still selling up a storm, women were beginning to hear a great deal about "simultaneous orgasm." Although many authorities acknowledged that frigidity was a real issue for women, some sex "experts" disregarded this possibility, emphasizing instead that a couple time its orgasms so they happened together. Most of the women we spoke to who were married in those years remember all too well the experience of faking vaginal orgasms just as they sensed their husbands were beginning to climax.

As one woman told us "I think it made him feel better to think we were normal."

And then of course, there were all the issues surrounding birth control and abortions. These days when they sell condoms in the corner grocery store, it's difficult to remember that as recently as 1965, women who lived in states such as Connecticut could not expect their gynecologists to offer contraceptive advice or fit them for diaphragms. It was illegal.

In the 1960s, as far as women and sex are concerned, much changed. The birth-control pill was marketed, and for the first time contraception became simplified, bringing with it a new sexual freedom for women. Now women could have sex with almost as much freedom as men. And they began to act on that freedom. In 1966, Masters and Johnson published *Human*

Sexual Response; it stated publicly what millions of women already knew privately—their orgasms were not vaginal. One woman told us that until then she had never heard the word clitoris, even though that's how she had been having orgasms.

Further, Masters and Johnson gave women the verbal approval necessary to start being in charge of their own orgasms when they stated: ". . . no two women practice automanipulation in similar fashion. Rather than following any preconceived plan for stimulating his sexual partner, the male will be infinitely more effective if he encourages vocalization on her part. The individual woman knows best the areas of her strongest sensual focus and the rapidity and intensity of manipulative technique that provides her with the greatest degree of sexual stimulation."

In 1969, Kate Millet published *Sexual Politics*, and the women's movement began in earnest. Books such as *Vaginal Politics* and *Our Bodies, Ourselves* told women to assume responsibility for their own genitals and to stop relying upon male authority figures. In 1972, Barbara Seaman published *Free and Female: The Sex Life of the Contemporary Woman*, and then in 1976, Shere Hite published her first book, *The Hite Report on Female Sexuality*. It was a much more accessible book than Masters and Johnson's *Human Sexual Response*, and the average reader could clearly see that other women were assuming personal responsibility for their sexual satisfaction. This was an amazingly radical departure from the view, popular only a few years before, of women as passive sexual receivers.

Although American men have obviously experienced the changes wrought by the sexual revolution, these changes are mostly attitudinal and nowhere near as drastic. When you interview a man of 70 and a man of 20 about their sex lives, the personal and physiological experiences of both are amazingly similar. Chances are that both of them began experiencing sexual arousal at about the same age; they began masturbating at about the same age; and when, decades apart, they started having sexual relationships, they had essentially the same expectations: They knew what is was to have an erection; they knew what it felt like to have an orgasm, and within their sexual relationships, they knew that if nothing else, they expected arousal and orgasm.

Probably the single most important major attitudinal change that has taken place in the male sexual perspective is the way men perceive women's sexual expectations, and how they view their role in helping to fulfill these expectations. In short, many men now realize something that they suspected all along—their wives and lovers are not having orgasms from intercourse. Further, when straight intercourse fails to provide the woman with an orgasm, there is no need for negative judgment. It does not mean that the man is a "bad lover" or that the woman is "frigid." What it has come to mean is that the couple is free to explore other mutually pleasurable ways of achieving climax for the woman.

Differences in women's attitudes toward sex and orgasm are clearly reflected in the differences in the sexual histories of the women we spoke to. The typical woman in her fifties told us that although she enjoyed sex when she was in her twenties and thirties, she didn't expect orgasms, and that oral sex or genital manipulation, if it took place, were considered foreplay and not a regular part of lovemaking designed to facilitate the woman's orgasm. However, many women who are now in their twenties told us that they were experienced in oral sex and orgasm often before they had experienced penetration.

The sexual histories of the following four women reflect the ways in which these changing attitudes have been incorporated into changes in behavior. All four women are from similar socioeconomic backgrounds.

Lois, 50, divorced, living with a man, two grown children

"I think the first time I was sexually excited, I was only 12 or 13. All the kids would talk about certain books that were in the library, and I took one of them out. I can't remember the title—*God's Little Acre* comes to mind, but I don't know if that's what it was. Anyway, while reading it, I definitely felt something in my genitals. By then I was kissing boys and playing games like post office. We would go on hayrides, believe it or not. I liked the kissing, but

I had a different feeling from it, a diffuse body and emotional reaction.

"By the time I was a senior in high school, I had a steady boyfriend; I went with him straight through college. We were very proper, and so we didn't really start heavy necking until we were both in college. I remember spending nights just stretched out in the backseat of the car, the windows all steamed up. We didn't even pet for the first couple of years. We necked. But it got more intense as we got older, and I guess more sexually mature. In any event, that's how I had my first orgasm, necking in the backseat of a car. I loved it, but I was embarrassed and didn't want my boyfriend to know, so I would pretend nothing was happening. He must have realized that my body slacked up after one of them. It was so thrilling. I still remember positioning my body so that my clitoris (only I didn't know what it was then) was right up against his erection, which I could feel through his pants. Sometimes we were even wearing winter coats, so that gives you some idea of how complicated it was. This whole rubbing stuff taught me how to masturbate, and that's what I would do on those nights that I didn't see my boyfriend. Of course, I tried very hard not to masturbate too often because I thought it must be sinful.

"Eventually we broke up because he went away to graduate school, and I wanted something more . . . who knows what. I met my husband right after graduation. He was almost ten years older and "experienced," which meant he expected sex. He talked me into going to bed with him. I don't really remember the first time except that it hurt a little and wasn't much fun. I guess then he felt guilty because he proposed. I felt guilty because I had been to bed with him, so I married him.

"I must tell the truth, I didn't find sex with my husband anywhere near as sexy as necking with my boyfriend. However, when we had been married three or four weeks, my husband and I spent a Sunday afternoon in bed. He took his time, and even though I wasn't particularly turned on either by him or the situation, I had an orgasm. I remember that it wasn't even that difficult to do, probably because I was a hot young girl. It was only about ten minutes of intercourse, straight missionary position. The orgasm, however, was no-where near as good or intense as the ones I had alone while masturbating or, for that matter, with my coat on with my boyfriend when my whole body would burn.

"Of course, my husband didn't know the difference, and he was very excited that this had happened. You should know that my husband and most of his friends were big into Freud. He considered it a big deal that I was able to have an orgasm through intercourse. He even called a couple of his "Freudian friends" to tell them. I think he thought it proved something about him, and about me.

"I should mention now that that was the first and last time that happened in our marriage. He never again took the time to bring me to orgasm. It's sort of amazing, but true.

"In any event, within a short time I was pregnant because I had inserted the diaphragm incorrectly, and within six months we were having sex maybe once every two weeks. Then somehow I got pregnant again—I didn't think it was possible so soon after having had a child. By the time the second child was three months old, we were really having almost no sex. All the sex we did have was fairly standard stuff. Once I believe he went down on me—I didn't ask, he just did it. But afterward he said he didn't like the taste. He never did it again. I was vocally unhappy about the lack of sex. It made me feel ugly and just awful—although to tell the truth, I wasn't any more interested in him than he was in me. I also masturbated when he wasn't home, and tried to fantasize about other men, but it really wasn't the same anymore. I think I was just depressed.

"He did me the favor of having an affair, which I found out about, so I started having affairs too.

"I was very attracted to the three men I had affairs with, but in every instance the sex was pretty blah. None of these men particularly tried to give me an orgasm. I liked all three more than they liked me. One was married and he lied about it, so I stopped seeing him. The other two really rejected me after a few encounters. They weren't interested in me; I guess it was strictly conquest stuff. With all of them I pretended to

have an orgasm or at least to get very excited. It seemed to
be the thing to do. You have to understand, I *was* very excited
about the prospect of getting excited by them. It was just
never relaxed enough, or lasted long enough to let it happen.

"In the meantime my husband and I got a divorce. Right
after the divorce I got involved with a man who was a premature ejaculator. He was in the strictly wham-bam school.
He acted as though his behavior was totally normal, and he
did nothing to compensate, not even cuddling.

"And then I met a man with whom I had a long, four-year
relationship. Sex was fabulous because I really loved him, and
he could sustain an erection for a very long time. I think he
also loved me in his way. Again, however, I didn't have orgasms. After about forty-five minutes or so I faked them. By
now I was in my thirties, and he was ten years older. I didn't
want him to have a heart attack. I think I had two or three
real orgasms through intercourse in all those years, but that's
all. One I believe was when I was on top. I think he thought
I was having dozens from my carrying on. It would be false
to think I wasn't enjoying the sex, though. I loved it, orgasm
or no orgasm.

"With all of these lovers I didn't expect an orgasm. It was
not written into the contract. I had grown accustomed to not
having orgasms, and I can't say that I really missed them all
that much. Of course, I continued to masturbate, sometimes
every day, sometimes every other day.

"When my children were grown, I entered into a long
relationship with a man and moved into his house. He's the
first man who manipulated my clitoris during intercourse. It
was real easy to have orgasms that way. The only problem
with this relationship was that he was technically a great lover,
but otherwise he was a washout. He didn't have a romantic
or truly sensual bone in his body. He would get on top and
get the job done, for both of us. I felt like I had a service
contract. I must say, however, that I stopped masturbating.
Eventually we split up.

"I guess I should tell you that several of the men after my
husband would try to go down on me to have oral sex, but I
didn't let them. I just felt too inhibited, and I remembered
my husband's reactions.

"Finally in 1985, I ended up with the man I'm with now. I'm in my fifties, so I'm nowhere near as sexual. I don't want it as often; I'm not as turned on. My lover is close to my age, and we will probably get married one of these days. In the meantime we live together in a co-op we mutually own. I have orgasms with him most of the time, primarily orally or through manipulation. I guess I got rid of my inhibitions; something about him makes me feel very secure, and he seems to like doing it a lot. I never have orgasms during intercourse. He doesn't really have enough control to stimulate my clitoris simultaneously—certainly not enough to watch me do it. The sex we have once or twice a week is pretty breathy and hot. He's a very tender and romantic lover and I love him, so I love the sex. Also, he makes sure I come, so I don't feel frustrated. But don't forget I am older. . . ."

Madelyn, 41, married for the third time, no children

"I didn't find out about orgasms until I was in my middle or late twenties. You have to remember when I grew up, people were doing things and lying about them. In high school I had a steady boyfriend, and we necked and petted in the back of his car. I would be fully clothed, but I would manually stimulate my boyfriend to orgasm. I really hated it, but it was sort of expected that if you were going steady, that's what happened. Once I had to take a blue plaid wool skirt to the cleaners, and I was mortified. It had all these dried-up sticky white stains. I knew what they were, and I was sure the cleaner knew too.

"I graduated from college in 1968, and when I was in college, we were all sleeping with boyfriends and saying we were virgins. It all changed a few years later. The people a few years after me were fooling around like crazy, but my friends only had sex with men who said they loved us. I don't think anybody was sleeping around. If you were pinned or engaged, it meant you could have sex. We needed a label to justify our actions, but no one talked about it or admitted that they were doing it.

"I started sleeping with someone I was engaged to, but I knew nothing about birth control; it was just luck that I didn't get pregnant because I was doing nothing. My mother had told me nothing about sex. A close friend did become pregnant that year, and it was very traumatic—for everyone. I don't know if the other women, or their boyfriends, were using something, because we never talked about it.

"I married the second man I slept with. I don't know why except that I thought one was supposed to get married, and he was very appropriate. In six years of marriage I can't say I had one decent sexual experience with him. I don't think it could have been pleasurable for him, either—I was one of those looking-up-at-the-ceiling, when-is-it-going-to-be-over people. I can't imagine a man with any sensitivity enjoying it. There was no intimacy in the marriage on any basis, sexual or emotional. At that time I had never had an orgasm, alone or with him. We got divorced, and I remarried soon thereafter, and I had the same kind of relationship. I guess I always hated change.

"I remember that right before I married my second husband—I was in my late twenties—I was sitting in the kitchen with my cousin, who is my age, and we were talking about men. Her sister, who is four and a half years younger, joined us, and she started to talk about the pleasures of masturbation and orgasms, and we sat there with our mouths hanging open and our eyes bulging. She said, 'If you can't find a guy, just masturbate.' We looked at her like she was from another planet. I had never heard anything like that before. I was shocked, but I think that's what encouraged me to try masturbation.

"My second husband was much more experimental sexually. He encouraged me to try oral sex—both ways. I had never done either before that. I remember talking about it with a woman friend and thinking how much we had all changed; we were beginning to talk to each other about sex in a way that hadn't been possible just a few years before. Everybody seemed to be screwing their brains out, and people were openly acknowledging it. For the first time I had a sense of more permission. I think my generation fell on the cusp as far as having a sense of freedom. I watched *Father Knows Best* and thought that was the way it was supposed to be. Life changed for me in a natural progression, going away to school, getting married, having children, getting divorced, and having a sense that other people were doing the same thing.

"I eventually divorced my second husband because he had affairs, and I couldn't handle it. The marriage disintegrated, and with it our sexual relationship. When I found out about it, I stopped being able to respond to him. Nothing was the same. I tried to forgive and forget, but I couldn't. I couldn't be in bed with him again. My whole sexual response is emotional; if I can't be there emotionally, I can't be there. I had loved him, by the way, but I had never had orgasms with him. But the act of sex itself was wonderful. I loved it, loved being with him. I felt satisfied. I would, however, fake orgasms. It seemed to me to be what he wanted. He was older than me; he expected me to have orgasms from sex. I think he would have been devastated if he knew. Younger men are different.

"I was very lucky to meet my third husband, and I have very satisfying sex with him. I love it, and I love him. I have very deep, very full orgasms when I masturbate, but I can't say that is happening when we have sex. It's my fault, really, because I know that he would be responsive to anything I told him, and I know I could show him how to do it so I could have orgasms. But I can't talk to him about it. This is not his fault—he's the most open, accepting person imaginable. I just can't do it. I'm simply too inhibited. I can't do it."

Donna, 31, happily married and the mother of a two-year-old son, hopes to get pregnant again soon.

"I began to fool around with boys when I was 15 or 16, and by my senior year of high school, I had a steady boyfriend. We didn't have sex, but we did a lot of messing around. Usually we would spend whole afternoons or evenings hanging out in bed. By the time we were seniors, we would take off most of our clothes and we would hang out, necking and petting. We kept our underpants on—that's it. I'm pretty certain my boyfriend had orgasms, although we didn't talk about it. He would put his hands down my panties and rub. It felt good, but nothing really happened. I think some of my friends were going 'all the way,' but I'm not sure. When I started college in 1976, I was still a virgin. The school I went to had a totally coed dorm and few restrictions or curfews as far as socializing was concerned.

"It seems as if all we talked about at school was sex—morning, noon, and night. We would stay up talking about our experiences. Not how to do it, but whether we had and with whom, and whether it was good or bad. For example, there was a lot of talk about whether or not you should sleep with someone who lived in the same dorm, and could friends sleep together and still just be friends? We also talked about birth control a lot. I think there was a certain amount of peer pressure to lose one's virginity. This didn't come from the boys but from one's friends. Everyone was running off to Planned Parenthood to be fitted for a diaphragm. If you weren't doing it, you felt as though you had nothing to contribute to all those conversations.

"I lost my virginity in my freshman year; I was eighteen. My eighteen-year-old boyfriends didn't know much about women's anatomy and orgasms, but they were willing to give it the old college try. They would try to manually stimulate me, and certainly there was oral sex—both ways—but even though it was warm and fun, something was missing. I wasn't having an orgasm.

"In the meantime in the dorm, there was also a lot of talk about orgasms. I remember my friends asking each other, 'Have you had one yet?'

"I decided I had better figure out how to do it myself, and that's what I did. I'm not sure that I knew what was supposed to happen, but I masturbated until I had an orgasm. Once I had managed to have one, it was easy to have others, and I started having them with the guy I was seeing, either through oral or manual stimulation. After about a year of that, in my senior year, I remember I had one through straight intercourse. It's interesting that even though I was having orgasms, I never told my boyfriend, and we never discussed them.

"Thinking back, I can't believe how casual and relaxed we all were about sex. I don't remember anything traumatic or unpleasant happening. Most of the boys I went out with were a little more experienced than me, and it was all very easy.

"After college, in the early eighties, we were just very sexual. Sex was fun and easy and not necessarily out of love. I think I went to bed with a lot of people just to be experimental. My friends were all pretty indiscriminate right after college. Now I'm shocked at how casual we were. Remember there was no AIDS, and everyone was doing it, so it seemed okay. If I cared about somebody, sometimes I would be more reluctant to sleep with him, because it was more important. I think I was very fortunate to have had the sexual experience of my teens and twenties. In my late twenties I met my husband, and now I'm happily married.

"My husband and I have a very relaxed and satisfying sex life. I think he is in love with me, and he certainly tries to please me sexually. I have orgasms both through clitoral stimulation and through intercourse. The orgasms I have through intercourse feel more diffuse, and they may last a little longer. The orgasms I have through clitoral stimulation are more intense. Probably the easiest way for me to have orgasms is through oral sex."

Lori, 22, engaged

Lori was born in the year that *Human Sexual Response* was published. She says she heard people talking about orgasms when she was in . . .

". . . junior high school. That's where I first heard about orgasms, but I didn't know what they were. Then I had one—in gym class. I must have been about 14. We were doing these exercises where you tighten up your abdomen, and wow! I wasn't totally certain, but I figured that's what it was. It was sort of amazing. Then I didn't have any more. I didn't really know about masturbating, and I wasn't doing it.

"In high school I think most people were having sex with their steadies. Sex was very in, and the girls were always talking about orgasms. You were weird if you didn't know what they were, and even if you didn't know, you pretended you did. Most girls pretended they were having them, although I think they probably weren't.

"When I was 16 I started dating, and my boyfriend and I would do a lot of necking and petting. You know, a lot of touching and feeling. We would take most of our clothes off by the time we were finished, down to our underpants. It was sort of silly—I don't know what stopped us from going any further. I think the guys would have always done more, even though the girls wouldn't. The boy I dated and I didn't do anything oral or do anything to bring about an orgasm, for either of us.

"Then when I was 17, I had sex with an older guy. It was nice, but I didn't have anything resembling an orgasm. I thought I had a problem. You know, I had heard so much about them. Most girls lie and say that they do, but it's all just talk, but I didn't know that then. I really thought there was something wrong with me.

"Then one day I was home watching Phil Donahue on television. He had a show about women and orgasms. That Donahue show taught me how women have orgasms; I learned that women need external stimulation, and that they're physically turned on from the outside in—not the other way around. I discovered that most women were like me and had trouble having orgasms. Afterward I talked to my mother about it. I hadn't said anything before, even though she's really terrific and open. She told me that she was the same way, that she needed special stimulation. She told me exactly why and explained about the makeup of the female body and stuff, and of course I understood then. My mother said that it takes time, and that for most women to have an orgasm it takes somebody who knows your body and is willing to take time. When I met the man I'm with, I could be very honest, which I was. I explained to him, so he tried and tried. He did everything—oral sex, hands, straight sex, and eventually it happened.

"I think most women my age have the same problem and don't have orgasms, except through masturbation, which they don't admit. I think you need to know your partner really well.

"I'm very lucky because I've been with the same man for three years. We're getting married soon; I really love him and he loves me, but a lot of my friends are really affected by the AIDS thing. They've stopped sleeping around, and there is very little promiscuity. It really has to be worth the risk before most women will go to bed with a guy—and they are using condoms. I know most of my women friends carry them, just in case."

WOMEN AND ORGASMS

A common belief among men and women alike is that it takes women longer to reach orgasm than it does men. It seemed to us to be interesting to note that when Kinsey published *Sexual Behavior in the Human Female* in 1953, he questioned this notion, saying, "Apparently many females, even though they may be slow to respond in coitus, may masturbate to orgasm in a matter of a minute or two. Masturbation thus appears to be a better test than coitus of the female's actual capacities; and there seems to be something in the coital technique which is responsible for her slower responses there."

Thirty-five years later, most women are still having problems with orgasms and the coital technique. Unlike men, who can give clear-cut answers as to how often they prefer to have sex, how long it takes them to reach orgasm, how much down time they require between erections, etc., women tend to be vague and uncertain as to their own natural rhythms and patterns. When asked how long it takes her to reach orgasm, the typical woman responds with an ambiguous answer, usually indicating that it depends upon the circumstances and what is being done to her, and by whom.

This makes perfect sense when one takes into consideration that in traditional sex-role relationships, the rhythm and pacing of sex is still pretty much determined by the man and set by his sexual pattern and drive. The woman who is involved with a man who requires twenty minutes of hard thrusting before orgasm is going to have a totally different view from the woman whose lover reaches orgasm after two minutes of gentle stroking. For these reasons, even if a woman is able to reach orgasm through intercourse, which she can sometimes do only in certain positions, she is often extraordinarily unclear as to how long it takes her to do so.

Even those women, whose husbands and lovers regularly stimulate them to orgasm through oral or manual methods, are dependent upon the man "finding the right spot," determining the motion and rhythm that work for the woman, and continuing it long enough for her to climax. In reality, all these factors often produce stumbling blocks or a kind of stop/start activity.

The only experience that seems to provide a woman with a clear-cut view of her sexual responses is masturbation, either manually or with a vibrator. Among the women we spoke to, those who are uninhibited about their needs for orgasm and who have chosen to masturbate to fulfill their sexual needs tended to know exactly how often they wanted orgasm, how long it took them to reach orgasm, how many they wanted, etc.

Carol is an example of a woman who is very clear about her sexual needs. She was married and divorced when she was still quite young. After her divorce she had sexual relationships with several men before she settled down with a man who she says she adores.

"I'm Catholic. I'm 39, and when I was growing up, Catholic girls didn't have sex. What they did instead was grind against their boyfriends, with their clothes on, of course. I ground my way to orgasm pretty consistently, starting in my late teens and until I was married to my first real boyfriend. We had sex before marriage, which is probably why I married him. Anyway, after marriage, sex became a nightly affair. I really hated the sex, which became fairly perfunctory, because I grew to hate him. I was just all wrong for him. He wanted a wife who could clean, and I wanted a career. So he spent most of his time pointing out my imperfections, and I grew to resent his demands. Eventually we divorced.

"I began to date and quickly got involved in a series of

relationships—some of which were very satisfying sexually, some of which were not. None of them were very gratifying emotionally.

"Somewhere in all those years I bought myself a vibrator, and since then I have never been sexually unsatisfied. It's wonderful. I use it every morning and every night—no matter what is happening in my life. I discovered that I like an orgasm, sometimes two, before I go to work. The same thing is true at night. So that's what I have.

"I think my vibrator is partially responsible for the happiness of my current relationship. I adore Gary, who is the best man in the entire world, the kindest, the sweetest, the most thoughtful. He does everything he can to satisfy me sexually, and I do everything I can to satisfy him. But if I were to depend on him for all my sexual satisfaction, we would have split up a long time ago. He has very little control, and he is often too tired to feel sexual. He is never too tired to be emotionally supportive or to make me dinner or massage my neck or make me feel good about myself.

"I've had enough bad experiences with men to be extremely grateful that I'm involved with a good man who loves me. I love him. But for sexual satisfaction, it's my vibrator, 'Old Faithful.' Every morning, every night."

Women who never have learned for themselves the full extent of their capacity for sexual pleasure, and have relied upon the sexual pattern and pacing of their particular partners, are often astonishingly unclear as to the extent of their own sexual drive.

Hazel, who is a happily married 47-year-old artist, lives in the Southwest with her second husband and the youngest of their five children. She was in her late thirties before she discovered that she was somewhat of a statistical anomaly in that she appears to be capable of reaching orgasm through a variety of methods.

"I grew up in a different era. All my mother ever told me about sex was to keep my legs tightly crossed and nothing would happen to me. She actually told me to practice by putting an aspirin between my knees. My family is Jewish; although they weren't Orthodox, they were still fairly religious and quite repressed. I remember that I had some strong sexual feelings as a teenager, but I didn't know what they meant. I think I tried to masturbate three or four times, but I was guilty about continuing, and I don't remember having an orgasm. I knew somehow it was a bad thing. You must realize that until I graduated from high school I honestly thought you could get pregnant from letting a boy lie on top of you, even if you were both fully clothed and nothing else happened.

"In my junior year of college I fell madly in love with a boy in my class. That's the first time I really necked. I thought I was going to marry him, so in my senior year I let him touch my breasts. I was so excited that I had an orgasm—but it was not that intense an experience. Shortly after he touched my breasts, he rejected me because I didn't know what a quiche was. Once, in a restaurant, a waiter asked if I wanted to try the quiche. I didn't know what he was talking about. My boyfriend said he wanted to marry someone who understood the finer things in life. I guess I flunked his test.

"All this meant is that I was so heartbroken that I got involved on the rebound, with a young man in the Army. I didn't really know him, and I spent very little time with him because he was in the service, but he said he loved me, wrote me long letters, and proposed. We engaged in *no* sexual experimentation before marriage except some light necking, and on our wedding night I was a true virgin. I had no idea what to expect, or what I should do.

"My mother had sent me to a gynecologist. I guess she thought the doctor, a woman, would fill me in on the facts. The woman said I was too tight and that my husband would never be able to break my hymen, so she did it in the office. It hurt so much that I screamed.

"My first husband, Ben, and I had a religious ceremony and a small reception. Then we went to a resort for our honeymoon. That first night I remember getting dressed for bed and lying down. Ben came into the room and proceeded to start performing oral sex on me. I had no idea what he was doing. I couldn't believe it. I thought he was some kind of nut! Then he entered me, pumped a couple of times, and had an orgasm; it was definitely less than a minute. A part of me was glad that it was so short, because it really hurt. My husband was, as they say, very well-endowed. It was long and thick.

"Maybe it hurt for everyone then because we expected it to hurt. There were two other couples honeymooning that we became friendly with, and when the three wives got together, we would go tee-hee and talk about how much it hurt, and how much we hated it. As a matter of fact, I don't remember any young wife saying anything else. Of course, nobody shared any of the details.

"For the next ten years my husband and I had basically the same kind of sex. He never lasted longer than a minute, if that long. But I didn't know anything else, or expect anything else. I thought it was normal. My husband never in any way indicated that it was abnormal. After about two years of marriage I started to have orgasms from oral sex with my husband. They were very tiny and shallow, but they were still orgasms. In the meantime the sexual revolution was happening around me. I read a few books, saw a few magazine articles, etc., and somehow I got a vibrator. I don't even remember how. I must have been so embarrassed that I blocked all the details, but I had this vibrator and a small stack of semi-erotic literature. I hid everything, and about twice a month, while my husband was at work, I masturbated with my vibrator. I was pretty guilty about it, and I would usually have one orgasm each time, if I was lucky. But my orgasms from the vibrator, although they were better than the ones from oral sex, were nothing to write home about.

"We had three children. I started painting, and he played golf. We could have gone on this way except that after ten years he became impotent. And I became upset. I didn't understand it. I thought he was rejecting me. I thought he was having an affair. I thought he no longer found me desirable. So after about the tenth time it happened, I exploded. I didn't know that anger is the worst thing you can do with someone who is impotent. It just made it worse. We continued this way for about a year. He would have a couple of months where he could perform, and then about six months when he couldn't. He kept telling me that it wasn't me, but I didn't believe him. I started wearing different clothes, tight pants and low-cut jerseys and lacy underwear. I just wanted to appear sexual.

"In the meantime, at my suggestion, Ben had seen a urologist and a psychiatrist and an internist. Finally someone suggested Masters and Johnson, and that's when my life changed.

"First of all, the therapists at M and J asked how long sex lasted. When I told them, they told me about premature ejaculation. My husband had had a problem, and I hadn't even known it. I learned a lot about sex at Masters and Johnson. I learned that I could be oral with a man, and it wasn't dirty and it wasn't a sin. I learned that it was okay to have pleasure from sex. And I learned how to communicate my needs and my feelings.

"Masters and Johnson were trying to treat Ben for both the impotence and the premature ejaculation, and they gave us exercises. We were supposed to stimulate and arouse each other. The problem was that when I managed to arouse Ben and he got an erection, he was so excited that he had an orgasm in a few seconds, often before penetrating. By the time we left Masters and Johnson, I knew I didn't want to stay with him. He had made me feel bad by his impotence —to this day I think he was having an affair and was guilty about it; although I felt sorry for him, I couldn't deal with it any longer. It was awful. Half of the time when I would touch him, he would turn white and his hands would get all clammy and he'd start perspiring. He was that anxious at the idea of touching me. It was awful.

"We separated, and I think actually Ben was grateful. I had known Al, my present husband, for a long time because his daughter and mine were friends, and after his wife died, we would see each other when the girls got together. We got pretty friendly. Once we even double-dated. We were both with other people. I thought we were just friends.

"Finally we figured out that there was an attraction between the two of us, and we went out. I had already told him all about Ben's sexual problems, because I needed a male friend, and he was very supportive.

"Well, the first time we went to bed, Al couldn't get an erection. Well, you can imagine the way I felt. I became hysterical. Here he was, the second man I was going to bed with and he was also impotent. I decided it had to be me, and I began sobbing. Al tried to reassure me. He said it was because I was very important to him. I liked hearing it, but I didn't believe it. He was telling the truth because sixteen years later, that was the first and last time he had problems. We finally made love the next morning. It was okay, but it was still awkward.

"We started seeing each other seriously, and I definitely fell in love with him. We made love a lot in the next two months and the sex got much better, but I wasn't having orgasms. I don't know what happened, whether I just became less tense or whether I had grown to realize that I could take Al's sexuality for granted. There was nothing fragile about his sexuality. I didn't have to worry about whether he was going to get it up or keep it up. He was always interested and acted like he really wanted me sexually, and he could keep it up as long as I wanted him to. So I began to relax. Then one weekend we went away; we spent most of the weekend in bed, and I had what I call the first genuine orgasm of my life. It was incredible.

"From that point on, there was no stopping me. I discovered that I could have amazing orgasms. I became like a crazy person. I wanted them all the time. I drove Al crazy too. I didn't let him go to work in the morning. I kept him up at night. It's funny, but he would sometimes plead with me to let him get some sleep already. I really became like a nymphomaniac. For a while I was upset—I thought there was something wrong with me. I even went to a doctor to make sure that something hadn't happened to my body. I thought maybe something had slipped and was in a different position. I couldn't figure out what happened. That year I discovered that I could have orgasms in a whole batch of ways. I can even have orgasms when I'm with him when he isn't even touching me, just because I get so hot. Now I can easily have six or seven orgasms in an hour of lovemaking. I have to build to each one, but it only takes a few minutes. I think my orgasms are vaginal. That's what it feels like to me. They're like explosions. I also release fluid when I reach orgasm. I know they say this is impossible, but I can feel it. There is an accompanying feeling of heat. It's a fantastic sensation, but I've become more restrained. I don't need them, or want them, every day anymore."

WHAT WOMEN SAY
ABOUT THEIR SEXUAL RESPONSES

Most Women Say That for Them
Sex Is Emotional as Well as Physical

When you ask enough women about their sexual responses, you quickly notice that you are getting two different kinds of answers. Some women tell you how often they need and want the satisfaction of sex and orgasm. Others tell you how thrilled and responsive they are to the emotional connection of sex with an intimate partner.

When asked about the importance of an emotional response, Marcie, 32, a divorced single, had a typical answer.

"For me, sex is both emotional and physical. To tell the truth, I think my body, or the physical part of me, is always ready for sex, but I keep it on a back burner and don't act on that part until I meet somebody who I respond to emotionally. When I go to bed with someone, I give emotionally as well as physically. It's too painful for me to sleep with somebody unless there is that dual connection."

We were genuinely surprised that we heard so few women talking about sex for sex's sake, without an emotional component. We had thought that more women, particularly the younger women, would have given us different answers. Several women did tell us that they went through brief periods, usually when they were in their early twenties, when they acted on many of their purely physical urges, but with the exception of one or possibly two atypical women who described periods in their lives when they preferred to have casual sex with anonymous strangers, the women we spoke to were clearly uncomfortable with such behavior.

Most Women Also Say That They Don't Need to Be Emotionally Attracted to Feel Physical Attraction. They Just Prefer Not to Act Out on Most of Their Purely Sexual Responses.

However, most women also pointed out that they didn't need to feel emotionally involved or "in love" to want sex—they just preferred to disregard sexual feelings unless the emotional component was also present. The average woman we spoke to said that she was able to distinguish between love and lust, at least at the beginning, but she preferred not to go to bed with a man unless there was at least some potential for a more serious involvement. Women gave two reasons for this. The primary one: Many women still say that once they give in to a purely physical urge, they find that their emotions come along with their bodies, and that after the fact, they have a harder time separating the physical from the emotional. And for women, there is also always the realistic consideration of pregnancy. Nina, a 28-year-old woman who went through a brief period of promiscuity, described the way she felt.

"I thought I would be able to just mess around and forget about it, but that wasn't the case. I went to bed with a couple of guys who were totally inappropriate just to satisfy some sort of romantic ideal of the totally free woman. It didn't work for me. I still believe in it in principle, but if my body responded to someone, I would start to have feelings. Then, if the man was detached, I would feel hurt. It was sort of silly. I remember one guy, a 21-year-old beach-boy type with a terrific body. We picked each other up at a sporting-goods store—we were both very flirtatious. Well, one thing led to another and we ended up in his room. He was clearly a kid but he was a pretty good lover. Enthusiastic, you know. Afterward, for some reason, he began to talk about his girlfriend, and I, believe it or not, felt hurt. It was just stupid."

In short, many women still say that when they responded physically, they wanted to give emotionally, and in many situations these feelings were just inappropriate.

And then, of course, there is the possibility of pregnancy. Women told us that despite the liberalized abortion laws and newer contraceptive techniques, spontaneous sex with the handsome stranger often leads to shoddy birth-control methods. As one 29-year-old woman put it: "One night of sex does not compensate for two weeks of anxiety about pregnancy. Sure you can get pregnant with someone you're involved with, too, but when there is a relationship, the relationship is more likely to be worth the risk. Also, you tend to be less careless with someone you know."

And finally, there are the issues surrounding AIDS and other sexually transmitted diseases. Women seem to be much more concerned about the possibility of being exposed than men, and for the most part, single women told us that they were conscientiously avoiding casual sex.

However, quite a few women have told us that over the course of several years they have ended up having sex with many men with whom they don't have an emotional connection. Diane, 25, said, "I've slept with a couple of dozen men, but usually it's because I want more of a relationship to develop. When it doesn't, I have no desire to continue a relationship based upon casual sex." Diane and other women state that they have no way of knowing which sexual encounters are going to develop into serious relationships, explaining that sex is part of the natural progression that a relationship takes. Diane also said, "Not all sexual encounters turn into relationships or marriages, but some of them do, and how do you know what's going to develop, unless you take a chance?"

As another woman told us, "Sex is one of the things that happens between two people who are developing a relationship. Unless you sleep with a man, how do you know whether or not you want to continue? There is an element of risk there, but sometimes you have to take it."

THE EMOTIONAL RESPONSE— WHAT WOMEN MEAN

Women frequently talk about "needing to feel an emotional connection." We asked women exactly what they meant. Here are some of their responses.

"When I was first married, I was very impressed with my husband, and very emotionally involved with him. I wanted to know everything about him, what he did, what he felt, what he thought. Then sex was thrilling. When we went out together, I would be proud to be with him, and I couldn't wait to go home and go to bed with him. Gradually I discovered that he wasn't the person I thought he was. He was stingy and cheap and completely selfish. I turned off on him, and with that I turned off on sex."

"I've learned the hard way that what counts most for me is the emotional connection. That's what makes me melt. Maybe it has to do with trust. I don't know. I *do* know that those times that I've gotten into relationships with people where I didn't have a true emotional connection, even though there was a strong physical attraction, I've ended up really hating them, and hating the sex."

"My whole sexual existence is emotional. It's the intimacy that excites me. There are times when I've felt as though I was having an out-of-body experience, but it's always because of what's happening in my head, not my body. . . . I love the eye contact, and the sense that the sex is bringing us closer together."

"I'd like to be able to say that I had a purely physical response, but I know it's not true because I'm too easily hurt by a lover."

"I don't know what it is to just want to have sex with someone. If I want to sleep with a man, it means I want to share a lot of things. It's never pure sex with me."

"I was married to a man who used to sleep around. When I found out, he would tell me that it was just sex, that it had nothing to do with me. I couldn't understand what he was talking about. It would never be just sex to me. His affairs made me feel abandoned, and I didn't want to sleep with someone I couldn't trust with my feelings. I got divorced so I would be able to look for someone else who didn't make me feel bad. I want the whole ball of wax with one person—I can't separate love from sex."

HOW WOMEN HAVE ORGASMS

The fact is that some women have an easy time having orgasms and can have them under almost any circumstances, anyplace and anytime, and some women have a tremendously difficult time having orgasms and can have them under only the most ideal conditions. Most women are someplace in the middle; they can have them most of the time, as long as they are receiving the kind of physical stimulation they require.

Women and Masturbation

Statistically we understand that there are women who cannot have orgasms under any conditions whatsoever, but we didn't talk to anyone who couldn't reach orgasm through masturbation. This is not to say that these women don't exist, but clearly they are rare.

As far as orgasms are concerned, for many women masturbation is the method of choice. Lots of women, even those who are in satisfying relationships, find that masturbation is the only sure way to reach orgasm. A few of these women sometimes masturbate in front of their partners after sex, but most of the time the women masturbate in privacy.

The scenario that Joanna, 28, describes is familiar to many women.

"I don't always have orgasms during sex. Sometimes I do, but sometimes I don't. When I don't, sometimes my boyfriend helps me come, usually manually. We sort of both do it together. But much of the time he seems to want to think that it's not necessary. Sometimes I say something like, 'Honey, could you get me some tea?' and I finish quickly by myself. Other times I wait until he is asleep and I get out of bed and go into another room and masturbate. I'm pretty excited by the sex with him, so it doesn't take more than a minute."

Many women who are not having sexual relationships depend upon masturbation as a regular means of sexual satisfaction. Several books, including *The Hite Report,* have described the different ways in which women masturbate, and as Masters and Johnson pointed out, no two women appear to use exactly the same method. Some women lie on their backs, others lie on their stomachs. Some women masturbate using a stream of water in the shower or bathtub; some use one hand, others use two; etc.

And, of course, there are women who prefer vibrators, saying it is less effort and more efficient. Other women said they thought vibrators were too mechanical and distracting.

How often a woman masturbates depends upon the intensity of her sexual drive and varies from woman to woman. Obviously there are periods in every woman's life when she is masturbating more than others. A fair number of the younger women who talked to us said that they masturbated at least once or twice a day.

Orgasm from Intercourse Without Clitoral Stimulation

As most of us know, Freud made a big deal about the so-called vaginal orgasm. Shere Hite, among others, has pointed out that a very small percentage of women reach orgasm without some form of clitoral stimulation. And we did talk to a few women who said that they regularly had orgasms from penetration alone. These women said that straight intercourse was the preferred method of reaching orgasm.

Further, these women indicated that their orgasms were extremely intense; three of these women said that they felt that they released a fluid, somewhat in the same way that a man ejaculates, when they reached orgasm. A couple of these women were quite adamant in defending the vaginal orgasm, saying that although the vaginal orgasm may be pure myth for many women, for them it was a reality. As one woman in a long-term happy marriage said, "I'm a penetration lady. It's always been strictly penetration for me, and it is the method that has always worked, through thirty years of marriage. I know that it's not supposed to be possible, but that's the way I am."

However, the vast majority of the women we talked to said that they required clitoral stimulation, and except in a few rare and isolated instances, they did not and could not reach orgasm from penetration alone. Maria, a 38-year-old single woman, said, "It's never happened and I don't expect it to happen. I think I would know by now if it was going to."

As for the isolated occasions, several women said they had reached orgasm through penetration a few, very rare, times. Liz, 42, said:

"In an entire lifetime of sex, with two marriages as well as a dozen other partners, I've only been able to reach orgasm through intercourse five times. I remember all five instances quite clearly.

"Once when I first started sleeping with my second husband, we had been making love on and off for about two days. I didn't feel I knew him well enough to suggest oral sex or to tell him that I wasn't having orgasms. So I was pretending to have them—faking them, which wasn't hard because I was extremely hot and very excited by everything about him, the way he looked, smelled, felt, etc. He was just a fabulous lover, so it was easy to make noises and act thrilled. It was genuine. Finally on the second afternoon after two days of intense excitement, he was exhausted. He just couldn't have another orgasm himself, but he was still erect . . . and he just kept going. Well, I had my first orgasm through intercourse. With nothing else . . . no clitoral massage."

Among the women who don't regularly orgasm from intercourse, all indicated that the orgasms were not as gratifying as those they have with clitoral stimulation. Liz told us: "The truth: It was a major disappointment. It just wasn't as great as the buildup. As a matter of fact, none of my five orgasms from intercourse have been that spectacular. All were sort of a letdown. And all of them were a lot of work."

Orgasm Through Intercourse with Clitoral Stimulation via Positioning

Many women said they were better able to reach orgasm when they were the person on top. These women told us that there were essentially two reasons why they found it easier to reach orgasm in this position.

First, a woman is able to position her clitoris in such a way as to receive direct stimulation from her partner's body.

Second, in this position a woman is able to establish her own rhythm and pace the sex to her satisfaction, thus maximizing her chances of bringing herself to climax.

But as several women told us, just because they find it easier to achieve orgasm in this position doesn't mean that they want to do it this way all the time.

Debbie is an example of a woman who finds it "very easy to have an orgasm as long as I'm on top. But it's boring to do that all the time. I also like the sensation of a man on top, or lying on my side. It's different, but no less enjoyable. I figure that if I don't come during sex, I can always get off orally. I sometimes prefer that."

Another thing that women mentioned about the position of being on top is that a fair number of men seem to resent it. A few women told us that they had known men who had complained when the woman wanted to be on top. One woman said that her lover said that he felt as though he was being used: "If I'm on top and moving so that I can have an orgasm, he will complain that I'm using his body to masturbate on. He doesn't like it."

Orgasm Through Intercourse Combined with Direct Clitoral Stimulation

This is the position that many women describe as the "no miss" for orgasm. In this position, once penetration has occurred, either the man or the woman simultaneously stimulate the clitoris directly. One woman said, "I like the feeling of my vagina clutching something. So it resolves that. And it puts extra pressure against the genital area, which helps. It's sort of like everything that needs to be touched gets touched. There is almost no way to miss."

Women have a whole variety of preferred positions. Some women swear that this is best done in the missionary position, while the woman stimulates herself. Other women suggest lying on their side, or with legs crisscrossed, while the man rhythmically touches the clitoris. Other women say that it is easiest when they are on top, in which case either the man or the woman can comfortably touch the clitoris. A couple of women said that they preferred a positon in which the man achieved entry from behind, and then either the man or the woman simultaneously stroked or manipulated the clitoris.

Women reminded us, however, that there are men who seem to resent either touching a woman or having a woman touch herself during sex. Some men actually will push a woman's hands away from her clitoris.

One woman told this story: "My ex-husband was always extremely upset that I couldn't climax during sex. I had been with a man who would touch me while he was in me, so I tried to indicate, without telling my husband how I knew, that I would be able to reach orgasm this way. I said that I had read about it in a women's magazine. He got all huffy and said that that wasn't real sex—it was masturbation. He didn't want to try it. I think he felt threatened by it."

Of course, other men are turned on by watching a woman touch her clitoris, or by doing it for her. One man mentioned that he finds that it intensifies female vaginal contractions, and hence increases his pleasure.

Some women say that they use their vibrators to stimulate the clitoris during penetration, in which case the man also receives an additional sensation. One woman describes the method she and her husband employ: "This is the easiest, quickest way for me to have an orgasm. While we are lying on our sides and he maintains a position inside me, we put the vibrator against my clitoris. For me this is so simple; it is an orgasm with no real work."

Oral Sex

"I like it best because it's warmer, wetter, and more intimate."

—*38-year-old single woman*

And that sort of sums up the feelings of the fans of oral sex. Some talk about the highly charged and intimate quality; other women say that nothing else makes them feel more vulnerable while still being in control. Several mentioned the emotional satisfactions of having a man perform oral sex.

"If someone does that, it sort of indicates that he really cares. It makes me feel loved and tended to; it's also a great way to get off. If I can relax long enough, chances are it's going to work because there is so much stimulation."

Other women point out that so many problem factors are avoided.

"If my husband is willing to take the time to bring me to orgasm orally, then it really doesn't matter how much of an erection he has, how long it lasts, or what he does with it. Knowing that oral sex is there as an option makes me much less anxious about my orgasms and takes the performance pressure off him."

Quite a few women mentioned that they had been with men who absolutely refused to perform oral sex, or who did so and then complained about it. This kind of experience often left the woman feeling inhibited about trying it again.

On the other hand, other women told us, and men indicated, that there were oral-sex junkies, men who were practically addicted to it. At least two women complained, only half jokingly, that they were involved with men who wanted to perform oral sex all the time and wanted them to have orgasms from it all the time. One of these women said that she could only have one orgasm, but her boyfriend was determined to prove that she could have several. The end result was that she often found herself feeling pressured.

Several men made a point of mentioning how much they enjoyed oral sex, saying that they were particularly good lovers because they were very knowledgeable about bringing women to orgasm this way.

These men said that they preferred to use oral sex to bring the woman to orgasm before penetration because they felt it was a turn-on for them and it made the woman very responsive.

A fair number of women said that their favorite method of reaching orgasm was through a combination of oral sex and manual stimulation. One said, "If my lover uses his tongue and then inserts one or two fingers in my vagina, I'm a goner."

Orgasms Through Manual Manipulation Alone

Many women had problems with this method and said that it only worked "when the man had great hands." Many women felt that most men did not have great hands. Some typical comments:

"The average man acts like he's playing some sort of exotic sport. They just don't get it. They think if they do it harder it's better, or if they do it faster it's better."

"Some women find it intensely painful to have direct pressure applied to the clitoris directly. I'm one of them. I've tried telling guys that. They always act like they understand, and then the next time . . . same thing."

"My husband acts like he's sawing wood with his fingers. He's a klutz in that department."

"There is, of course, the exceptional man who has hands of velvet; however, they are few and far between."

How Many Orgasms Can a Woman Have?

As foolish as this question may seem, it is one that is often asked, so . . . the answer is that it depends, as illustrated by the different answers we received from women:

"I can only have one orgasm. It's a very nice orgasm, but it's only one. Afterward I am just incapable of reaching a second climax."

"I have a terrible time reaching the first orgasm, but once I've had one, the second is easier. Then sometimes I even have a couple more small ones."

"My husband and I have counted because I have so many. One night I had twelve. Each one of them is separate, and I have to build to all of them, but I can keep going until I'm totally exhausted."

Not Having Orgasms Does Not Equal "Frigidity"

The whole notion of using the word *frigidity* to mean inorgasmic is not just old-fashioned; it is also totally incorrect. Frigid means cold, and as just about any woman can tell you, it is possible to be really "hot" and still not have an orgasm. An absence of orgasms does not mean an absence of pleasure. Some comments from women:

"I've had some very, very good sex without having an orgasm. I remember being as hot as a firecracker and still not having an orgasm. Being hot means being totally turned on, on fire, sizzling. Having an orgasm can be completely mechanical, you know, like playing pinball."

"Being excited by someone and enjoying the sex is an emotional as well as a physical experience. Orgasms are a lot of work sometimes, and for me they can mean turning away from the pleasure of the sex and concentrating on the one spot on my genitals which will produce an orgasm. I don't always want to do that—I'm having too good a time."

"I've never had an orgasm during sex. But I want you to know that I really love sex."

Not Having Orgasms Does Not Equal Not Wanting Them

However, even though a woman can enjoy sex without having an orgasm, most women want to be able to have them with their partners. The typical woman we spoke to said that it is infinitely more gratifying and intimate than having them alone.

The experts say that if a woman can have an orgasm while masturbating, she should be able to show her partner how to do it for her. That is, if he is willing to follow her lead.

But a lot of women say that they are too inhibited to show a man what to do unless he asks. But they do wish that he would ask. Other women say that they try to indicate what they need, but their partner doesn't pay attention:

"I reach orgasm through masturbation every time. I don't reach orgasm, or at least a good orgasm, through sex most of the time. Why? We always have sex according to his rhythm and his way. I don't have that many problems, and I know he wants me to have an orgasm, but he wants to do it *his way*, through fucking. His way doesn't work for me. He never brings the subject up, and I don't know how to."

"My husband is pretty liberated and I know he would do whatever I wanted, but he never asks, and I don't know how to tell him. I always reach orgasm, either orally or through manipulation, but it's a fairly weak orgasm because I really need simultaneous vaginal penetration or pressure applied to the outside of the vagina to have a satisfying orgasm. I don't know what to tell him."

"I've been with men who ask, but they always ask as if they don't want to know, or else they become so clinical or voyeuristic that I can't communicate."

"I've heard men complain about women who give instructions. I don't want to be like that. But to be honest, I've given up on having orgasms with my husband.

"Let me tell you what it's like. Up front, you should know that I love my husband, that I'm very attracted to him, very turned on by him. I feel as if he loves me a lot, and basically I'm a very happy woman. But as far as orgasms during sex with him . . . forget it. Here's what happens.

"We get into bed, and we start kissing and petting. I love performing oral sex on him until he gets erect, and that's what we do. It gets me very excited. That's when we start having problems. He starts to either perform oral sex on me or manipulate me, and he does it wrong. I've tried moving his hands to the right place. I've moaned and put my fingers where I want them. He pushes them away. He wants to do it himself ! His way! By now, instead of getting more excited, I'm getting more annoyed, and I'm beginning to get physically irritated. So I indicate I would rather have him inside me. He gets inside me, which I find very exciting, and if he just spent a minute on my clitoris, or let me do it myself while he was in me, I would have an orgasm that way. But no! Again, I try to indicate that's what I want. But if he does it, he does it for maybe ten seconds, and if I try to put my hands there, he pushes them away, which makes me feel very inhibited. I'm afraid that if I masturbate in front of him, he'll get turned off or upset. And he acts as if that's what would happen when he pushes my hands away.

"Also, you have to understand, my husband doesn't have any sexual problems or anything, but he's not a major stud.

He's not one of those guys who gets hard in a second and stays hard no matter what. He's very sensitive, which is one of the things I like about him. How can I start criticizing what he's doing in bed without making him feel bad? And he never asks or follows my lead when I try to show him. I love the intimacy of our sex; I love it when he gets excited and when he comes. I love the expression on his face. But I've given up on orgasms. I don't complain, it's not worth upsetting what we have by complaining. I wait till he takes a shower, then I masturbate. I have better orgasms by myself. I get more turned on with him, but I have better orgasms by myself."

Women Who Have Never Reached Orgasm with Men

We talked to a few women who said that they had never had an orgasm during sex with a man, no matter what the man did—oral sex, manual manipulation, protracted intercourse.

These women were, however, capable of reaching orgasm through solitary masturbation.

Linda, for example, says that she is quite open with her current lover and has told him that she thinks it is practically impossible for her to reach orgasm with a man: "I've had four lovers in my life, and although I enjoy sex a great deal, I seem to have a hard time when it comes to orgasms. My parents were very repressive about sex, and I think I'm inhibited. I have orgasms using a vibrator, so I know I'm orgasmic. I never fake orgasms because I think it's dishonest, but I know that my boyfriend is bothered by it; he tries everything, and sometimes I think I'm going to come, and then inevitably something happens—like the phone rings, or I get a cramp in my leg, or my boyfriend has to change positions."

Patti, who is in her early forties, said: "I can't say it's my husband's fault. He would do anything I asked. He's very open and very connected to me. It's me. I'm just too repressed to tell him what I need. I fake orgasms. I always have."

Orgasms, Emotions, and the Control Issue

As far as the connection between orgasms and emotions, we heard two diametrically opposed points of view. Some women definitely felt that orgasms were purely mechanical. If someone pushed the right button the right number of times, they would eventually climax. One woman who felt this way said, "By the time my marriage ended, I hated my first husband, hated him. And I was never that attracted to him. However, even though I wasn't all that excited, he automatically hit the right spot, and it was real easy to have orgasms. I love my current husband and am very attracted to him, but I often end up faking orgasms because I don't want him to feel bad."

Others were equally adamant that they had to be emotionally tuned in. One 36-year-old woman who has had several long-term lovers said, "In order to really climax, I always have to feel as if I am in love. Then I'm a sexual pushover. Without that feeling I'm just never involved enough."

The women who could not reach orgasms with their partners mentioned the fear of losing control. One of them said, "I have to believe that there is a control issue with me . . . that if I were to release to a man the one thing I can do for myself and allow him to bring me to orgasm, I would be giving up total control. As long as I am the one who controls this, then I am the boss. I accept the fact that I'll never be able to reach orgasm through intercourse, and to trust a man to bring you to orgasm through oral sex is giving over even more power. It makes you so much more vulnerable . . . I don't think I'll ever be able to do that."

HOW DO MEN REACT TO THE FEMALE ORGASM?

"When you first start sleeping with women, you're too worried about *your* orgasm to pay much attention to theirs. You just don't know. Guys talk about it, but not with any real detail, and usually just to show off what great studs they are. I slept with a lot of women and I don't know if they got off because I don't think I was doing it right. Finally one really showed me what to do. You know, it's like having a baseball, having a bat, having cleats and a diamond. It's not until someone coaches you and you play a couple of seasons before things start really coming together, before you learn the difference between a curveball and a slider."

—*26-year-old single male*

Men tell us that they are confused, not only by how women have orgasms but also by their attitudes. The average man doesn't understand it when a woman doesn't have an orgasm. To him it means that she's not enjoying sex, even if she says she is—and it implies that he is an inadequate lover. Most men expect to have orgasms from sex, and therefore they can't believe that women don't feel the same way. For some men the idea that the woman isn't having orgasms seems to be very threatening. How does the individual man deal with this? From the men and women we have spoken to, there are several definite patterns.

The Man Who Doesn't Get Very Specific About Orgasms

This man is essentially noncommunicative about sex. He doesn't know how to raise the essential issues, and he has often been conditioned by women who "fake it," or by women who are equally uncommunicative. It isn't that he would prefer not to know if his partner isn't having orgasms, it's just that he doesn't know how to deal with the answer. His partner often is equally not forthcoming. Here are just a few examples:

"I'm not entirely sure that I'm satisfying my wife. I think I am. She tells me that the sex is fine, but she never tells me much more than that. I realize that she's not very verbal, but I can't help but worry whether she is telling me the truth. I always ask her if there is anything else I should do, and she always says, 'No, I'm fine.' But I don't know what that means."

"My wife tells me that her friend can't have orgasms from intercourse, and that her friend's husband has to do special things after or before sex. I don't know whether this means my wife wants special things too. I try to ask, but we don't ever really seem to discuss it."

"After ten years of sex I discovered that my wife was faking orgasms. I discovered it because I read *The Hite Report*. She read it, too, and she left it lying around, so I know she wanted me to see it. We didn't discuss it, but I started taking more time with her clitoris. I figured she was faking them to keep me happy, so I never said anything, but now I'm sure she has them. We've still never talked about the difference. But I think she likes me more."

The Man Who Is Willing to Try Everything

Some men are genuinely gung ho on women and orgasms. Their enthusiasm is overwhelming. Some typical comments:

"When a woman has an orgasm, it makes you think she's crazy about you, which is probably a big lie, but it's a terrific feeling. When a woman doesn't have an orgasm, I feel bad. It's not that I feel like I failed. I realize that it's complicated, that it's nowhere as easy as it is for a man, but I like to do everything I can."

"The second woman I was with was an expert on how she came. She showed me everything, and so now I do the same thing with every woman I'm with. I ask her to show me, to show me how she would do it for herself. Then I take my cue from that. It's the best way to do it."

Some of these same men complain, however, that women are sometimes not particularly helpful, and recount long, drawn-out sagas of trying to bring a woman to orgasm.

"It was very easy getting Barbara to climax through oral sex, but she didn't want to do that. She wanted to do it the

old-fashioned way, so I suggested she get on top, because
some women have an easier time that way. So she would
get on top, and then she'd complain that the angle hurt her,
so we changed angles. Then my penis would slip out. It
seemed as though the only angle that worked for her is one
that didn't work for me. So there was a lot of hurting and
slipping, slipping and hurting . . . then we would change
positions.

"So I would get on top, or the side or whatever she felt
was the best angle of penetration. 'That's good, that's good,'
she'd sometimes say. I would think maybe it was working.
Then ten minutes later she would say, 'Maybe you could
change position and try something else.' So we'd do that. She
would seem like she was heating up, which in turn would
heat me up, and I would get closer to orgasm myself. Then
once again she'd say, 'Let's change positions, and maybe you
could go a little slower this time.' All this talking about positions makes it difficult to maintain an erection, and there is
a point at which a guy shuts off. If nothing seems to work,
you get insensitive about it. Like I said, Barbara could always
have orgasms through oral sex, so I don't know why she was
so all fired up about orgasms and intercourse. I was with her
seven years . . . and no position worked. She said once that
it was easier with her last boyfriend, and I felt like saying,
'Yeah, it was easier for me.' "

"You know, I was with this woman once, and after the third
or fourth time we had sex I realized she wasn't having orgasms,
so when we started, I said, 'Let's see if we can do something
that feels a little better for you.' It seemed like a reasonable
suggestion to me. So I went down on her. Thirty-five minutes
later my jaw was sore, my mouth was sore, my tongue was
numb, and my neck was really starting to hurt. So I looked
up. I couldn't tell if she was loving it, hating it, or just putting
up with it. She wasn't giving me a clue."

Some Generational Differences

Among the men we spoke to, some of the younger ones,
but not all, seemed to be more aware of women's sexual needs

than the older men. Exposed to books and television shows, and women who are verbal about their physical needs, they tended to have a greater awareness that each woman is a little bit different and that part of being a loving partner is mutual exploration. You can see the differences in some of the following responses.

"It took us about a year before we figured out how Sue has orgasms, and then it was by accident, although we had tried a lot of things. I lie on the floor on my back and she gets on top. I would have assumed that she would have the same results on the bed if she's on top, but no way. She says that on the hard floor she can get more leverage and the extra tension she needs."

—26-year-old man

"My wife doesn't have orgasms through intercourse. It's always oral, and I usually make her come before I do, although sometimes we reverse the procedure. It's fun both ways."

—32-year-old man

"My first wife and I were married in 1954. Sex was infrequent, and I don't think she enjoyed it much. Seven years into the marriage, she said she'd never had an orgasm, but when I tried to talk about it, she said that she had changed and now she was having them. I think she said that when she saw I was upset, to make me feel good. I think she tried to act excited, but I didn't believe her. I married my second wife in 1976. Early in the relationship, she told me she didn't have orgasms from intercourse. I manipulate her until she comes . . . she coached me on it."

—57-year-old man

"When we were married back in the early sixties, I was very upset that my wife didn't have orgasms through intercourse. She needed oral stimulation or manual manipulation. I think I thought this meant that she was frigid, that she didn't like sex. I thought there was something wrong with her, and consequently with me. It definitely affected the marriage badly."

—56-year-old man

"I've slept with maybe fifty or sixty women. One of them could have orgasms through intercourse alone. That's it. All the others needed something extra. I like doing it."

—32-year-old man

SEX AND THE SIZE ISSUE

Here's another way in which everybody is different: It would appear that while everybody's genitals are slightly different in size and shape, everybody also has different levels of insecurity as to whether he or she is "built normally."

What do the sex manuals say? Most of them don't. And if they do address the issue of size, they often say that any man or woman can be a satisfying lover and can overcome all obstacles, as long as he or she is mentally fit and cares. Many of the more prominent sex therapists don't address the issue of size at all, except in the most general terms. Nonetheless, men and women tend to be extraordinarily sensitive about the size and shape of their genitals.

Men are distinctly more vocal than women in articulating their concerns about genital size. As a matter of fact, when we asked our interviewees if they had any questions they would like to ask the opposite sex, younger men invariably asked, "How much does size matter?"

Several posed the question as that classic existential dilemma: "So I want to know, is it the meat or the motion?"

Barry, a 36-year-old married man, said that he first started thinking about his penis size when "I was about eleven or twelve years old and I went to camp for the first time. That's when I found out how important size really was. They had what they called a camp tradition—it was called the Great American Boner Contest. All the guys in the bunk would take out their dicks and measure them. At the end of the summer we'd see which dick had grown the most. I remember the little guys would get really embarrassed."

The average man knows his penis is an average length and not the twelve-inch "weapon" or "tool" glorified in various men's publications; he also knows that one doesn't need or even necessarily want to be significantly oversized. However, several men said that when a man cares for a woman, he wants her to think, regardless of what she has seen before, that his penis is her favorite. They want to know that it measures up to what she expects.

One happily married man of 36 said, "Before I met my fiancée, I was never that involved with a woman, so I never worried about size—I figured that it was big enough for me, and that's all that mattered. But now I think about it because I want to be what she wants. And I've even asked her, 'Am I big enough for you?' That's one of the few questions I have asked her."

Although a man typically can be expected to "size up" the size of his own penis, he doesn't want anyone else to take the same liberty. One man remembers being "turned off" by a woman who was, as he put it, "too practical," by evaluating his erection.

"This was a woman I just met, and it was the first time we went to bed—and the last—and I remember her looking at my penis and going, 'Oh, very nice.' The tone of her voice was so practical . . . it was like the way she'd look at a car or a chair. It was clearly an object to her, and I hated that feeling."

Large/Small—a Size for Everyone

Most women say size does not matter to them. There were, however, exceptions in both directions. We were surprised to discover that women are more likely to be troubled when a man is very large because some of them then find sex painful.

Paula, who is now happily married, remembered her second lover: "He was huge, just huge, so huge that it didn't work no matter what we tried, and we tried everything. It was the classic 'there was nothing to do but throw my arms around it and weep.' I remember that someone told me about the Kama Sutra, and I went out and got a copy. It attributes animal types to different genital sizes. I decided that I was definitely a rabbit, and he was a bear, and that in the future I would avoid all bears."

Many women mentioned the physical repercussions that can occur as a result of having sex with a man with a large penis. One woman said, "I was really in love with Bradley, and the first time we went to bed, I was genuinely excited when I noticed that he was very big. I thought it would be particularly satisfying. Well, it was, and it wasn't. It was fun, but something about the way he was built and the way he hit me inside gave me bladder infections. During the time I was going with him I lived on antibiotics and cranberry juice. He really excited me as a lover, but I had so many physical repercussions that I began avoiding sex. The relationship eventually ended for other reasons, and my feelings of loss were not as intense as they might have been, because I honestly thought, 'Well, at least now I won't always be in pain.' "

Among women, when the conversation turned to size, bladder infections were a recurring theme. This is something few men take into consideration or acknowledge as a serious problem.

As for the question of "too small," women had very rarely encountered men who they thought were too small. In most cases the women said that the man's size didn't drastically affect their sexual relationship. Several women also mentioned lovers with particularly small penises who were extremely satisfying lovers.

Pamela, a 32-year-old fashion consultant, remembers . . . "my ex-husband was very small. The first time we had sex, I was worried that I wouldn't feel anything, but that wasn't the case; it felt fine. He was extremely sexual and very, very passionate, so the sex was terrific. The marriage would have ended sooner, but the sex held us together. We broke up because he wouldn't move to the big city and I couldn't spend one more day in the country, no matter how satisfying the nights. We continued to sleep together for a long time even after we separated."

There are women, of course, who prefer men who are large. Liza, a 31-year-old manufacturer's rep, says that "too small" is a problem in her current relationship right now, but there are other problems as well, and at 5'10", she is much taller than her 5'4" boyfriend.

"I'm a giant, and I know it, and Bobby is obviously too short for me. His penis is also small for me, and it bothers me. He is a good lover, and I always have orgasms, but I would prefer it if he were bigger, all around.

"I must admit, though, that when the relationship was really working, I wasn't as disturbed by the size problem. Now I'm angry at him for a lot of reasons, not the least of which is that he's been unfaithful—many times. The way I feel: If he were loving and kind to me, I could overlook the imperfections, but since he's not, I don't want to have to put up with the fact that he's a shrimp. You know those small mushrooms that float around inside Chinese food? Well, that's what his penis looks like. When I loved him, I loved him despite his size. He's been so mean to me that now I hate him, even though I'm dependent on him, and I resent everything about him and the way he is."

We spoke to several other women who said they greatly preferred a large penis. These women said that a larger penis enhances pleasure. A couple of women mentioned that they found it more exciting because it fulfills some fantasies, such as those that center around being overwhelmed by a man and his desire. One of the women we spoke to stressed that she felt she preferred "large" because that's what she had become accustomed to: "Dean is so huge that I think he ruined me for anyone else. I definitely think he stretched me. Even if he didn't, I feel as though a man who is a normal size won't be able to satisfy me anymore."

Her Screams Were Not the Kind I Wanted to Hear

A number of men also talked about situations in which the women they were with complained about sex being painful because the man had a large penis.

Greg, a 35-year-old doctor, remembers that his last girlfriend complained incessantly that he hurt her: "It was really awful. She was always grimacing and twisting. She would say that I hurt her. I didn't know what to do. We tried different positions and different ways.

"After a while you stop enjoying it. Every time it began to feel good to me, and I was getting the kind of physical sensation I wanted, I would look down at her and she would be twitching or retracting. Sometimes she even said, 'Ouch.' The sex ended up being so convoluted because the positioning was so complex. I'd find myself on my side somewhere half off the bed, not able to hold her, not getting enough penetration, and just not doing it. Oral sex was the only sensible solution, but we both missed intercourse.

"When the sex is not that pleasurable, it certainly makes you look at other problems. It didn't make me want to leave her, but it did weaken the bond."

Women's Size Concerns—Anxieties About Being "Too Large"

Women are sometimes worried about the possibility of having a vaginal canal that is "too large." Although no men mentioned this as a problem, both men and women remembered dirty jokes from junior high that emphasized this possibility. One man did say that he had been with a partner whose vagina he felt was "too large" for him. But in this case he also felt that it was a total misfit physically. He is a slender man of about 5'6", and the woman, who is nearly 5'11", was large-boned and husky.

Too Tight and Other First-time Jitters

Many women remember being "too tight" the first time they had sex, and more than a few men remember experiences with women who they were unable to enter. Unfortunately, when that happens, often the woman thinks she is malformed or peculiarly built, and the man thinks he is inadequate.

One man remembered that the woman he was involved with was beyond entering: "We just couldn't have sex. We're talking *Ali Baba and the Forty Thieves* here. I clapped my hands and said, 'Open sesame!' Nothing worked. She was as tight as the safe at Fort Knox. We must have tried everything but a crowbar. I know it must have worked with her and the guy she married because the last time I saw her, she had two small children—but for the two of us, it was impossible."

Meredith, 41, remembered the first time she had sex: "I had no idea it would be that painful. I just couldn't go through with it for several weeks. It was awful. Finally I went to a doctor, and he snipped away, and then everything was just fine."

Both men and women report feelings of panic when first-time sex is extremely difficult. Often both partners have totally unfounded fears that when the man finally manages to enter the woman, he will be stuck.

Gail, 36, remembers her fear: "There was this story going around in the town I grew up in when I was a kid. It was about how some couple was fooling around in the balcony of the movie theater. They said that he got stuck in her, and that somebody had to call an ambulance and take them to the hospital to separate them. It was awful. I remembered it, and the first time I had sex, that's all I could think about. I thought, 'Oh, no, we're going to have to roll over to the phone and call the doctor, and I'm going to die of embarrassment.' I didn't relax and stop worrying about that possibility until I had been having sex for about six months. Now, of course, I think about it and laugh."

So Does Size Matter?

Men and women both seem to agree that a good fit matters. That good fit has to do with height, weight, and lot of other facts besides genital size. It is certainly a factor, but among

the people we spoke to there were very few instances where
sex wasn't working because of "fit," and in those cases the
individuals were quick to report that other things in the relationship also were not working, and that those other issues
were creating the major problems.

Size does seem to be a temporary issue among young people
having sex for the first few times. Sometimes it takes a little
more effort than anyone anticipated, and anxiety about size
becomes a real issue. But these concerns should evaporate
after a little bit of experience.

So does size matter? Like many things in life, it would
appear that it matters when it matters, and then it can matter
a great deal. But most of the time it doesn't seem to matter
at all.

5

What Really Happens in Bed: Talking About Birth Control, Masturbation, and Sexual Motivation—Conversations That Rarely Take Place

EMBARRASSMENT, SELF-CONSCIOUSNESS, AND THE SOUNDS OF SILENCE

When it comes to talking about sex, almost everybody is embarrassed by something. Contraception, masturbation, and sexual motivation are three "somethings" that we chose to focus on because they are very real and very fundamental aspects of human sexual behavior and rarely are talked about in any meaningful way.

First there is contraception; the method to be used, or not used, is perhaps the most important decision a couple can make together. Yet from the people we spoke to, it seems apparent that many men and women, in both long- and short-term relationships, are clearly avoiding the kind of specific discussion that something this serious merits.

Then there is masturbation, the single most widely practiced form of sexual behavior. Most of the people we spoke to, both single and married, agreed that they were doing it . . . but they were extremely self-conscious about talking about it and often communicated feelings of guilt and conflict.

Finally there is sexual motivation; that is, the many ways in which we can complicate our lives for the sake of sex and then come up with a dozen good rationalizations, pretending to the rest of the world, and often to ourselves as well, that our motivation was based on anything and everything but sex.

BIRTH CONTROL—WHO'S TALKING?

Typically, women of childbearing age are concerned about birth control. Some are even anxious about it. This is understandable because it is a real and very important issue. Women talk to each other about birth control a lot. They also talk to their gynecologists. Who *don't* they talk to about birth control? Their partners. From the men and women we've spoken to, it would appear that very few thoughtful, in-depth conversations about birth control are taking place in American bedrooms. Why don't these conversations ever take place? Men and women, married and single, say that there are several reasons.

As one would expect, nobody wants to start talking about birth control right before sex. People say it ruins the spontaneity and disrupts the flow. But what about less intense moments? Many men and women, including long-term happily married couples, told us that they have rarely discussed which birth control method to use, and what that means in terms of advantages, disadvantages, and side effects; if they have, they say that the conversations were very limited. Some women say they don't like to bring it up because they don't want to appear overly clinical. Other women don't initiate conversations because they think it makes them appear whiny or less appealing. As one woman said, "Birth control isn't very sexy."

Men said they are often embarrassed or peculiarly shy when it comes to asking appropriate questions. Some also admitted that sometimes they don't want to hear all the answers.

A report published in the March/April 1987 issue of *Family Planning Perspectives* presents research on estimates of the proportion of American women of reproductive age who experienced unintended pregnancies, unintended births, and abortions. The data are based on figures from the 1982 National Survey of Family Growth and the Alan Guttmacher Institute's 1981–1982 national survey of abortion providers.

The report states: "We do not know whether current abortion rates will continue, but if they do, then nearly half of U.S. women can be expected to undergo an abortion at least once during their lives; furthermore, if the lifetime rate of unintended pregnancy remains at the 65 percent level estimated for women aged 40–44 in 1982, then current abortion rates imply that about 70 percent of women who experience an unintended pregnancy will have at least one abortion."

We spoke to so many women—and men—who told us about being part of an unintended pregnancy. In some of these instances birth-control failure was directly related to a failure of communication often caused by a woman's embarrassment about appearing overly experienced, clinical, or nonromantic by disrupting the spontaneity of sex.

The Myth of Spontaneity and Out-of-Control Birth Control

Sex manuals often encourage spontaneity, and yet, as any sexually experienced adult man or woman knows, spontaneity and contraception are not the happiest mix. Birth control requires planning, consideration, and partner cooperation. That's the only way it works. As many men and women have learned through experience, those spontaneous, middle-of-the-night nudges, sexy though they may be, are conducive to real pregnancy.

When Does a Woman Get Pregnant?

There are two times when a woman can get pregnant: when she wants to get pregnant and when she doesn't want to get pregnant. And at least one woman told us that the

only time she didn't get pregnant is when she was trying
to make it happen.

We promised we wouldn't try to present statistical information, but we were so bowled over by the fact that more
than half of the women we had spoken to had experienced
at least one, if not more, unplanned or accidental pregnancies, it seemed worth noting. Many of these women then
had abortions. Some of these women, including several
health-care professionals, then went on to have another unplanned pregnancy.

From the newspapers it sometimes seems as though the
only women with accidental pregnancies are teenagers living
in inner cities. But these weren't the people we were interviewing; from the experiences of these men and women
it seemed as though accidental pregnancies and abortions
were very much a part of the psychosexual scene for all eco-
nomic groups. As we unfortunately know, underprivileged
teenagers often become pregnant accidentally. Who else gets
pregnant accidentally? Here are some examples from among
the women who talked to us.

"I had four accidental pregnancies in my twenties, and
four abortions. Two in my early thirties—I had one abortion
and decided to have a child, who is now 14. After my child
was born, I got pregnant twice again; after the second abortion I had my tubes tied. It really broke my heart to have
two abortions after having a child—then I knew what a child
was, but I had no choice."

—Emily, a 45-year-old ceramics instructor

"I have five children, all of whom were conceived because
of human error. I also had one abortion. My husband says
if it happens again, he'll divorce me. He acts like he had
nothing to do with it."

—42-year-old social worker

"My husband and I have had five pregnancies—two children, three abortions."

—35-year-old lawyer

"My husband was my first lover, and I got pregnant the first time we made love, at 18. I had an abortion."

— *70-year-old-grandmother*

"I had four pregnancies by the time I turned 26 and four abortions. I think I finally learned."

— *32-year-old nurse*

"I had grown accustomed to the pill. When I could no longer take them, I switched to an IUD. When the IUD gave me problems, I had it removed. I had never before had to deal with unprotected sex. I just didn't think I would get pregnant that easily."

— *31-year-old filmmaker*

Among Single Women, Embarrassment Is Still a Major Factor in Unplanned Pregnancies

"I'm ashamed to admit it, but I got pregnant twice, not once but twice, because I was too embarrassed to stop the preliminaries and go off and put on my diaphragm. I was carrying it in my pocketbook, but I didn't put it on."

— *Nellie, 29-year-old editor*

Why is an intelligent, reasonably cautious, and basically non-self-destructive woman prepared to risk an unplanned pregnancy rather than admit that she is "prepared" for sex? Nellie said:

"Look, I'm usually careless the first time, not because I'm careless but because I'm basically shy, I think, and I don't want to appear to be overly eager. You feel funny saying to a man that you came prepared for sex, even before he raises the issue.

"I met Joseph at my summer house, and we went out to

dinner a couple of Saturday nights in a row, at the beach. The first time we were with other people. Then the second Saturday after dinner we walked back to town along the beach. It was ridiculously romantic, and we necked and talked on the beach. He talked about his last relationship and said that it ended because the woman wanted to date other men. I was very attracted to him, and I thought it could be a real relationship. I didn't want to appear to be overly aggressive or threatening, or do anything to jeopardize a potential future. The necking we did was sexy, but it was very sweet. I mean, he didn't grab my clothes off or say anything that made it clear that we would go to bed the next time we saw each other. Yet I knew that that was what was going to happen. He invited me to his apartment in the middle of the week. He said he would make me dinner and we would rent a movie. When I got there, of course, we forgot about dinner. I had the diaphragm in my pocketbook, but the right moment to excuse myself never came. It made me feel funny to say, 'I knew we would end up in bed, so I brought my diaphragm.' I guess it's the old I didn't want him to think I did this all the time. If he had said something like, 'Do you have a diaphragm, did you bring it?' I would have put it on. I kept expecting him to raise the issue and suggest putting on a condom, and he didn't do it. Then, at the last moment, I told him that I wasn't wearing anything and asked him to pull out. So he did, but not fast enough. Now, with the AIDS thing, I think I would be less embarrassed about asking someone to use a condom—but I'm not sure. I don't think I would be able to carry one, even now."

Among Both Married and Single Women, an Erratic Sex Life Is Often Implicated in an Unplanned Pregnancy

Among the women we spoke to, the ones who had the highest number of individual unplanned pregnancies were those who had neither a regular partner, nor a partner with whom they had a regular pattern. Single women with erratic

sex lives said they were often reluctant about making a commitment to birth-control pills or IUDs because they believed that they were having too little sex to warrant the inconvenience, the health risk, or the expense of a visit to a gynecologist. Many prefer to wait until they are in a regular relationship before getting serious about birth control, sometimes with disastrous results.

Emily, a typical example, was very certain that the absence of sex in her life made her careless when a sexual opportunity suddenly presented itself . . . .

"I didn't have a regular method of birth control for several reasons. The first and most important is that I had sex so infrequently, I was inexperienced with the diaphragm; and I used it so seldom that I always either stored it someplace and couldn't find it, or it was so old that the rubber was cracked. I didn't have a permanent method because the pill made me ill, gave me headaches and flashes before my eyes. I had used it during my early twenties, but my doctor advised me to stop. I had a coil inserted, but I had such heavy bleeding, it had to be removed. If I was in a relationship, I guess I would have found a way to practice birth control like a normal human being, but when there's no consistency . . . I know it's no excuse, but it's the truth.

"All of my abortions were pretty much the result of one- or two-night stands. In all the cases, I was physically turned on, because it had been such a long time between sex, and in at least half the cases I felt uncomfortable about stopping to go find and put on a diaphragm. I also felt uncomfortable about asking the guy to use a condom. I figured if I stopped long enough to even think about birth control, the mood might pass, for both of us. My body was demanding this of me. It wasn't my head. I think on all the occasions when I got pregnant, I was a little high, even though I'm not normally a drinker—but that contributed to the mood. There were a couple of years during which I had sex only twice, got pregnant twice, and had two abortions."

Bobbie, another single woman in her late twenties, said, "I'm not really using anything, which is stupid, but I'm not having a regular sex life. I trust the guy to pull out or wear a condom. Then I worry, and when my period is due, I'm always rushing into the bathroom every couple of hours to see if it's starting. I should know better because I had one abortion from a guy who didn't know how to pull out."

Eve, a married woman in her thirties, said that she can't expect her husband to use a condom because he only gets partial erections and sometimes has a hard time maintaining them. She says that they have never discussed the way in which his sexual pattern affects birth control: "My husband has a very low sex drive, and I guess I don't want to discourage him when he feels turned on, but I also can't put on a diaphragm every night in the hopes that he'll want sex, which he does very, very infrequently, and there is no pattern to it. It's really stupid, because I got pregnant that way. He says I should have stopped him; I say he should have asked. I've never been able to be fully forthright about the birth-control issue because I don't want him to feel inadequate because of the sexual problem. I still have hopes that it will change sexually, and I don't want to do anything to create more psychological stress."

Many Men Say That They Don't Fully Understand Birth Control and/or How Easily Some Women Become Pregnant

"I guess I knew intellectually that I was perfectly capable of getting a woman pregnant; yet on another level I don't think I ever believed that it could really happen to me. Years of using the "shotgun" method, i.e., pulling out at the last minute, only reinforced my sense of being safe. Then the method failed."

—Philip, 27

Men are certainly involved in as many unplanned pregnancies as women, yet they are often confused about the

various ways in which women use or don't use birth-control methods. Many men think that they are "safe" because it hasn't happened so far. Others assume that if the woman is willing to have sex with them, she is "doing something" because "it's her body." If they don't know the woman well, they are often reluctant to ask exactly what that something is.

Men told us that they rarely initiated conversations about birth control; instead they waited for the woman to say something. Most of them said that they wanted to do the right thing, but they assumed that the right thing was to follow the woman's lead. Others said that if they initiated a conversation, it was very vague and nonspecific—usually some variation of "Is it safe?" or "Can I do this?" Surprisingly, although many men said that as adolescents they would buy condoms in order to practice getting them on, a couple of very sexually experienced single men said that until the AIDS epidemic, they had never used a condom and didn't even know how to put one on; they had always expected the woman to provide birth control.

Yet men often become very upset when they are involved in an unplanned pregnancy.

One 31-year-old man described the degree of guilt and distress he felt when a woman he was with got pregnant this year. He says he remembers quite clearly the conversation they had the first time they had sex. . . .

"The situation was becoming very intimate, and I realized that in a few minutes we would find ourselves in bed, having sex, so I said, 'Should I use something?'

"She said, 'It's not necessary.'

"Now, when someone says to you, 'It's not necessary,' you assume they mean it's not necessary either because she can't get pregnant, or she is doing something not to get pregnant, like taking the pill or using an IUD. You don't assume that 'It's not necessary' means the woman is prepared to take a crapshoot.

"So once you think you are protected, you don't think about it anymore. There is a complete change in attitude.

A man feels one way if he thinks he is going to have to withdraw before climaxing, and another if he thinks it is safe to climax in that woman. One is total paranoia and pulling out at the slightest twinge, but if you think you can relax, you become reckless about it all. P.S. She got pregnant sometime that first week. When she told me, I was stunned. I felt totally betrayed. It changed the relationship. It changed my attitude toward sex with her, and it changed my opinion of her. It was so stupid. I never wanted to be responsible for anybody's abortion."

Single men are not the only ones who feel responsible for unplanned pregnancies. Some married men manage to stay very detached from the process of birth control and sometimes even regard it as a major inconvenience . . . until it all becomes real.

Neil, a married man, says that his wife got pregnant when she didn't want to, and in retrospect, he realizes that it was his fault.

"There were times when I would grab her and get sexy, and she'd say, 'I have to go put on my diaphragm,' and I would look annoyed.

"So I guess once when I grabbed her, she figured that it was an okay time of month, and she didn't want to stop me with the diaphragm business. It really was my fault."

Inexperience and Unplanned Pregnancy Sometimes Go Together

Quite a few women told us that they had become pregnant when they were quite young and just beginning to experiment sexually. They simply didn't have adequate information or adequate protection. End result: unplanned pregnancy. Some of these women had more than one pregnancy within the first two years in which they were having sex. Some of these women had abortions, but in other instances they were forced to marry, causing both partners

to radically alter life goals; in others, the women were already married but had to disrupt career or education plans.

Young men can also be inexperienced and poorly informed. Tim, a 25-year-old graduate student, remembered that he was very insensitive with his first long-term girlfriend: "I just didn't understand. You know, we would start fooling around in bed, and then she'd say she had to go put her diaphragm on. I guess she had a tough time doing it. But that would leave me staring at my hard-on for a full five minutes. Or what was left of it by the time she came back. I was really insensitive and selfish. But I don't think she understood the way I felt, either. No, we never talked about it. I wish we had, because in retrospect I'm grateful to her; it would have been a disaster if she'd gotten pregnant."

Do Single People Discuss Birth Control Before or After They First Go to Bed?

According to the people we talked to, more often than not such discussions take place *after* the first time. Why? Here are some reactions.

"It seems so cold, so unromantic and inappropriate."
—34-year-old woman

"I'm on the pill, so I don't have to talk about it."
—23-year-old woman

"I suppose I should, but I assume if the woman doesn't say anything, it is taken care of."
—43-year-old man

"I never used to say anything, but then I got somebody pregnant, so now I always check."
—34-year-old man

Do These Same People Think About Birth Control Before First-time Sex?

Here are some reactions.

"Of course I do. I'm not stupid. I just don't know how to talk about it."

—34-year-old woman

"Of course I do, that's why I'm on the pill."

—23 year-old woman

"I don't think about it much. I just pray a lot."

—43-year-old man

"I used to think about it; now I think harder."

—34-year-old man

Are Couples Communicating Honestly About Birth Control?

Yes and no. We talked to several young couples who clearly had honest and open conversations about birth-control practices; these people rarely, if ever, "took chances." But most of the people we spoke to indicated that they were not really talking.

Men, for example, are not regularly included in their partners' gynecological visits and are often blissfully unaware of the intricacies of various birth-control systems. Many don't fully understand the difficulties that can be associated with the pill, and even the most sympathetic husband has been known to get annoyed by a woman who is complaining about reactions to the hormones it contains.

As a rule, neither men nor women were sharing their feelings about the inconvenience of several birth-control methods. We found that men complained about the diaphragm in a way that would surprise many women. Contrary to common belief, several said they could often "feel" the diaphragm, and repeated physical contact with it during thrusting resulted in soreness and discomfort. They had never mentioned this to their partners.

The women, in turn, had no sense of this. We asked one woman who was a diaphragm user for some twenty years whether her husband ever complained about "feeling" the diaphragm, and had the following conversation.

"He can't feel it."

"Are you sure?"

"Absolutely. If anyone says they can feel it, then the woman is inserting it incorrectly. Everyone knows you can't feel a diaphragm."

The following day the same woman phoned to say, "You're right. I'm wrong. I asked him, and he says it often bothers him, but he didn't want to upset me by saying anything."

Both men and women complained about many of the contraceptive jellies, used either alone or with a diaphragm. Not only do people say that they taste terrible, which is a real deterrent against oral sex, but also some men and women say that they are sensitive to certain chemicals in some of the brands and have developed skin irritations. Women who are more accustomed to discomfort from contraceptive methods tend to assume that there may be some small irritation from the jelly, but men are not that familiar with the problem. As one man told us, "If you start itching and burning after sex, you imagine who who knows what." Beyond that, chemical spermicides used as birth control without a diaphragm are relatively unreliable.

It would also appear from the couples we spoke to that when the diaphragm is the method of choice, the couple does not work out together when it is going to be inserted. The diaphragm and spontaneity clearly don't go together.

One woman said: "I've been married five years, and I still never know when to put it in. I don't want to walk around wearing it, but short of that, I don't know what to do. Also, I'm never sure at what stage to put it in. If he's going to want oral sex, the diaphragm is a problem because the jelly is icky. If I had a clue ahead of time, I would know what to do."

Several women said that they preferred to insert their diaphragm and contraceptive jelly, then take a shower or bath, thus washing away the external traces of the jelly or cream. But they also said that unless they knew when their partners were going to make overtures, this was difficult to do.

Women also spoke of making a man feel sexually pressured. They said being always prepared made them feel as though they were more eager for sex than their partners. One woman said, "I would wear my diaphragm all the time, but when I do I think it makes him feel pressured to have sex."

Condoms and Birth Control

When condoms are the method of choice and the man is in charge, a whole different series of problems emerge.

As one man said, "Of course I don't like condoms. But I've never told her how much I hate them. Sometimes I don't initiate sex just because I don't want to have to roll the damned thing on. They're just no fun." Perhaps the phrase *no fun* oversimplifies the whole condom issue. When you talk to enough men, you get a very clear sense of some of the drawbacks that condoms present. All of the following condom-related complaints were voiced by the men we interviewed:

- Loss of sensation (the raincoat effect).
- Loss of erections because of the interruption and unpleasant physical sensations from the condom.
- Pregnancy risks via breakage, spillage, etc.
- Complications surrounding stop-and-start sexuality.
- Awkwardness of actually putting it on.
- Women complain about them.

Some married women are also sensitive to the condom issue. They worry whether it's reducing pleasure for their mates.

We did talk to two women who had been using condoms as their primary form of birth control for many years, long before AIDS became an issue. They said that they preferred condoms because they felt that they were efficient and easy. One of these women said that she always kept them in her bedside table in case she had sex with an unprepared partner, and that condoms were very much her method of choice. She was very matter-of-fact about it: "I don't care if someone thinks I'm not being romantic. I'm very practical, and that's just the way I am."

Sterilization

Right now sterilization is America's most popular form of contraception, and we spoke to several men and women who had made that choice. All of them were close to or over forty and already had one or more children. Two of the women said that they were not totally thrilled and regretted losing the option of having another child, and at least one husband said that he was very disturbed when he discovered that his wife had undergone sterilization without his agreement, even though they wanted no more children. Everyone commented that it definitely took a great deal of the anxiety out of sex.

One man said that he had been so irresponsible with the women he had been with in terms of contraception, two of his friends persuaded him to have a vasectomy, with the additional incentive that they would pay for it. He said, "They gave it to me as a birthday present. I think the underlying message was that I was getting too old to be doing this kind of stuff. I should have had it done years ago."

We also spoke to several younger women who had married men who had already fathered one family and, not wanting another, had undergone sterilization. Both of these women were ambivalent about the finality of that decision; one couple was looking into the possibility of having it reversed. Both agreed, however, that it was great not having to think about birth control. In those cases spontaneity was definitely a possibility.

Fact: Some Forms of Birth Control Do Interfere With Spontaneity

There is no way around it. It takes time to insert a diaphragm or roll on a condom. This time clearly can disrupt the mood, contribute to loss of desire, loss of erections, and loss of "the moment." This is something that happens to everyone. And there are no easy answers. However, the statistics on unplanned pregnancy should convince everyone that carelessness in the name of spontaneity is no answer.

The sexual revolution had a profound effect on America's sexual behavior; however, it was unable to alter the fact that the ultimate physiological end point of sex is the continuation of the species—i.e., making babies.

The fantasy notion of sweeping, spontaneous, unbridled sexual passion with no repercussions doesn't mesh with the gritty, real details surrounding the machinations we humans have to endure in order to avoid pregnancy. But as too many of the men and women who spoke to us have discovered, the sort of out-of-control behavior that causes one to avoid those details often results in a very real unplanned pregnancy, which, unlike the movieland concept of spontaneous sex, is no fantasy.

MASTURBATION—EVERYBODY'S SEXUAL SECRET

Everybody's doing it . . . and doing it . . . and doing it. And nobody's talking about it. Men and women, married and single . . . if there's one thing almost all of our interviewees had in common, it's masturbation. Granted, frequency may vary, style may vary, and attitudes certainly will vary, but it's almost always there, tucked away in the most private corner of our individual sex lives.

But try asking about it, and the most open and honest men and women suddenly turn reticent. Sometimes they even turn red. But most often body language and a sudden clamming up are the clues that the questioner has gone too far, trespassing into private territory.

The fact is that except for a few notable exceptions, nobody wants to talk about masturbation—not with these interviewers, not with their friends, and especially not with their partners. Sure, many of us will joke about it or allude to it, but when it comes to revealing the specifics of what we do when we are totally alone, people would prefer changing the subject.

Note the following conversation with a 29-year-old man who up until this point, as you can see, had been extremely forthcoming in describing a relationship.

"I'm big on locations . . . the beach, on a mountain. I remember once we were in this hotel room with a balcony, up in the mountains. It was a gorgeous night, and suddenly the urge hit, and we went for it, right there. It was late, but there were two guys in the pool, and we could see them jockeying for position to see what was going on. It was the best we had."

"Did you ever repeat it?" (interviewer)

"No. That was the end of the relationship. Our Super Bowl."

"What about your 'private sex life'?" (interviewer)

"Huh?"

"Masturbation." (interviewer)

"Oh, boy . . . oh, boy. . . . Now you are getting intimate. What about it?"

"How often do you masturbate?" (interviewer)

"Oh, um . . . not that much."

"What do you think about when you do it?" (interviewer)

"What do I think about? People who give me pleasure . . . situations that give me pleasure. Women I know."

"Pornography?" (interviewer)

"No. Usually . . . oh, God, if I ever run for public office and this gets out, I'm dead. It's funny. It's not the act itself that does it, it's usually something prior to that . . .

undressing, fondling, rolling around on the sofa and/or floor."

"But usually with women you know?" (interviewer)

"Yes, definitely. I'd say ninety-eight percent of the time."

"Could you be more specific about how often you masturbate?" (interviewer)

"Christ, I don't know."

"Could we have a rough estimate?" (interviewer)

"Let's say twice a week. You don't believe me, do you? Okay, it goes in cycles . . . you understand. I'm not a robot. Sometimes more. Sometimes less. I'll say it averages out to two or three times a week. Do you really need to know this?"

Masturbation and the Myth of Sexual Immaturity

Most people have seen studies or reports indicating that masturbation is a process that many people continue throughout their lives. And these same people are aware of their own masturbatory pattern. Yet for many of them, even if they themselves masturbate, it still conjures up images of teenage boys in the bathroom with *Playboy* magazine, and young girls feeling guilty every time they touch themselves. As one single man said, "Admitting you masturbate is like saying you can't find anybody who'll go to bed with you. It's like saying you're still a horny 16-year-old boy with no options."

Many of the people we talked to had constructed such protective walls around their masturbatory pattern that over time they have come to believe that they are the only ones left "doing" it, and that everyone else had grown up and outgrown masturbation. This attitude was especially common among the men we interviewed.

Masturbation Isn't Really a Substitute for Sex

No matter how much anyone may enjoy solitary masturbation, it would appear that it in no way replaces intimate human contact. Most of the people we spoke to were fairly clear about the difference. One man said, "It's just different. My orgasm may be better, but it's not as pleasurable in other ways. I think just body contact gives you a certain physical release, and I like the way another body feels."

Women tended to stress the fact that there was little emotional satisfaction in masturbation, and that it didn't replace a real partner.

Masturbation and the Single Life-style

One would expect men and women who are not in ongoing relationships to masturbate regularly, and they do. One would also expect that when these men and women enter into sexual relationships, they would masturbate less. This is not always the case.

Several people pointed out that they sometimes masturbate more. Why? One 25-year-old man said, somewhat apologetically, "When I first meet somebody I like, I'm usually totally turned on. It's silly, but that's the way it is. So not only am I having a lot of sex with the woman, sometimes I go home, fantasize about her, and masturbate. Sorry. . ."

Several women said essentially the same thing.

Women, but not men, also stressed that with the fear of AIDS, they were becoming more dependent upon masturbation as their sole sexual outlet. One woman in her late twenties told us, "Sometimes I would have sex that could only be described as casual or recreational. I won't do that now. I've had my AIDS test; it's negative. No more chances for me—from now on it's me and my trusty vibrator."

Some older women told us that they were resigned to masturbation as a sexual choice because they felt they were limited in terms of appropriate partners. One 56-year-old woman said that she was astonished at how sexually satisfied she was: "As I've grown older, I have less sex drive, but I still have very good orgasms. I bought my first vibrator in the seventies, almost as a joke, because I always had trouble with orgasms, and I read somewhere that masturbation was a way to learn how to have them. For me it was. I don't expect to find a man to be with. Occasionally I have a small fling, but it's never really for sex anymore. It's for companionship or something else. Masturbation works for me. It makes me feel as though I will never be desperate for sexual satisfaction, which is something I worried about when I was younger."

Masturbation and Marriage

Happily married men and women are masturbating, and unhappily married men and women are masturbating. In some marriages the partners are practicing mutual masturbation. But most of the people we spoke to were masturbating alone and not telling their partners.

The most interesting thing to us was that with only a few exceptions, the married men and women who told us that they were masturbating also told us that they were fairly certain that their partners were not. The following interview with a 42-year-old married man is a good example of the kind of exchanges we had.

"On the average, how often do you masturbate?" (interviewer)

"Maybe once a week, sometimes more . . . if my wife is away, more."

"Does your wife know this?" (interviewer)

"No. I mean, I don't think so. I certainly wouldn't do it when she's around or anything."

"Does she masturbate regularly?" (interviewer)

"I have no idea. I've never asked her, but I doubt it. Knowing her, I really doubt it."

Many women are equally certain that their husbands are not masturbating. Others are not certain; and a few women said that they asked their husbands and had been given yes for an answer. One woman said, "If you had asked me that question two months ago, I would have said absolutely no, you don't know my husband, but now I'm not so sure, because I was away for a few days, and when I got back, I discovered that he had taken out some soft-porn videos, which he had neglected to return. I'm sure he watched them alone, and I can't imagine why he did it unless he wanted to get turned on."

In some marriages, one of the partners is masturbating because he or she doesn't want to pressure a spouse, whom they love but whom they perceive as having a less intense sex drive.

Some men said they masturbated simply because of the ease and speed of it.

Tony, who is 31, has been married for four years. He finds that he continues to masturbate regularly, no matter what is happening in the marriage: "Even when sex is great, and it often is really superb, just what sex is supposed to be, yet there is a time when I want to masturbate. It's quick, it's easy, it's what I want. It's like fast food when I don't want a full-course meal."

A couple of husbands said they masturbate because they are too tired to initiate sex. One told us, "Sex is real work. It takes time, effort, etc. If I'm exhausted and just want sexual relief, masturbation is a two-minute satisfier."

Almost all the men and women said that they did not want their partners to know that they masturbated. Several men said that they felt their wives would get upset and feel rejected. And in those few instances when we spoke to women who had been with men who they knew were masturbating, the women said that they did feel rejected and upset.

Women also worried about telling their partners; they said they felt that their husbands wouldn't know how to deal with it, and they feared it might make the men feel as though they were inadequate lovers.

Masturbation and How Its Status Has Changed

Not that many years ago, even therapists were telling people that masturbation was not advisable. They said it would make it more difficult, particularly for women, to adjust to a "normal" sexual relationship. We also remember all the myths about warts and insanity.

Now all that has changed. Many, if not all, sex therapists

are encouraging women who have problems with orgasm to use masturbation as a learning process in developing more satisfactory relationships with their partners. Some men are also being counseled to masturbate in order to learn erection and ejaculation control.

When Kinsey published his famous works, almost none of the older respondents admitted to masturbation. In a more recent survey of men and women over 60—done in the late 1970s by Dr. Bernard Starr and Dr. Marcella B. Weiner and reported in *The New York Times*—approximately 50% acknowledged that they masturbated.

SEXUALLY MOTIVATED AND SEXUALLY DRIVEN—EVERYONE'S COMMON CONFESSION

"What's really amazing to me about those years in which I was sexually obsessed by a married man is that most people thought I was a normal person. I went to work, went to meetings, talked about what was going on in the office, but in my head all I could think about was that relationship. In reality I knew he was wrong for me, but I was so overwhelmed and turned on sexually that I stopped thinking clearly. A whole part of my brain just shut down—the smart part. I was a longing mess. I discovered that when I'm that attracted to someone, my hormones are in the driver's seat. I cease to be rational."

—36-year-old woman

Almost every man and woman we spoke to said that at various life stages he or she felt totally out of control and completely motivated by sex. A great many people talked about how "stupid" they had been. When they were involved with someone, or wanted to become involved, they talked about the kind of foolishness they had engaged in because of desire. When there was no sexual involvement, they talked about how an absence of an ongoing sex life altered their moods and affected their well-being.

Further, many said that all too often they had made major

life decisions based totally upon sexual motivation. Many of them referred to themselves as having been "sexually driven," particularly in the years under age 40.

Perhaps nothing tells us more about sexual attitudes than the way in which all of us make important life decisions based on sexual events or sexual hopes, and then hide the fact that we have done just that. As we talked to people, we couldn't help but notice that just about everyone's personal history was littered with stories about times during which sensible thinking and rational considerations were overwhelmed by sexual needs or sexual shame. The stories were interesting, but here's what we found most fascinating: The people we interviewed confirmed that when these events were taking place, they concealed from the outside world, including their closest friends, the full extent to which they were motivated by sexual considerations, be it sexual need, sexual response, sexual shame, or sexual confusion.

Some of these sexually motivated situations were just amusing diversions and had little long-term impact; others involved major life decisions and were far-reaching, long-term, and occasionally devastating. Here are some examples of both.

Teenage Lust

Who can't identify with the sexual urges of an adolescent boy or girl? Thomas, 40, said that's when he discovered . . .

"I was sexually driven. I did the most amazing things for sex. My first girlfriend? I was 15 and living on a farm in New Hampshire. She was two years older, and even more sexually crazed than me. The relationship only lasted three months because she nearly killed me. She wore me out. She lived three or four miles away, all uphill, and her parents didn't want her to see me. So I was getting up at dawn to feed the cows and do chores, and then in the afternoon, on my free time, instead of hanging out at the old swimming hole, I was riding my bicycle three miles up- and downhill to her place, and she would meet me in the bushes in what is now a state park. So for the next two hours we'd have sex in the bushes.

That's how I accidentally discovered oral sex. In the bushes. I couldn't tell if she was enjoying it or having an epileptic fit. I was down on her, and my ass was totally exposed, and something was always biting it.

"Having sex in the bushes is not as romantic as it seems. First of all there are not only all these damn hikers, but there are creepy crawlies, and poison ivy, and even some stray cows. You'd have a hell of a time telling your parents how you got the hoofprint on your ass.

"When we were finished, I'd ride home back up and down the hills, just in time to help my father for a couple of hours. He'd given me tennis lessons as a birthday present. I played tennis from four to five, went home for dinner, and then after everybody was asleep, I'd sneak off—back on the bicycle up and down the hills—to meet her. After three months I was covered with bites and poison ivy, and I could barely walk. Winter was coming, but I was prepared to freeze to death in that damned bush. Fortunately for my life expectancy, around about that time her parents decided to send her away to school to protect her from the local riffraff like me."

The Wrong Vacation

Ted, a 32-year-old salesman, describes his irrational pursuit of a woman he thought he was attracted to.

"I have engaged in more moronic behavior because of sexual lust! Typical? I once saw an incredible woman at Logan Airport, tracked down her luggage, found out her name and that she was a travel agent in Miami. Then, three months later, I was still thinking about her, so I planned a Miami vacation. I have no friends in Miami. I had nothing to do in Miami. I had no other reason to want to be in Miami. I convinced my friends that it would be a good idea to check out job possibilities in Miami.

"I certainly wasn't going to tell them that I was stupid enough to spend a couple of grand for a boring vacation I didn't want just so I could track down some unknown female in the Sunbelt. There was nobody else in my life, and I was unhinged."

Choosing an Apartment

Larry is a 29-year-old art director who recently moved to New York from San Diego. About a year and a half ago he broke up a long-term relationship because he found that he was "attracted to other women" and wanted to date, and sleep with, more women before settling down into a permanent relationship. He says he has a specific physical type of woman to whom he has always been attracted. He had one brief affair with a woman who fit this description when he was in his early twenties, but since then the women in his life have not "really been his physical type." When he first came to New York, he said he had a "sexual agenda" planned; this agenda included a woman, or women, who fit his fantasy. What he didn't take into account was the difficulty that one can encounter in fulfilling such an agenda.

Larry says that he "bores friends" with his stories about how rarely he meets the right women. What he does not tell friends, or anyone else, is how determined he is to find his "type," and how much time he devotes to looking for a sexual relationship. . . .

"I have to admit it. Everything—every place I go, where I have my coffee, the way I plan my week—everything is structured to maximize the possibility of a sexual relationship. I feel foolish about this, but I don't know what else to do.

"Let me tell you a story of how dumb I can be sometimes. When I moved East and was looking for an apartment in Manhattan, I went to this party, and there was this really great-looking woman there. She heard that I needed someplace to live and came over to me and said that she shared an apartment with two other women, but one of them was moving out. Would I be interested in a roommate situation? Would I be interested? I immediately made plans to see the apartment the next day. I was so excited, I couldn't sleep. There was one problem to start out with. I wanted an apartment in Manhattan, and she lived in Brooklyn. She was certainly good-looking enough to get me to Brooklyn, even though I'm not comfortable on the subways—I just haven't been in the city long enough to know where I'm going, or where I'll end up.

"Well, I got on a subway, anyway, and it turned out that she lived way out in some godforsaken place. The subway was a nightmare, the local subway station was a nightmare, and when I got up on the street, I realized that the neighborhood was home to more drug dealers than I had ever seen before. But when I got to the apartment and was greeted at the door by this absolutely adorable creature wearing this cute outfit . . . she was so cute that I just thought to myself, 'I could spend a year here, hiding with this woman.'

"It was a nice building, but the room I would have was small and dark, with a tiny window eight feet off the ground overlooking an air shaft—I know because I pulled up a chair to look. Oh, yes, even though it was in Brooklyn, it also cost more than the apartment I share now on the Upper West Side of Manhattan.

"So guess what? Even though it was all wrong, I took the apartment. But first I had to convince the landlord that there would be no funny stuff going on between me and either of the women! It was so stupid. And what did I tell my friends? I convinced my friends that the reason I wanted the apartment was because the building had a garage, and I could keep a car. I don't even have a car.

"Well, I moved in, and you got it—she got engaged a couple of weeks later and moved out to be with the guy. So I was stuck in Brooklyn with the other roommate, and we had to split the rent two ways until we found somebody else. Eventually I managed to move out, but I was so nuts, I still can't believe it."

Other Sexually Motivated and Oft-regretted Acts

Margaret, a 40-year-old schoolteacher, says she has a list of things she did, all of which were almost totally sexually motivated. She regrets them all.

"I have this list of things that make me feel as though I want to die from embarrassment. I can't believe I could have been so stupid.

"One: When I was in graduate school, I let this guy I was desperately attracted to use my mailing address as a drop for packages of marijuana. It meant I got to see him when he came by to get his mail. . . .

"Two: I got this fabulous job with this great school, and I convinced the director to hire my then boyfriend for a job for which he was uniquely unqualified by exaggerating his qualifications. The director didn't know that he and I were going out. I thought I would get to see my boyfriend more often.

"Three: I decided to leave my husband, but not because I really wanted a divorce. What I really wanted was to have an affair with a guy who lived sixty miles away. I thought it would be easier for us to get together if I wasn't married. I never told anybody."

Marital Choices

Harry, who is a 57-year-old accountant, has a story of a sexually motivated marriage back in the fifties:

"When I was 24, I got married, against my parents' best advice, to a really pretty and really spoiled girl. I can't say that I didn't know that she was 'born to shop.' I did. I just didn't know what it meant. She gave new meaning to the word *only*, as in, 'It's *only* $2,500.' The only parts of the paper she read were the department-store ads.

"People honestly told me that after the first six months or so I would wake up one morning and stop thinking about sex and have to face the fact that I married a spoiled brat. I told them that I was sincerely in love and that underneath her spoiled exterior, she was really a simple girl. I thought I would always feel hot, all the time. Thirty years, two kids, and a messy divorce later, I wish I had listened to my parents. But who can talk to a 24-year-old guy who wants to get laid regularly?"

A New Career

Several women with solid careers said that they started on their career track because of relationships with men. Sarah, a doctor in a large hospital, related the following saga.

"How I got my M.D.? The truth? I wanted to be a lawyer, but in the middle of my senior year I became sexually obsessed with a married doctor. I had this fantasy that maybe we could work together and thus find time to make love. In any event, I had a lot of time on my hands because he rarely could get away from home. I switched gears, spent a year taking premed courses like chemistry, and applied to medical school. Everything I learned I learned because I wanted to impress him and to win him. Every time I studied late at night, I felt closer to him because he had learned all the same stuff; I would finish studying and go to my room and masturbate, thinking of him. It's nuts, but that's what happened. Eventually he took a job in another city.

"Now I'm a doctor, and I don't even know what I saw in him in the first place. I guess it's a classic case of sexual obsession. It could have been worse—he could have been a bank robber. Then I'd be in jail. Now I'm in a big-city hospital with a lot of cute male doctors who are dating nurses and flight attendants and *lawyers*."

Marriage and Sexual Shame

Roxanne, a 47-year-old real estate agent, remembers that she got married because of sexual inexperience, fear, and shame.

"I married my first husband because he raped me. It was date rape, and we'd been going out for a year. But still and all, it was rape. . . . I was too embarrassed to tell anyone. I was a Catholic, and I thought if you slept with someone, you had to marry him. I was also worried that I had gotten pregnant. So I dropped out of college and married him. . . . I did get pregnant, within a month. We had two children, and my husband left me when the oldest boy was 5.

"I moved back with my parents, went back to school, and eventually was able to support the boys, but I often wonder what would have happened if he hadn't forced me to have sex. The only other person I've told about the rape is my second husband. I was too ashamed—I thought it was my fault. But it sure did change my life."

Part II

Sexual Life Patterns and Stages

~

Introduction

Sex . . . it is our passion, sometimes even our obsession. It inspires high drama or perfect prose. It is the stuff that dreams are made of . . . that is, until we start having it on a regular basis. Then it's almost frightening how quickly it can become a weak second choice when weighed against the latest episode of L.A. Law.

It used to be that there was one basic sexual pattern, and it was followed by most Americans. It used to be that men and women were single and mostly celibate until they were in their early to mid-twenties. Then they married and got to sleep together. It has been said that men were supposed to insist upon their conjugal rights, and women were supposed to submit to and tolerate, but not enjoy, the act. Then everything changed.

Now young men and women often start having sex while still in their teens, and it is not uncommon for members of both sexes to have several sexual partners and to decide upon a living-together arrangement before marriage. As a matter of fact, an article in the *Wall Street Journal* in June, 1988, was headlined, SOON MOST PEOPLE MAY HAVE "LIVED IN SIN" and goes on to report that a survey, financed by the National Institutes of Health and carried out by University of Wisconsin researchers, "found that almost half of all Americans 25 to 35 have at some time 'lived in sin'—lived with an individual of the opposite sex outside of marriage . . . whereas only 11% of Americans marrying between 1965 and 1974 had cohabited before their first marriage, 44% of those marrying between 1980 and 1984 had. Cohabiting between marriages is even more normal; 58% of recently remarried people have [done so]."

The same survey found that within a few years most couples who live together either marry or separate; and three fifths of those cohabiting for the first time end up marrying each other.

But whether men and women live together before marriage or not, as we all know, soaring divorce rates indicate that after a few years of marriage many of these same men and women find themselves single once again, and once again sexually interacting with several partners. Average citizens get married, divorced, married again, have affairs, get divorced, become celibate, get happily married, etc. Each of these stages, by definition, changes one's attitude toward sex.

From the people we talked to, it quickly became apparent that many of us, if not most, are sexual chameleons. So many of the people we talked to had individually gone through all of the sexual stages and acted out many of the most common patterns, including serial monogamy, marital monogamy, marital affairs, full-blown promiscuity, and complete celibacy.

It would seem that one's attitude toward one's own sexuality is largely dependent upon the stage one currently occupies. Today's hypochondriacal, albeit sex-starved, single searching for a suitable partner is tomorrow's couch potato, too tired for sex and refusing to yield the remote control to his equally overworked supermom mate. And at the flick of a divorce decree, the same man and woman may find themselves with a heightened sense of sexuality, going through a temporary period of sexual activity that some people might define as promiscuous.

6

What Really Happens in Bed: The Single Life and Temporary Sexual Solutions

SINGLE AND SEARCHING

"If I, or for that matter most of my friends, thought it was going to be this way forever, you would have a lot of very unhappy, or very frightened, people."

—33-year-old man

One of the first men interviewed was a burly, young Southern bachelor, a civil-service employee named Jack. "As long as you're single," Jack said, "you can't take your sex life for granted."

After interviewing singles by the dozens—young, old, divorced, widowed, and confirmed—we've come to the conclusion that Jack knows what he is talking about. We're willing to concede that somewhere out there exists a single who has found a way to have both freedom *and* a sex life that can be taken for granted, but we didn't meet him or her. The facts seem to indicate that to have a secure sex life you need a secure, stable relationship with two committed partners, and the absence of this kind of relationship is what being single is all about.

Ask any group of singles. They'll tell you that being single is worrying about taking off your clothes in front of a total stranger, and it's worrying about whether you'll ever again have the chance to take off your clothes in front of a total stranger. Sometimes it's the loneliness and despair of a solitary bed and screaming hormones, or the intolerable frustration of trying to work out a sexual relationship with someone who isn't interested. Other times it's the trembling anticipation and spectacular sex of a new affair.

Single sex can be the best or the worst, or anything in between. Some of the singles we talked to, for example, were waiting for romantic love and relying on masturbation as a means of finding temporary satisfaction; others had a more active approach and were turned on by the excitement of searching for love, while often settling for sex, with the perfect, or flawed, stranger; others were in highly charged affairs with partners who for one reason or another were emotionally unavailable; and still others were drawn to a series of semi-serious relationships in a style that has become known as serial monogamy.

If the act of marriage implies commitment to one person and a permanent sexual arrangement with a reliable pattern, the single state conjures up images of fleeting encounters and temporary sexual solutions where the only discernible pattern is the insecurity of it all.

THINKING ABOUT SEX THE SINGLE WAY

"I think about it all the time, but I'm embarrassed to tell you how little sex I actually have. I have this recurring fear: that by the time I find somebody to marry or sleep with on a regular basis, I'll be so old that I'll have lost all desire or all ability."

—31-year-old single man

"My single friends break down into two categories: those who think about sex all the time, and those who try not to think about sex all the time."

—34-year-old single woman

It's a truism that you are more preoccupied with sex when you can't take it for granted, and it seemed to us that no other group thinks about sex quite as much as the men and women who are not in committed relationships. For these red-blooded single men and women, trying to find comfortable ways of resolving their personal sexual dilemmas takes up a great deal of time and thought.

Most of these individuals told us one of two things: they hadn't found that certain someone to whom they wanted to make a commitment and hence are always engaged in either searching or compromising; or they had found the person to whom they would like to make such a commitment, but the situation was lacking in reciprocity, and the absence of fulfillment with their would-be soul mates was exacerbating their frustration.

The men and women we spoke to said that this sense of not being able to count on a loving sexual partner has the effect of intensifying sexual feelings so that they become paramount. For these reasons it appeared that the elements of extreme compromise and sexual frustration are often part and parcel of being single.

Singles, both men and women, complained about spending too much time in anticipation, waiting for sexual events that sometimes never take place. A 43-year-old single woman said, "I still think about sex all the time. I'm really happiest when I have someone to sleep with every day. The fact is that I have to look at my life so far and say that my single greatest disappointment is that I've never had an ongoing sex life."

Age does not seem to be a factor in these thoughts. A recently widowed 64-year-old man said, "I'm obsessing about sex now like I did when I was a teenager. I never spent this kind of time worrying about my sex life when my wife was alive."

What does all this concern with sex mean in terms of day-to-day living? One 29-year-old man put it very succinctly: "The fact that I am unfulfilled and frustrated keeps me off-balance much of the time."

This sense of a life that is lacking in balance is a common source of distress for many singles. Some said they felt that without an ongoing, committed relationship, they couldn't work efficiently; others complained about wasting time; and still others said that sexual daydreaming was their prime source of recreation.

Temporary sexual solutions may be far more appealing in the abstract than they are in reality. We understand that it's not all fun and games, but is any of it fun and games? That obviously depends upon a lot of factors, such as age, gender, level of sexual interest or disinterest, and, of course, attitude. People have different attitudes toward temporary sexual solutions. Most of the people we talked to didn't like them, but others were having a nice time; still others were trying to make do.

"I'm making the most of it, meeting as many women as possible, sleeping with as many as I want, getting experience and having a good time. I figure I'll settle down in a few years. In the meantime I want to make the most of it."

—*23-year-old man*

"One of my friends walks into bars, and women come up to him and ask him to take them home. I can't get over it. Last week some girl came up to him and asked him if he wanted oral sex. . . . Nothing like that ever happens to me. *Nothing* happens to me. Believe me, I wish it did!"

—*28-year-old man*

"I hate waking up alone, hate going to bed alone, hate always thinking about sex, and hate never having any."

—*40-year-old divorced woman*

"I'm too old to have to take my clothes off in front of strange women."

—*64-year-old widower*

"The first time I was single, I was in my early twenties, and I didn't know enough to enjoy it. Now it's fun— maybe not for forever, but for now I'm having a good time."

—*44-year-old divorced man*

"I can't believe men still find me attractive, but they do, and I'm enjoying it, at least for the time being."

—*70-year-old woman*

"Yeah, I have enough sex, but I've come to believe that sex without love is boring . . . and I don't love anybody, at least not anybody who loves me back."

—*34-year-old man*

As many single men and women told us, the single person's frame of mind could shift from day to day depending upon whether or not he or she had just had a good weekend or had just met a potential new love interest. There were a lot of variables, and although many said they were sometimes elated by the sense of freedom and unlimited potential in terms of possible mates, they stressed that more often they were depressed by their single status. And it goes without saying that any one person's attitude can change drastically many times, depending upon the time frame during which he or she is single, how long he or she has been single, and the events leading up to their single status. Some men and women who lost partners through death or an unwanted divorce were obviously depressed at the idea of being single again.

But the one common theme that runs through all of our conversations with singles is the notion that these frustrations are, thank God, temporary. This is the reason why some singles can put up with so much from unsatisfying sexual partners; why others can forsake so much in their personal lives, clinging to almost monastic existences; or why some can themselves deviate so far from what they perceive as acceptable personal behavior. You see, almost all singles—young, old, male, female—are convinced that their single sexual patterns will not be permanent. It is this belief in change and the possibility of future love, commitment, permanence, and steady sex that gives them the strength to get through it all, even when their own actions or misactions, relationships or lack of them, do not live up to their expectations of what life is all about. No matter what, they are convinced that it will improve or be shed once they are finally in a permanent sexual relationship. In the meantime they are prepared to look for temporary solutions.

LIVING WITH TEMPORARY SEXUAL
SOLUTIONS—SOME MEN/SOME WOMEN

Karen

Karen, 27, has been divorced for three years. Born into a large Catholic family, she lived in a small town in Illinois until she was 21 when she married Timothy, her first lover, a young man who came from an almost identical family background.

"I dated him for more than two years before I slept with him. . . . At first the sex was fairly intense, and we would find ways to be together three or four times a week. It was very exciting, and I always had orgasms, but I knew, even then, that my strong response was as much a function of my own sexuality as of anything he was doing. I loved him and felt close to him, but I always had my reservations about him as a life partner. He was like my brother. Nonetheless, at first I honestly felt emotionally that I had to marry him because I slept with him. So we got engaged. By the time the wedding rolled around, I was no longer as guilty about the sex. However, I was totally guilty about my parents, who had put up all this money. I had to go through with it.

"We got married at a Catholic Mass. I was in white. My sister's daughter was flower girl, etc., etc. As I walked up the aisle I was thinking, 'Why am I doing this?'

"The marriage sex was basically boring, although my husband was technically a very good lover. He was very well 'hung,' so it was easy to have an orgasm with him, but there was absolutely no passion. Frequency cooled down; we had sex maybe once a week. Because I was no longer turned on to him, I began to hate it, even though I always had orgasms. I began to avoid sex; I think he may have been doing the same thing.

"We were friends and buddies, and eventually he accepted my feelings and we got divorced.

"Right after my divorce I slept with a lot of men and was

quite wild for about a year or so. I was going out with a different guy every night of the week; I slept with maybe two out of five. It was sort of fun, and very different from the way I had been brought up, but not something I would want to repeat. Now I'm much more careful.

"As a single woman, I think most of the men I've dated don't understand women's orgasms; several men have been intent on 'giving' me multiorgasms. I don't want several orgasms. I want one good, big orgasm. When a man keeps going down on you to get you to come again, it's a little like having someone force-feed you double chocolate-chip ice cream. It's not really fun and becomes annoying. Men always say things like 'Doesn't that feel great?' and I keep saying no.

"For the last six months I have been dating, and sleeping with, two guys. One really cares for me, and we have sort of a mini marriage on weekends—friends, picnics, parties, etc. He's a lot of fun, a caring lover, and I'm pretty sure he's monogamous, but I'm dissatisfied with his goals and I'm starting to turn off, even sexually. He's like old faithful, and it bothers me that I'm no longer that interested; it is so similar to what happened with my husband, but I can't change what I feel.

"The other man I'm still turned on to, but it's a very unsatisfying relationship because we spend no real time together. I only see him during the week, and I think he also has somebody else he sees on weekends. I never ask him, and he's very evasive about his schedule.

"Although we have more in common, and we talk about everything, this relationship is really a sexual attraction. We get together to have sex. He works hard and often he's tired, so we meet at his apartment, order in some food, open up a bottle of wine, and we go to bed. We make love and watch television. That's sort of all we do together.

"It's interesting that I find him so much more appealing, because he really has a lot of sexual problems. He doesn't always get erect, and when he does, he doesn't always come. I don't really think it's my responsibility to excite him, but

I get turned on by turning him on. I should also add that he has a definite 'performance' attitude—he *always* has to make me come first.

"For his birthday I made him dinner at my apartment, and I got this really terrific lacy underwear. I put it on with a garter, high-heeled shoes, and a big bow on my head. Nothing else. I wrote 'Happy Birthday' across my bod in pink icing. When I opened the door to let him in, I thought he would die.

"Sometimes, though, nothing works. I mean, there have been nights when I have spent what seems like hours sucking on him, and he just doesn't get erect. I don't really think it's my fault; I think he's just tired."

Karen is particularly concerned about AIDS, and she says that her anxiety is one of the reasons why she continues with these two men; she feels that they are both safe.

"I got really worried about AIDS about six months ago. One of my first lovers after my divorce was a guy who said he was bisexual. I just didn't think about AIDS then, but I've worried about it a lot since. Finally I went and got an AIDS test, and it was negative, thank God. I had been sleeping with both Rob and Frank for over six months at the time. Neither of them have been wearing condoms, so I figure they are both okay. I haven't really spoken to either man about a need for AIDS prevention. It seemed wrong and out of place somehow. My friends tell me I'm crazy to feel that way about Rob because I know nothing about anybody else he goes out with. I think they are right, but . . ."

Karen says that she thinks she is quite sexual. However, she rarely masturbates, and that has held true throughout her life, even during her marriage when sex became infrequent.

A typical week in Karen's life:

Monday night: "Rob and I had a date. I went home after work, put on my diaphragm, showered and changed. I always use a diaphragm and jelly, which I usually insert before I leave the house and before I shower—sometimes the jelly irritates me, which is a nuisance; otherwise I have no problems with it. I met Rob at his apartment. I picked up a video of a movie that I liked and that I knew he hadn't seen. When I got there, he opened some wine, and we ate cheese and talked for about forty-five minutes—you know, sort of a catch-up, mostly about his work and mine. Then we started to kiss in the living room, and eventually we moved to the bedroom. We made love—sort of standard, traditional sex . . . some oral first, then straight intercourse for about ten minutes. I know he always wants me to have the first orgasm, so sometimes I have to fake it; otherwise he seems too controlled and he doesn't let go. I prefer sex when the man is more passionate and focused on his own pleasure. Otherwise it's too mechanical. There's still a lot of electricity between us, so it's good. It feels intimate and sensual. Afterward he ordered in Chinese and we ate in bed and watched the movie—a sort of typical evening. We went to bed early. He woke me up at about six-thirty and we had sex again."

Tuesday night: "I had dinner with three girlfriends and we talked about men."

Wednesday night: "I saw Frank. We went to a movie with another friend of his whose wife just left him. Afterward we had a pizza. He spent the night at my house. He's a very good lover, very skillful, and he spends a lot of time trying to please me."

Thursday night: "I went home, ate carrot sticks, watched *L.A. Law*, and went to bed."

Friday night: "I was home alone. Sometimes I see Frank all weekend, but I'm trying to see less of him."

Saturday: "Frank and I drove out to the beach and spent the day. We went back to his house, made dinner, and watched television. We had sex before bed, but we were both tired and it was quick."

Sunday: "Frank drove me home Sunday morning, but he came back later and helped me put down new linoleum in my kitchen. I made him dinner, but we did have sex first. I really didn't want to, but I didn't want to be rejective because I really like this guy, even if I'm not passionate about him. Frank went home after dinner because he had to get up early the next morning."

Anne

Anne, 24, broke up with her boyfriend a few months ago. Now she is dating again. She says she is . . .

". . . really nervous about AIDS and really angry. I wanted to have a freer time of it and date some and experiment some before I thought about marriage and babies. I've only had two lovers, and I didn't want to marry either of them. I feel like AIDS is cheating me out of a period in my life that I wanted to have.

"Perhaps the reason I feel this way is that I come from a fairly traditional background. I'm sure my mother was a virgin when she married my father, and also my older sisters. I heard a lot of preaching against sex when I was growing up, but it didn't take. I don't think I was as sexually precocious as some of my friends who were sleeping with their boyfriends in high school; I waited until I left home and went to work. I met an older man, and he sort of initiated me into sex. That lasted a very short time, but I realized that I really liked sex.

"The guy I just broke up with wanted to get married, but I wasn't that much in love with him, and I figure I'm too young to compromise. I don't want to settle down like the other women in my family. But right now I don't like my choices. I met a man at a party a few weeks ago. We've been out a few times, and I'm sure he is thinking of asking me to sleep with him. I know I'm thinking about him. But I'm going to ask him to use a condom. I'm nervous. So are all my friends. I think there is much less casual sex than there used to be. One of my best friends had an AIDS test because she went to bed with somebody who was bisexual and didn't find out until afterward. The guy wasn't even the one to tell her. Someone else did. I just don't think you can trust anyone."

Joan

Joan, 38, has never married and has been working for the same company since she graduated from college. She is now fairly well paid and successful, although she feels she has never been truly career-oriented. She says that she basically was working until marriage, but marriage has never happened.

"I guess I have a career by default. I thought I would graduate from college, meet Mr. Right, and get married. It didn't work out that way. I was seeing someone rather seriously in college, but we broke up shortly thereafter. It just wasn't going anywhere, and he was all wrong for me. He was, however, my first lover, and we were both young and easily excited.

"After the breakup I made a major mistake. I had an affair with my boss. This is one of those don'ts that I did. It was just stupid, and it took up four or five years of my life. It was the typical alone-on-weekends-and-holidays syndrome. Sex wasn't even that good; it was boring, and he had problems. I think I was just excited by his power. Also, because he was very involved with the company, I became a workaholic, and some of my marriage goals were replaced by career goals.

"Right now I'm sexually involved with a man who isn't sleeping with me—I mean, isn't having sex with me often enough. I don't really understand why. He's a heavy drinker, so that may have something to do with it. Sex was fine for the first two or three months we were together, and then it started slowing down. Now we have sex maybe twice a month.

"When we do, I can't say it's very gratifying sexually, but I'm very, very attracted to him, and it's very exciting; the intimacy is exciting. I just wish it were more often. He's older than I am—he's in his fifties, which may have something to do with frequency, and he's an old-style lover. Totally into penetration. He was married to the same woman for twenty-five years, and I think they had a boring sex life. He rarely goes down on me, although he likes me to do it to him. He's just inexperienced and uneducated as a lover. I'd be happy to teach him, but at this rate I don't think I'll get a chance. I haven't told him how dissatisfied I am, but how could he not know? I'm afraid to bring it up because I don't want him to think I'm demanding, and I don't want him to feel bad. Maybe he's giving me as much sex as he's capable of. Maybe he doesn't find me attractive.

"He stays over at my place four or five nights a week, but he doesn't touch me. I don't know what to do about it. Some nights I get in bed next to him, and he's asleep in two minutes, and I just lie there. I've even gotten up and gone into the living room and masturbated because of the frustration. Then I get back in bed and curl up next to him. I'm glad he's there, I just wish he were more there.

"In the mornings, however, we cuddle up and have coffee in bed. He's sweet and good to me. A younger lover would probably be more interested in sex, but with a younger lover, I'd be more worried about AIDS—of course, I'd also have to think about that with any new man."

Cindy

Like many of the other women we spoke to, Cindy, who is a 26-year-old aerobics instructor, is concerned about AIDS. She says that she became pregnant last year and had an abortion. The experience made her very aware that bad things could happen to her too. She said she doesn't want to take any chances but that she really misses sex.

"I'm not happy sexually. I would be if I had a great lover, but I don't have a lover. I don't have anybody. I used to go with this older guy—he was in his mid-forties; I started sleeping with him when I was 21, but now I find him boring. He was an okay lover—very energetic, you know—and at the beginning I was very involved with him, because he was an intellectual, and I liked that, but he really didn't give very much emotionally. He was very distant and not affectionate, except in bed. Otherwise he was cold. He was like this really successful photographer, and I loved him and respected him. But he hurt me so much; I got so emotionally turned off that

I turned off on him. He would see other women and would tell me about it. He would tell me that they were terrible in bed, that he liked me better, and that I was better in bed, and more beautiful. He'd usually discuss this over lunch. That made me initiate sex more and chase after him because I was jealous. I wanted to be loved.

"So for a while, even after we broke up, I would call him when I wanted to have sex. We don't do anything else because all he wants to do is watch TV. It didn't bore me so much when I was totally turned on to him, but now that I'm not, I just don't have the patience. But I'm not calling him anymore because he still goes out with too many women, and he was never that careful about who he dated. He thinks he is but he's not. I'm really paranoid about AIDS.

"When we were together, we'd have sex for five or six hours straight. He was very insecure and always wanted me to tell him how fabulous he was. I was with him because I loved him, not because he was the best lover in the world. The best lover I ever had was totally crazy, except in bed. Sometimes you have to get out of bed.

"I can deal with sex that is just for sex, but I don't think most men can. When I've gone to bed with somebody with a free and open spirit, no strings attached, I've usually discovered that the guy thinks he's using me for sex. I don't like that feeling. I had it with a man who was all hung up and involved with some woman who wouldn't sleep with him, or wouldn't go down on him or some such. But he said she inspired him. It was too weird. I was supposed to be the sexual person, because she was some kind of asexual saint. Once I met him, at his suggestion, at his place. We had sex on the couch because he didn't want to do it in 'their' bed. I couldn't handle all the neurosis.

"I had some questions about a man I went to bed with, so I had an AIDS test a month or so ago. It came back negative. Lots of men find me attractive, very attractive, but it's like playing Russian roulette. From this point on I don't go to bed with anybody unless I'm sure. I've masturbated so much, it's terrible. I'm not happy about this, but I don't know what else to do. I would love to meet somebody with whom I could have a good relationship; it doesn't have to be marriage. But I'm not meeting anybody."

Fran

Fran, who has two school-age children, has been divorced for a little over a year.

"I just celebrated my thirtieth birthday, and two years ago, if someone had told me I would be alone for it, I would have called them a liar. I didn't know there was all that much wrong with my marriage. My husband wasn't as interested in sex after the kids were born; maybe I wasn't, either. I was tired, but so was he. Some people say we just got married too young—we had been together since we were 20. He was my best friend, so I was real shocked when he said he wanted a divorce. I wanted to go to counseling, but he wouldn't do it. He's with someone else, you know, someone younger, thinner. He met her three weeks before he left me. Some men just have affairs, but I think he was too honest to do that.

"My friends tell me I have to go out and meet people, but I don't know how to do it. How do you meet men with two young kids and a full-time job? Even if I had somebody, I don't know what I would do if I liked him. I certainly couldn't bring anybody home with the kids. I had one date three months ago with this creep that my sister-in-law's cousin dug up. He took me out to dinner, which was nice, and then he brought me back here. My baby-sitter went back home, and I offered him some coffee, and he tried to start up with me in the living room. I told him that we couldn't, that I was worried about waking the kids, but he didn't believe me. It was awful. I sort of had to fight him off. He kept trying to put my hand on his crotch. I couldn't believe it was happening to me. I'm one of those women who thought I'd be married for life. I still miss my husband a lot. He's still my husband to me; of course I miss sleeping with him. I masturbate some, but it's not the same.

"I have another single friend, and she goes with a lot of men, and she keeps offering to find me dates, but I think I'm just not ready for it. I don't want to go to bars to meet men

—that's what she does sometimes. When I'm ready, I want somebody who is good to my children. That's the most important thing to me. Although I'd like him to be cute too. My husband was real cute."

Allison

Allison, 35, agreed to meet with us but said she couldn't understand why we would want to hear "my history of saying no."

"I come from a very religious fundamentalist background, and what that means is that I don't drink, smoke, or fool around. I want very much to get married and have a family, and when I do, I want to be a virgin in spirit as well as in body. I keep to both the spirit and letter of the law. It's not easy, believe me, but I do it.

"I had my first kiss at 17, and I've been dating ever since. I went to a religious college, but I made the mistake of going out with boys who were not always of my faith. Consequently I think while I was wrestling and trying to convince some guy to change his ways, the young men who were serious about settling down were settling down. The restrictions on sex means that a lot of people in my church marry very early.

"In my twenties I moved to Florida, and I dated a lot of men who were very worldly. Now I wish that I had resisted my impulse to date worldly men. It was a mistake for me, because most of these men ultimately rejected me because of the sex issue or the religion issue.

"A lot of my evenings have ended in what I call a classic conflict situation.

"I say, 'I'm sorry. It's not you. I can't do it.'

"He says, 'You're wrong about this. Sex brings a couple much closer together.'

"I say, 'No.'

"He says, 'It's a natural thing to do.'

"I say, 'I'm sorry, but no.'

"He says, 'It's a wonderful way to express affection and devotion for each other.'

"I say, 'If it was just between you and me, I would certainly want to go to bed with you . . . but I have to think about something more. I have to think about my relationship with God.'

"Then he says, 'I certainly respect you. I do have tremendous respect for you. But I'm never going to ask you out again.'

"I have had several relationships that lasted longer than six months. Some were with men of my faith; a couple were not. With these men, we hugged and touched and were close. We had good friendships. With men of your faith it's easier. They have the same frustrations, but at least they're on your side. I've necked with these men, but my rule is that I stop when I start getting very turned on. One man I went out with calls once a year to see if I'm still a virgin.

"One man attempted a date rape. It was fairly unpleasant. I thought he was a nice man, even though I didn't know him that well. I was with friends at his apartment for lunch. Everybody else had to leave, and he asked me to help clean up. I didn't see any reason to say no. It was really stupid of me. Then while I was doing dishes, he excused himself. When he returned, he didn't have any clothes on, and he was fully aroused. He tried to assault me. He tore my clothes and twisted my arm. Somehow I did manage to get out of there. It was like a scene in a movie—racing up an empty street with no way to get home. Now I'm more careful. I also took some courses in self-defense.

"In the seventies and early eighties, people really gave me a lot of flak; they thought I was extremely weird. Guys used to always ask me if I was frigid. Give me a break. I am positive I will love sex. I am very responsive and I can't understand anyone not liking it. I'm very much looking forward to it.

"Times have changed, you know. For a while I think my inexperience was a real negative—men wanted someone who had more experience, but now I think more men realize experience can be gained quickly. I feel my stock has gone up in the world. In other words, I think more men are looking at me and saying, 'Well, she's got that religious stuff, but at least she's disease-free.'

"I really want to get married. I joke and tell people that I will consider anyone who can use a fork, but I guess I'm looking for what I've always looked for. I plan to stay in my faith."

Evelyn

Evelyn, who has been divorced twice, is in her mid-fifties. She says that she has had a great deal of sexual experience, both good and bad. Right now she is having a relationship with a man in his early forties. It has been going on for about two and a half years.

"I am having the best sex! Tender, loving, intimate, sexy sex. It's fabulous. I can't believe this is happening to me at my age, but it is. Mel is much younger, and he has custody of his son, who is just a child, so I don't see him all that often. We get together once a week, sometimes twice; we're on the phone about three or four times a week; and we see each other for special occasions, like holidays and birthdays. He is very much there for me, even though he's not always with me—I know I can call him, for instance, for just about anything. But he has the child, and he just started a new business, and we're both busy.

"I've made it clear also that I don't have the strength for a young child—the boy has a mother. Mel and I have talked about maybe living together when the boy gets older, but we still have our age difference.

"When we see each other, often the first thing he does is start taking my clothes off. Sometimes we make love in the living room, standing up. All the lights are on, and I used to worry about his looking at my body and noticing all the ways in which it's aging, but when I look at him, usually his eyes are closed. I don't think he notices or cares. I don't know if I would be so all-accepting, but he is. He can have sex for thirty to forty minutes, and we usually do. He's changed sexually in the last two years: He used to be fairly standard missionary position; now he's very experimental. He used to be more inhibited about oral sex, but that's changed; now he seems to love it. The sex is truly fabulous and very close. Afterward we usually go out for dinner. Sometimes we'll go to a movie, but most of the time we just have dinner and talk. We talk like crazy."

Evelyn says that in the past she has often slept with more than one man at a time, but that age has also changed her.

"I've been basically faithful for the last two years, with a couple of small exceptions. I went to bed with an old friend. We met again at the wedding of a mutual friend's daughter, and we had too much to drink. At least I did. One thing led to another, and we decided for old-times' sake to go to bed together. To be honest, I started it. I said to him, 'I've always wondered what you would be like in bed.' He said, 'No time like the present to find out.' Afterward I was really upset with myself.

"As I've gotten older, I find that I've changed sexually. My orgasms are still very good and very intense, but my desire is not nearly as intense. In a way, it makes life easier."

Dorothy
Dorothy recently helped her oldest grandchild celebrate his twenty-first birthday. Dorothy will be 72 in a few months. Her husband died two years ago, and she began dating only within the last eight months . . . primarily, she says, because of sexual frustration.

"My husband and I had a very satisfying sexual relationship until the last six months, when he became ill. After his death I found that I missed male companionship and male sexuality. I like men. I like being with them, but I've come to enjoy living alone, and I'm not sure I would ever want to marry again. I had a wonderful marriage, but this is a different part of my life, and it allows me to be perfectly selfish. I like it. I have a country house I go to on weekends and in the summer. I like gardening and swimming. I have friends. I'm not rich, certainly, but I'm comfortable. I certainly don't need a man to provide for me; my husband did that. But I do miss a regular sex life.

"That's probably what brought me back into a dating scene at my age. The first man I met was almost ten years younger than me. He was extremely seductive and very attentive. After we had been to bed together for the first time, he told me he was married. It was sort of shocking and surprising, but I decided to continue seeing him, anyway, primarily because of a sexual attraction. He was sort of an aging refugee from the sixties; he didn't wear bell-bottoms, but he looked as though he wanted to. He was the first man I had ever been with except my husband, and he wasn't as satisfying a sexual partner as my husband, and he had a few sexual problems, which I think were age-related. We spent a couple of wonderful weekends in bed—I don't know what he told his wife, and I didn't ask him. It ended after a few months because I think he was very neurotic. I got the impression that he had always had affairs, and that he enjoyed them while they were new, and tired of them quickly. It was an odd experience for a woman my age—you know, running off to meet a married man in motels and hotels. I became quite hooked on him sexually.

"While I was still seeing him, I met another man, who was a few years older than me, and we started an affair also. This man had sexual problems, also, and was impotent much of the time. However, I discovered he could still have orgasms, and he was very attentive and made love to me in other ways. The sex is okay, but I don't think I'm going to continue to go out with him. He is quite demanding and emotionally immature; it's ridiculous. He's in his seventies and he's like a teenager. I don't want those kinds of demands made on me.

"I recently met another man, with whom I have not started a sexual relationship. We're having a nice, rather formal friendship, doing things together. He's a widower. So far he hasn't come near me except to peck me good night, but the relationship may have long-term promise."

Connie

Connie, 43, was married once, at 27, to a man who was a couple of years younger; they were divorced when she was

32. During the last ten years she says she hasn't had a "regular sexual diet. . . ."

"It's been so intermittent that I almost wonder if it is worth it. There are times when I am almost totally turned off sex, and when that happens, I think I'm happier. It's more comfortable not to feel anything. It's awful walking around feeling sexy when there is nobody there.

"What's happened in my life? Not much, let me tell you. The love of my life, who I met when I was 35, lived in another state. We would see each other once a month for a weekend. We would spend the weekend in bed; it was perfect. Perfect sex and perfect understanding, I thought. When I met him, he was separated from his wife, who he said didn't want to sleep with him. Finally they reconciled, even though he said she still wouldn't sleep with him. He called me a couple of years ago, and he told me that he and his wife were still not having sex. I think he was telling the truth.

"The other men in my life recently have all been marginal. I went out with one man, who is still a good friend, for about a year and a half. We made love all the time, but he drank too much and he never really got hard. He thought he did. I didn't. But that's not why we split up—I just didn't love him. I don't have orgasms from penetration alone, anyway. I always need clitoral stimulation. It's funny, but every man I've been with has made sure that I've had the first orgasm. That's always amazed me.

"Then another man I've been seeing is older, and he can't have orgasms. I think it may be age-related, but we never talk about it.

"I went out with a married man briefly, but I knew his wife, and I just felt too guilty about it. He calls all the time.

"Then I guess I should tell you that I'm also having an affair with somebody I went to summer camp with thirty years ago. He's also married, but I don't know his wife. He's from out of town, and we see each other maybe twice a year. He used to be much more passionate when he was younger, but he's still fun.

"It really bothers me that I've never had a long-term, fulfilling sexual relationship. I hate it."

Mick

Mick, 25, lives and works in the Midwest. He is thinking of getting engaged to Laura, 23. They have been going together for close to two years, and sleeping together for eighteen months.

Although Mick had as many as fifteen or twenty mostly isolated sexual encounters, this is his first meaningful sexual relationship, and he feels that he is intensely attracted to Laura, as well as in love with her. Laura is much less experienced, and Mick is her first real lover.

"We both still live with our parents, so our private time is *very* limited. About three months ago Laura's parents discovered we were sleeping together. She went to a doctor to get a diaphragm, and she left the bill where they could find it. They were very upset. They're conservative and religious, and the whole thing caused a major disenchantment on their part. They never in a million years thought their daughter would do anything like that.

"Laura and I had a lot of major discussions with them, and we went to see their pastor with them, and what we finally agreed, Laura and I, was that we would lay off talking about it for a while for the sake of maintaining a relationship with her parents. We don't want to be dishonest; we just don't talk about it. I think what they've done is kind of hope for the best and try to put it out of their minds; they feel strongly about saving yourself for marriage. We just do what we have always done, but we're more careful.

"We can never spend the night together, anyway, unless we go away for a weekend. We spent a weekend at her cousin's last month. It was great. Her cousin sort of made it clear that he knew we wanted to be together, and he left us alone.

"If I stay over at her parents' house, I sleep in the guest room, and we absolutely don't try to get together at night. Her parents would have a stroke.

"When we do get to be together, we do a lot of foreplay and sharing, a lot of feeling and caressing and stuff. I really love this woman.

"Laura hasn't had an orgasm yet. I've emphasized with

her that we're not going to make a big deal out of it; we're going to let it happen naturally. I've tried to focus on what will give her more pleasure. I'm anxious to learn what to do, and I'm very open. Let me tell you that if she hadn't been so open and hadn't told me that she wasn't having an orgasm, I never would have known it. She's very verbal and she seems very excited, and exciting. She's incredibly physical, and it's reciprocal.

"But I think she would like more oral sex, and I'm trying to spend more time on that. I don't think I've been as much of a giver in that area as she has with me.

"We talk on the phone every night for half an hour, and we have sex once, maybe twice a week if we can work it out. Sometimes our physical contact is very fleeting—like we took a two-hour-bus ride, and on the way back, most people on the bus were asleep, so we held hands and kissed and talked. It was a lot of fun."

Jenny

Jenny, a 34-year-old working single mother, says that she is currently sexually obsessed with a man she works with, a doctor.

"I'm a physical therapist—that's how I met Joel. He's 38 and divorced for the second time. He has two teenage kids with his first wife, but he barely sees them.

"He's not very good to me. And I guess the sexual attraction is what keeps me in the relationship. When he's with me, he's just overwhelmingly passionate. I feel like I'm glued to him.

"When I first met him, I just felt sorry for him. He seemed sad and lonely, and he was getting a divorce. I had been divorced for about two years, but I really hadn't gone out much. I'd had one small affair with a married man, but that had ended, so I was pretty open for something. Joel didn't ask me out at first. He would just always smile at me in the halls when he saw me. I work in his hospital two days a week. Finally he asked me out, and when he walked through the door of my apartment, he just stopped, looked at me, pulled me toward him, and kissed me. Like they say, it knocked my socks off. We went out to dinner—but who ate anything?—and he came back home with me and spent the night.

"It was my daughter's weekend with her father, and he spent the rest of the weekend in my apartment. He's a very experienced lover—he's also very passionate, very involved.

"The following week, he told me I had to be careful at work. He said he had had an affair with a woman there who was very jealous. It turns out he's still having affairs with not one, but two women at the hospital—one of whom is in a real position to hurt him professionally. I have a funny feeling that we all know about each other, and we all run around trying to protect him.

"When I was single the first time and didn't have a child, I never would have gotten myself in such a pickle. I'm more dependent now. I'm scared of losing him, even though there is nothing to lose. I let it continue because I'm so attached to him emotionally and sexually that when I see him, sometimes my hands shake and I hyperventilate.

"Fortunately I've only let him stay over once when my daughter was home, and then we got up before her and pretended that he had come by for breakfast. I'm ashamed to tell her or show her that he doesn't care for me. I think what a terrible example I am to her as a woman. Her father left me, and now this man is walking all over me. I really resent being this sexual pushover, and wonder if it has something to do with hormones or my age."

Mike

Mike, a 30-year-old single man living in Los Angeles and working as a commodities broker, also said that his relationship had an obsessional quality. He is, as he says, "emotionally attached" to a woman named Mary Jo, who lives in Houston; he "thinks about her a lot" and has no real interest in anyone else. However, because the day-to-day dynamics of the relationship are so unsatisfactory, he continues to date, hoping that another woman will make a difference in his life.

When asked what it is about this woman that has affected him so deeply, he says:

"I don't know. She's not that pretty, and she's not that brilliant, but something about her lights a fire in me that I don't feel anyplace else. I don't know what it is about her; she's just special.

"I have an incredible sexual relationship with Mary Jo—incredible. She's very passionate, very experimental. The problem is that when we started sleeping together, she was still married to my cousin.

"We didn't become lovers until after they started having problems; hell, I didn't even know that I was that attracted to her. They were both living in L.A. at the time, and I remember one day visiting at their house; my cousin was gone and we both went swimming, and she took her bathing suit off. I guess I knew I could have made love to her then, but she was married to my cousin, and I didn't think it was right. Then.

"But about six months or a year later, it became apparent that they were having problems, and I knew that my cousin was dating. Mary Jo was all upset and feeling crummy, and I took her out for a drink. She said she felt unwanted, unattractive, abandoned, and we kept drinking, and I kept assuring her that she was a very beautiful woman. Well, we started touching, and I kept saying, 'No, this isn't right. I'm not right for you.' Stuff like that. You have to understand that I thought I was still in love with my ex-girlfriend—she had split up with me about a month or two before.

"Anyway, I took her home, and when we got back to her house, as soon as I stopped the car, we started kissing, and the next thing I knew, she was sucking my cock . . . right under the garage light . . . it was movie stuff.

"I thought about her husband, my cousin, returning, but I couldn't stop it. It was incredible. First we were in the car, and then we moved out to the yard; we were lying in the grass and she kept sucking my cock. Finally I pulled her down on top of me and we made love.

"I think that's when I made my mistake. When we were

finished, I just sort of lay there and then I went home. If I'd known for sure that she and my cousin were going to get divorced, I think I would have gone for her right there. Instead I just felt funny.

"I went to bed with her again the following weekend, and again at her house. I knew my cousin was out with his girl-friend, so this time I spent the night. I remember 'cause when I got home, my cousin dropped in at my apartment; he said he'd been trying to reach me the previous night 'cause he'd had a blind date for me. He asked me where I'd been. I said it was none of his business . . . what could I say, that I'd been out poking his wife?

"Anyway, what happened is that my cousin moved back into his house, and Mary Jo moved out. She had found out that her husband, my cousin, was having an affair with her best friend—she sort of walked in on them. Anyway, she told him she was going to stay with friends, but she was staying with me. We were sort of lovers, and sort of friends, and she was sleeping with other guys as well. You see, at this time I was pretty much unobtainable emotionally because I was still involved with my last girlfriend, who had gone off with some other guy.

"So Mary Jo and I would have sex sometimes once a week, sometimes three or four times a day, depending upon whether she was there, I was in the mood, etc. I was still into my ex-girlfriend. I remember once Mary Jo was fellating me, and she stopped and said, 'You're not into this.' She was right; I was thinking about my ex-girlfriend, and I told her that. But my feelings started to change, and I suddenly began to feel like I was really beginning to fall in love with her. And it seemed that she was about ready to end all her fucking around, but at about this time she started an affair with her best friend's husband—he was the husband of the friend who was having an affair with *her* husband.

"Anyway, it sort of all blew up; I got angry, and we stopped sleeping together. She was going to look for another place to stay. Then the best friend's husband went away for a couple of weeks, and we started sleeping together every night, making love every night, but when he came back, she lied to me. She told me she was going to visit a friend; instead she went to meet this guy, and she didn't come home all night.

"Then she started sleeping with both of us but on alternate nights; it was pretty weird. Finally, after a couple of weeks of this, she moved and left town.

"She started writing me love letters, and I started telling her to stick it. I didn't answer her letters or anything.

"Then I met another woman, a really gorgeous, nice woman, and we started to go out, develop stuff—it was terrific. Too good to be true. I didn't know how right that was because within a couple of months Mary Jo came back to get some of her stuff. I heard from friends that she was back in town, that they'd seen her. And I started to feel those old feelings.

"The next morning I drove my girlfriend to work, and when I came home, Mary Jo pulled up in her car. All I wanted to do was hold her, to be with her. God. That day she came by at work to give me my house keys back, and we started to hold each other in the office. It was too electric.

"She called me when she got back to Houston and asked me to come visit. I don't know if I would have gone, but a couple of weeks later this girl and I split up. It was her idea, so I decided to go see Mary Jo. After all, I had just been rejected by this other woman, and I felt needy.

"Mary Jo picked me up at the airport and started telling me about how she had started sleeping with an old lover. I got angry. I didn't want to be in the apartment with her. I didn't even want to sleep in the same bed. But the next day we went shopping in this mall, and there was a song coming out of the Muzak, and she was standing behind me, and she started rubbing my back. It felt great. That reminded me of all the old feelings again, and that night we made love, and it was magic, like always.

"I'm the only man she really has good orgasms with; she takes a long time, and oral sex is what really works. She says that other men have given up on her, and there were times when I gave up too. I had to . . . I couldn't continue. Remember that scene in *Annie Hall* where Woody Allen is sitting there rubbing his jaw, and Shelley Duvall is saying, 'Sorry it took me so long,' and he says, 'That's okay, I'm sure I'll be able to speak normally in a week'? Eventually I got it right, and now I can make her come every time."

Mike is one of the few men we spoke to who discussed his reactions to a woman giving him specific instructions on how to bring her to orgasm. He says:

"After a couple of months she would start telling me what I was doing wrong sometimes. At first I resented it. It was like, 'Oh, boy, I feel great . . . I'm doing this for you, and you're criticizing.' But I went with it, and eventually it developed into a very good communication. She is very open, and the degree of candor and communication we have sometimes is amazing.

"She tried to fake orgasms a couple of times, but I figured it out and just kept at it . . . until she really came.

"It's interesting, because a combination of oral sex and manipulation is the only way she can come, and I don't really come from oral sex. I like intercourse. It's my surefire method. I like to make Mary Jo come before me. I love having intercourse with a woman who has just come. They're really receptive to anything.

"Anyway, after I went back to L.A., she got more involved with that guy she had started seeing. He wasn't really that interested in her; he just wanted sex. I went to see her on Thanksgiving, and it was the same old stuff. I walked through the door of her house, and I had a present for her. She said, 'Are you trying to convince me to go to bed with you?' and I slid my hand up her leg, and her panties were soaked.

"I was talking to her almost every day, but I didn't see her again until almost February. Then I went to see her. She was all depressed from this other guy. He just blew her off. She had gotten pregnant from him and had just had an abortion.

"I accidentally had a couple of women get pregnant with me, so I was sympathetic; these things can happen. We couldn't have sex, but we hugged and kissed, and finally she managed to bring me to orgasm through manipulation and sucking. It was amazing because it's really almost impossible for me to come that way. Then I made her come several times before we were through.

"Anyway, when I got home, I called her, and she was out. I called for several days and she was always out, and I said to myself, 'Who needs this?' So I started looking for someone else, and I met this really fabulous-looking woman who seemed to like me, and we started to go out. I went back to her apartment with her, and to make a long story short, so to speak, I couldn't get it up. No way. It was really strange. This woman was very understanding and all that—at least she said she understood, and we agreed we would just be friends. Of course, we ended up trying again, and it was the same story. No dice. I got really upset and depressed over my failures. I even went to a doctor—I thought maybe it was hormonal . . . but no, everything checked out normal. Even my testosterone levels were up there.

"So when I went to see Mary Jo again, I was really worried. I thought I wouldn't get it up. But she was very patient . . . she knew I was having problems, and it took a while for me to have an erection, but finally everything worked. You know, it's not just sex. We're also amazingly affectionate. We go to sleep with our arms around each other.

"I realize that I can't function with anyone but her anymore. I don't seem to be attracted to anyone else. But to be perfectly honest, I'm just not as sexual in general . . . and I'm having this real confidence problem, not just with sex. I don't know if it's depression or what. I don't even feel much of an urge to masturbate. I live here; she lives there. I don't know what we're going to do about it. We talk on the phone every day. Sometimes we even have phone sex. . . .

"I love kissing her breasts. She's just beautiful to me, she's really incredible, wonderful. I never fantasize with her because she's my fantasy come true."

Arthur

Arthur, who is 24, by his own admission is quite inexperienced. He says he thinks it is a direct result of his religious upbringing and a rather stern moralistic code. Nonetheless, he has yearned for an open sexuality and has constantly searched for the woman who will introduce him to the kind of nonrepressive experience he has heretofore only dreamed of.

"I don't really have an intimate knowledge of sex. I think one of the reasons is that I am blessed with starting up with the most screwed-up girls imaginable. They all had stories. Typical girl. Let me tell you about Jennie. I met her because she was sharing a summer house with my cousin. You want to know the first thing she said to me? I'm sitting in the living room minding my own business, and this blonde walks in in her bikini, looks at me, and says, 'My birth control pills are getting too expensive. Do you think they're tax-deductible?'

"I thought, 'This is great.' She hung around me all weekend, and she couldn't stop talking, with lots of sexual references; she told me how she lost her virginity at 13 at summer camp; she told me about the married man who only wanted her body, and she had all these bikinis—gold, blue, striped. I lost count. So I asked her out.

"Well, I took her out to dinner a few times, and to a show or a movie, and each time when I took her home, I would go to kiss her and she would stop me at the door. But all the while her clothes and the way she looked at me made me think she was as interested as I was. Besides . . . all those stories of hers made me think she was a really hot number.

"So I made reservations at this little inn about two hours outside of the city. It was a gorgeous fall weekend. I figured we had nothing to do but make out and look at the leaves. Well, was I ever wrong! The first thing I did really pissed her off. When we go to sign the register, I tell the truth. My name, her name, not Mr. and Mrs. I'm sorry, I don't like to lie. Well, that got her. 'What's the matter,' she says,

'I'm not good enough to be your wife?' We had dinner, a
bottle of wine, a walk in the woods. We get back to the inn,
and I go into the bathroom to take a shower. I come out
thinking, 'Well, finally, this is it!'

"Instead, she looks at me like I crawled out from under
a rock. Every time I went to touch her, she started to shake,
as if to say, 'Don't touch me please.' You've got to understand,
I'd been thinking about this for weeks, and all she did was
shake."

Will

Will, 58, has been divorced for the last thirteen years.

"I've changed a lot over the years. I was wildly unfaithful
when I was married. After the divorce I had plenty of sex
with dozens of women. Then I lived with another woman
for a year, but I was unfaithful to her too.

"For the last eight years I've been seeing one woman; she's
a good deal younger than me—she's still in her mid-thirties.
I've been fairly faithful.

"We don't see each other that often because we both work
hard and she travels for her work. Then I still have these
children I go to see, every other weekend. Sometimes this
woman and I only get together every other weekend. I'm
alone most of the time. Nights I'm home alone. For a guy
who always had a very active sex life, now I have a very
inactive sex life. I masturbate a lot, and I talk to myself.
Sometimes I lose the difference between talking with myself
and talking with another person. Sometimes I take out sexy
videos. I suppose I could go out—several women are interested in me—but I don't have the confidence I once did.
I used to have great success and often was juggling two or
more. Now I think women think I'm an older man, and I'm
having a hard time dealing with it.

"I have less confidence as I've gotten older. I think your
confidence goes as your body goes. Even though I've made
love to scores of women, I've always had problems with erections the first few times I'm with someone. For example,
if I met an attractive woman tonight and I felt this woman

wanted to go to bed with me, I would immediately start thinking about whether or not I'd be able to get an erection. I'm very susceptible to my own suggestion—if I think, 'I wonder if I'm going to get an erection,' then there's a chance I won't.

"I remember one woman I was with who did everything, anything she could think of, and I was tremendously attracted to this woman, and she was very dirty . . . she knew everything. But it was like beating a dead man. I told her this often happens when I first have sex, but I don't think she believed me.

"I think a lot of men have erection problems at first, but I think women don't understand that; they think you're sexually inadequate, and then I think they begin to blame themselves. I think men don't understand how much that happens. A cruel man can use that against a woman. Another thing is that women are sexy only to the degree they like themselves. If they're having their period or if they don't think they're attractive, they're not going to be sexy no matter what you do to them.

"The other sexual problem I have is that I've overtrained myself not to come too soon. I start holding it back and holding it back, and pretty soon it's held back, and it's not coming, and they're thinking this guy's unbelievable, but all it means is that you haven't had a climax.

"I trained myself not to come too quickly, but I don't think any sexy woman will let you get away with coming quickly. I also don't think a truly sexy woman wants to blow you too much—because it means she will have less sex.

"When I'm with this woman I see, I think that my performance is as good as ever, but I probably don't have the same endurance I once did. However, I've never met a woman who needed as much sex as me on a daily basis. When I'm with this woman for four or five days, she usually says, 'Hey, enough, I'm getting sore.'

"Another thing I've noticed as I've gotten older is that I find fewer women attractive. I used to find every woman attractive. Maybe as I've gotten older I just realize I don't want to find somebody else and start again. I'm not saying

I couldn't do it, but the idea of beginning with somebody new . . . I don't know. It may be my age or it may be that I'm in love with this woman and don't want anybody else."

Drew

At 34, Drew says he has been in and out of a series of unfulfilling relationships.

"The longest relationship lasted two and a half years. And I guess I haven't really come all that close to marriage. I was in love, very briefly two years ago, with a woman who was very difficult. Everything was difficult—sex was also difficult. I say I was in love with her, but perhaps I'm confusing it and thinking that the harder something is to achieve, the more worthwhile it becomes, which if you stop and think about it is really absurd.

"Right now I've been with a woman for a little over six months. We have very, very good sex. For me, by and large, the sexual act never varies tremendously whether or not I think I'm in love. Many women have complained that I am distant, and that may be true.

"A part of me wishes that I were more sexually motivated. I like it, but I'm not obsessed with it. I think more sexual motivation would be more symptomatic of being a more passionate person . . . more in touch with my feelings.

"What happened this last week?

"I saw this woman on Monday and we had sex.

"I saw her on Wednesday and we had sex.

"I saw her on Saturday and we had sex.

"That's sort of our pattern.

"Birth control? Usually she uses a diaphragm. Some nights she puts it in when she brushes her teeth; more often she interrupts sex and goes into the bathroom. Last night, though, she forgot to bring her diaphragm with her, and she didn't tell me until after we started. She's had an abortion, so she's usually pretty careful. We've played Vatican roulette a couple of times, but not too often. Last night she said we shouldn't risk it. So the actual intercourse part was pretty short, but I brought her to orgasm that way.

"This woman can come to orgasm fairly quickly, but I've been with women who take a long time. When that happens, I usually manually stimulate them at the same time, which I find really advances everything. You know, if sex goes on too long, it's still fun, but sometimes it's like, what is this, an endurance test?

"I try not to think about AIDS too much, but I had a complete physical about a year ago and had an AIDS test with it. I wish this woman would have one. If she had AIDS, I would probably already be a goner, but she didn't strike me as the kind of person to have AIDS, which is just ridiculous. I know you can't tell who has AIDS."

Gene

Gene, 40, talks about being single for the second time: "It's sort of interesting because I'm doing the same things I was doing fifteen years ago. Like talking to women I would never be talking to except for sexual reasons.

"I've only been divorced for about eighteen months, so I don't want to rush into anything—not that there is anything to rush into. I got to tell you I've had two very bad experiences in the last year or so. What is it with women these days? It is very different from how it used to be.

"I met a woman last year, for example. I don't think I have ever ended up in the sack so fast, and she was the one who was pushing. But she was totally detached and really didn't seem to enjoy sex, and I was frantically trying to figure out what buttons I wasn't pushing. She wouldn't touch me. She wouldn't hold me. I took her away for a long weekend, and we had a lot of sex and fun, and I thought she was warming up to me. Then, when we came back, she said she didn't want to see me anymore. I thought about it a lot, and I guess I figured that she didn't like me that much.

"Then I met someone who acted like she wanted to get very intimate and close. Sexually she wasn't that great, but she seemed to care for me so much that I thought we would work it through. She couldn't have orgasms, but I've known several women like that. I assume that if you spend enough time, eventually it will happen—at least that's been my experience in the past. I thought this relationship had a future, but then I noticed two things. The first is that she started drinking. I guess maybe she always did, but I hadn't noticed it. And then the thing that made me most crazy is that this woman kept talking about her ex-husband, even in bed. It certainly took a lot of joy out of the sex. Then she wondered why I was less ardent.

"I'm used to a different kind of woman. My wife really catered to me. We had other problems, but I knew where I stood with her, or at least I thought I did. At the beginning she loved me, and she acted like she loved me. Her feelings for me were very clear. You used to be able to evaluate how much a woman cared for you. Now I just can't tell.

"I don't seem to be too interested in women my age. I don't want to think it's a superficial thing. So many of them seem so jaded. Yet on the flip side of the coin, there is all this other craziness with the younger ones."

THE EMPTY BED SYNDROME

We spoke to a surprising number of single men and women who were temporarily celibate. As one would imagine, none of them were pleased with this life-style. The men who were still under 35 were perhaps the most vocal. John, who jokingly described himself as your standard, depressed, sex-starved single male said, "What's happening in my bed? A lot of tossing and turning. I had a girlfriend two years ago with whom I had a good, fairly long-term sexual relationship, but that ended because I didn't want to make a commitment. Now there's been nobody for a long, long time. I sort of try to forget about sex. Sometimes I'm so tired that it's easy; other times I feel that life is just not worth living. I hope one of these days—soon—I meet someone and make up for this dry spell. Why the dry spell? I've never been able to just pick someone up for sex, even before I thought about stuff like AIDS. I need a relationship, and I just haven't met anybody. The women I've liked have been involved elsewhere, and the women who like me, I haven't been attracted to. It's bizarre, really."

Why do so many singles find themselves without sex? The reasons vary. By far the most common: "I only want to sleep with somebody I care about—and I haven't found that somebody."

Some men and women said they resist entering into sexual relationships unless it seems really right, because they have a tendency to get emotionally attached to the people they sleep with. One 35-year-old man said, "People think it's easier for men than it really is. You can shed your clothes, but you can't shed your personality or your sense of responsibility. You get involved. You may not want to, but you get involved. It's intimate, and you become intimate."

And one 36-year-old woman said, "You know, the normal way should be to get emotionally involved first and then go to bed with somebody. I've done it too many times the other way around. Sometimes the man is all wrong. As a matter of fact, *often* he is all wrong. End result: wasted years, a certain amount of heartbreak. I'm just staying alone for awhile."

Lisa and Adam are good examples of single people who are temporarily celibate:

Lisa

Lisa 34, works for an environmental protection agency in a rugged national park. She has always been an athlete and a serious climber. Her interests are what brought her to her current profession; in it she spends most of her time out-of-doors doing rugged physical labor. We met Lisa, who is tall, thin, tanned, and very elegant-looking, when she was on the East Coast visiting relatives.

"I've been celibate for well over three years. Well, that's not technically true. I haven't had a penis inside me for over three years. I had oral sex two years ago. That's it.

"I think I just don't feel comfortable about going out and meeting men and sleeping with them without anything meaningful.

"It may be easier for me to live without a man because I do so much hard physical work that I'm often exhausted. I love my work and the ruggedness of the environment I'm in, but I don't know how long my body can keep doing it, or whether I will start slowing down. Most of the people I work with are men, but nothing ever develops there. I don't know what it is, but the men I'm attracted to aren't attracted to me, and when they are, the relationship never seems to last. It's painful and frustrating. I'm just trying not to think about it and learning to live without sex. I have friends who go from one man to another. They seem to need constant companionship and reinforcement. I don't, and I think I'm lucky. But like I said, it is a celibate life.

"All of my sexual experiences have been enjoyable. Nothing bad or crazy ever happened to me. My first lover was warm and sincere, but he was seeing other women and we drifted apart. I remember him fondly—maybe if it was something I didn't enjoy, my thoughts would be different, but I enjoyed it. My last sexual experience was with a friend who was like a brother.

"Vacations? This year I'm going to go do some climbing in Nepal. Not being in a relationship allows me to be independent and to do things that many women can't. I want a relationship, but if it's not there, I know how to enjoy my life alone. I don't want to settle down just so I can say I have a husband. A man in Wyoming once put his hand on my leg and said, 'What I really want someday is to have a piece of land, a house, and a woman.' I wondered if he wanted to get a cow and a horse too."

Adam

Adam, 33, lives in a Midwestern city where he does research at a large university. He says he thinks about sex constantly, although it certainly isn't a part of his life.

"I read a statistic the other day that the average person has seven sexual fantasies a day. It's good to know that I'm above average in something. But there's probably a reason for my excessive fantasy life. It's been a while since I had sex . . . a few years. I think I remember that Johnson was president at the time.

"I'm joking but I'm not joking. I feel just awful about the

absence of sex in my life. Because it's not just sex I'm missing; I'm also missing a relationship. I feel confident that if I were in a relationship, sex would cease to be a problem. But I do feel that my youth is rapidly passing me by, even if I don't have the same biological clock as women do. I feel instead as if I have a biological stopwatch. It started the last time I got laid, and it keeps ticking and accumulating time until I finally meet someone again. The clock just keeps running. In the meantime everybody I know is getting married or into relationships. I'm still alone. It's like being the last guy to finish the marathon. You don't know if you're going to make it . . . and by the time you get into the stadium, you think it will be dark and everyone else will have gone home."

One would assume that it would be easy for an attractive single man to find women for sexual companionship—if that's what he wanted—but Adam says it really isn't so.

"By the time you reach my age, most of the women you meet want marriage and children. You can't just fool around with them. The last woman I went out with was very sexual. She was really into sex in odd places . . . you know, broom closets, moving vehicles. It was fun, but she wasn't just a sex object. She wanted love and a future, and I think I hurt her because I didn't want that with her."

When Adam was a few years younger, he was more apt to get into short-term relationships with, as he puts it, "a sexual component."

"Women who are age-appropriate tend to want to get married, and I haven't met anyone for whom I want to make that kind of commitment. I used to meet women I really liked, who were willing to get into sexual relationships that sort of drifted. But my last few experiences were disasters because the women wanted more. I find I can't just start a sexual relationship anymore.

"When you're younger, you're more apt to do things for

the express purpose of getting laid. I still have mental angst when I remember that when I was 23 I went out with this very inexperienced girl just because I wanted to go to bed with her. She was a virgin. I felt terrible because I wasn't in love with her, and had no intention of being in love with her. It wasn't a one-night stand or anything. I dated her for a few weeks before we did anything and we went out for about two months, but my attitude was not particularly admirable.

"I can no longer excuse that sort of behavior. I need something real, but I haven't found it."

Avoiding Sex as a Means of Avoiding Inappropriate Involvements

Several women said that they were being extremely cautious about having sex with someone because they had a history of becoming emotionally involved with almost everyone they went to bed with—often with disastrous results.

Didi, 32, told us that she had decided no more sex unless the man was perfect for her. "I used to joke and tell my friends that I fell in love with every man I went to bed with. But it's no joke. I have a rocky history of acting on sexual attractions to the wrong men. So I go to bed with the guy. Then because I went to bed with him, instead of being able to just have sex and forget it, in my head it becomes an emotional involvement. I decided it was easier to not have sex until I know whether or not it is real."

A great many women mentioned that they had rushed into early marriages because they were having sexual relationships. In many cases these women were over 40, and had been raised in a more sexually repressive climate. But an astonishing number of women in their twenties said they felt that having sex with a man clouded their judgment, causing them to view the man unrealistically and leading them to confuse lust with love. They were trying to compensate for this by being very selective in how they chose their sexual partners. In some instances this resulted in long periods of no sex.

Many women in their forties and fifties said that they were clearly going through dry spells as far as sex was concerned. As one 42-year-old woman said, "Me have a sex life? You've got to be kidding. I can't have casual sex anymore, and there is no one special in my life right now. I haven't been to bed with anyone in close to two years. I've sort of gotten accustomed to living this way. It's not so bad."

SERIAL MONOGAMY AND THE SINGLE LIFE-STYLE

Speaking to singles made it very apparent to us that serial monogamy had become a common life-style. What is serial monogamy? It is the practice of moving from monogamous relationship to monogamous relationship, and seems to be very much a by-product of the sexual revolution. In today's complicated sexual world there are many single men and women who are torn between their reluctance to settle down and their inability to remain emotionally detached in a sexual relationship. Often these men and women feel that a sexual relationship, by definition, is serious.

These individuals are perfect candidates for serial monogamy. They often enter into relationships that are inherently limited, yet they seem to be unable to extricate themselves until the relationship has run its course. It is often sexual intimacy that keeps them from walking away from something they know is not ultimately going to meet their needs for permanence and stability. Once in these relationships, these men and women are usually monogamous.

We spoke to a good number of singles who have gone from serious relationship to serious relationship; in some instances these relationships have included a living-together arrangement.

The following sexual histories are good examples of life-styles that lean toward serial monogamy.

Ralph, a 32-year-old businessman

"My first lover? It was my college girlfriend. She presented my with my first sexual experience as a Christmas present.

We were both very inexperienced. The relationship lasted a couple of years, and we had sex constantly. If anything, I think she was more interested in it than me; she would unzip my fly whenever I was trying to study. People were always around, so we would be having sex half clothed in the oddest places. The healthiest part of the relationship was the sex. That part was a lot of fun, but otherwise we fought all the time about everything.

"The fighting made us break up, which upset us both. The fear of not having a relationship, the loss of a constant sex partner—it really bothered me.

"After her there was no one for about a year, then I started going out with a virgin who freaked at the idea of semen. That freaked me. She also made it clear that she wanted a husband, and I didn't want to get married.

"Then there was nobody, and then I had the sort of series of funny things that happen after college when everyone is sharing apartments and also being a little more promiscuous. You know, oral sex in cars, petting in elevators and lobbies, brief dating, and having sex with casual strangers that you're not interested in. It lasted about six months.

"Then I moved to California, and on the flight out I met a flight attendant. In the beginning I wasn't seeing her exclusively, but within a short period of time it became fairly serious. The problem was that she lived in Houston, so there was a lot of letter writing and talking on the phone—fairly frustrating from a sexual point of view.

"She was a funny cross; although she had more sexual experience than me, she was very naïve about some things. For example, she had no form of birth control, and we never had a discussion about birth control, which sort of irked me. We used condoms.

"When she came to visit me, I would immediately want to have sex, and she would immediately want to talk to me and go sight-seeing. I don't think I understood that a lot of women understandably don't want to have sex the minute they see you. I was very insensitive to her need to be psychologically warmed up first. I was faithful to her, so I constantly felt starved. After about a year of this it was apparent

to both of us that the distance was a big problem that neither of us was prepared to surmount. We saw less and less of each other, and eventually it ended.

"About three months after I stopped seeing her, I met Alicia, who was working in a boutique near where I lived. She was a little exotic to me, and far more worldly than the other women I had known. She had briefly been an actress, and although she was only a year older than me, she was already divorced.

"I found her very appealing emotionally, although the sex was always a problem. We were just wrong for each other. She wanted no foreplay and I love that stuff—all the fondling and kissing and touching—and oral stuff too. All the other women I had known had really appreciated it; they gave me a sense that I was doing something other guys they had been with weren't doing. But Alicia seemed to be only interested in intercourse. She had a vibrator, which I was always trying to convince her to use in sex. I wanted it to get more comfortable and open for us, but it never did. Sex was just not that connected. Also, we used a lot of hit-and-miss birth control. Sometimes I withdrew; sometimes I wore a condom. I was always experimenting with condoms—ones with tips, ones without, ones that pulled on like socks, ones that rolled on, etc. With it all, she became pregnant. Her decision to have an abortion sort of sounded the death knell to the relationship, even though we continued on for close to another year. I was very upset.

"Also, we had little in common except an odd emotional connection, which is hard to describe. As different as we were, we had the same reactions to a lot of things—people, movies, current events. Through this period I should tell you that I was having a lot of work problems, and I used the relationship as a way of escaping from my problems. I think she did, too; we were hiding out with each other, and the relationship lasted for five years. I almost married her because we were used to each other, but she was actually pushing me in a different direction careerwise, and that caused a lot of friction.

"Eventually we were barely sleeping with each other, al-

though we kept seeing each other for close to six months
with little sexual contact before we finally split up.

"Then there was a period of nothingness . . . just nothing . . . a long, long period of no relationships, no women,
no sex. I think I had guilt over Alicia, that we didn't get
married. I think also I had kind of gotten turned off to sex.
I had become accustomed to turning off. My career was in
trouble. I felt as though I couldn't be involved with the
women I wanted to be involved with, and I didn't want to
get involved in anything that wasn't going to lead to marriage
because I didn't want to hurt anyone else. So for close to
two years there was just me and myself.

"Then my career started to improve; I began making more
money, and I guess I was feeling more positive in general.
I woke up one morning and decided that I was being crazy
with this masturbating alone stuff. So I started dating a lot.
That's when I met Teri. The one thing I do remember about
it is that it was the most anxiety-free sexual relationship I
ever had. First of all, she took care of birth control, which
was a great relief to me. Then she liked everything I liked
sexually, etc. There was one problem, though. Although she
was very comfortable with sex and could take the initiative,
it took her an extraordinarily long time to have orgasms. I
would try endlessly—it was a real chore, even for me. I like
oral sex and playing with a woman's body—remember, I
complained that there was too little of that with Alicia. Well,
with Teri, there was too much. It would become torture.
I tried to get her to show me what to do, where to go, but
she wouldn't. I just decided that if she wasn't going to help
me, I wasn't going to feel guilty. But it eventually started
to get better. The problem is that just as things were starting
to improve in that arena—she was beginning to have
orgasms—she announced that she was still in love with her
previous boyfriend and was going to give it another chance.

"I was stunned because I didn't understand how a woman
could be so intimate with a man and then turn off, but I
think I've always been kind of shocked that there are women
who can do that, who can separate the emotional thing from
the sexual thing. I always thought it was a masculine trait,

although I have a hard time doing it, and I've met a few women who seem to have no problem with it at all.

"Right now? I've started dating again; I'm probably looking more seriously now. I'm still upset about this last relationship, and there are also some new concerns. This AIDS thing. I've never dealt with it, and suddenly I find that it's creeping into my thoughts and changing my attitude—a whole lot."

Melissa, also 32, is a high-school English teacher

"My first lover was the traditional childhood sweetheart. After years of groping, we finally went to bed at the end of our senior year, and it was a huge disappointment, a real big letdown.

"Then right away in college, I met this older guy who was a graduate student. His name was Roy, and I was really impressed by his intellect, and flattered that he liked me.

"Roy was 26 and divorced. He had married his high-school sweetheart, and she had left him to pursue her own interests. He had been divorced for two years and was ready to get married again and start a family. I was a very naïve girl, but I knew I wasn't ready for marriage. In the meantime, that year my parents got divorced, and my whole world fell apart. I should also tell you that I became pregnant very early in the relationship; it was a birth-control failure. I didn't know how to use the diaphragm. Fortunately I had a spontaneous miscarriage, but all of it made me lean on Roy very heavily, and he was always there for me. I wasn't that attracted at first, but he seemed so kind and so smart that I got more interested. We started going together seriously. Then he said that unless I moved in with him and made more of a commitment, he was going to start seeing other women—he said he wanted a serious relationship. I wasn't old enough or smart enough to say, 'Well, you've got to do what you've got to do.' I had had enough loss that year, so I moved in with him.

"In retrospect I realize that sex was not a big part of that relationship, but at the time I thought it was a lot of sex. We were sleeping together almost every day. Also, he liked small sexual games like mild bondage and stuff. I didn't really get off on it, but I went along with it to please him. At first it seemed very silly.

"We started not getting along almost immediately because I didn't want to be there and was really itching to leave. I was still in college; I didn't know anything about making dinner every night and paying bills. It was just a rough time for me. I ended up staying with him, with one foot in the door and the other out until after I graduated.

"Finally he sort of encouraged me to move out. I think he thought that once I got a taste of the real world, I would come rushing back to him. We never really stopped seeing each other; it just sort of cooled off.

"In the meantime I had met somebody at work who I really liked but I didn't act on it until one day when Roy and I had a huge blowup. So I called this guy—he had sort of indicated that he wanted me to. His name was Derek, and his story seemed to be like mine. He said he was with a woman and was trying to split up with her. I remember he met me for lunch and we went for a walk down by the river, and the next thing you know, we were kissing.

"I was very attracted to him, and we immediately started this passionate relationship. He said he was going to break up with this woman immediately; she was about to take her law boards, so I—can you believe—told him not to do it until afterward. I said it wouldn't be kind to mess her up when she was about to take all those tests.

"I was head over heels in love. He called me at home; I called him at the office because this other woman lived with him.

"We would meet in private places, or he would come over to my apartment. It was very, very intense. Finally he said it was getting too emotionally crazy for him. He called me and said he was going to marry the other woman. I wished them well; I had to respect his decision to stay with her. I think he was genuinely torn.

"Actually I ran into him about six months ago, in a restaurant. He was with his wife. I was sitting at the next table. When I saw him, I was going to say hello, but he averted his eyes and wouldn't make eye contact or anything. All the feelings came back, and I felt really awful.

"After he broke up with me I was definitely pretty shaken. I didn't go out for a few months, and then I went out with too many people, a trifle on the slutty side. I was upset and just not paying too much attention to what I was doing. I guess I felt really wounded.

"Then I met Josh, and I became pretty gaga over him because he was so good and so moral and had all these values. One of them was no sex. He was a Mormon. I was raised as a Unitarian, which is very different, but I went along with his feelings, and for the next year and a half I went with someone who didn't have sex. We did everything but. We rubbed everything, touched everything, necked, petted, etc. He felt that if he didn't put it inside me, it was okay. He was definitely having orgasms. It's not as strange as it seems because we weren't together that much. Right after we met, he took this job in another state; we were about eight hundred miles apart—too far to get together more than once every month or two. So we spent a lot of time on the phone, and when he came to visit me, he stayed with his sister, and when I went to visit him, he put me up in a hotel.

"Eventually I realized that I couldn't live his Mormon kind of life, even if we were married. It was too hard for me; there were just too many things I didn't agree with or understand. The distance also forced me to make a decision. I didn't have the money to visit that often. It just wasn't working, and I didn't think it would work out. So I ended it. I think he was hurt, but I hope he is happy because he was a very good person.

"Then I met Hank, and he was married, but I didn't know it because he lied at first. I met him in June, and his wife had just taken this summer job teaching in Canada. She was gone, and he certainly didn't act married. I liked him a lot at first. He was very exciting and I was very attracted to him. Another friend told me he was married, and I didn't believe her. But I asked him, and he acknowledged it. He said he and his wife were more friends than anything else and that they had an open marriage.

"I didn't know what to believe, but I was already very involved with him. I thought I would figure it out at the end of the summer. When his wife came back, he stopped calling. He was a coward. By then I was crazy about him. Once I called him, and he came by at work and asked if I could see him on the sly. It seems his wife wasn't all that open. I did that for a while, but I couldn't continue. I felt guilty because I knew his wife loved him. They have since separated.

"By that time I was feeling fairly cynical toward men in general, and then I heard about this job, which was in another state.

"Three weeks after I got there—I was barely settled in —I met Victor. He was everything Hank wasn't. He was honest, sincere, and he wanted a real relationship. The only problem was that he was insanely jealous, and it affected everything, including the sex. He would have these intense moods and wouldn't even want to talk to me, let alone sleep with me for weeks on end. It was all very up and down, and too difficult. It lasted close to three years, and finally there was one fight too many.

"Right now Victor still calls me, and Hank calls me and says he wants to try to get more serious. I'm not sure if I can trust Victor's moods or Hank's intentions. There is another man asking me out. And I'm not sure what I'm going to do about it all."

SINGLES AND THE FEAR OF AIDS

The scene is Jones Beach on a hot Fourth of July weekend. Across the clear blue sky, a plane is etching its message in white smoke: FOR ALL THE RIGHT REASONS—TROJANS. We have no idea of what percentage of the singles on that beach were paying attention.

Carter-Wallace, Inc., the company that makes Trojans, commissioned a survey in June 1988 on condom use in this country. For this random telephone survey, Carter-Wallace interviewed two hundred men and two hundred women, all sexually active. (In the last year, 38% of the women and 56% of the men claim sexual relationships with more than one partner; 29% of the women and 31% of the men claim two or three partners; 25% of the men and 9% of the women have had four new sexual partners.) In this survey, 57% percent of the men and 53% of the women said that in their most recent sexual relationship they had discussed taking precautions against AIDS and other sexually transmitted diseases.

According to various studies conducted within the last few years, the female consumer accounts for 25–40% of all condom purchases. Yet a survey released by the Alan Guttmacher Institute, a prestigious private family planning research organization, indicated that only 12% of American women use condoms regularly, up only 3 percentage points since 1982. However, condom sales, as a whole, increased by 40% between 1986 and 1987. But how do all these facts and figures translate into the way sexually active singles are behaving? What do typical single people think about AIDS? Do they think they will be personally affected? Are they being more careful in general? What measures, if any, are they taking to protect themselves?

We have no hard facts and figures. But here's what single men and women told us.

By and large, women were much more anxious and concerned about AIDS than the men. Most of them introduced the subject of AIDS, and an astonishingly large percentage of the single women we spoke to had been tested for the AIDS antibody. Many times there was no real reason for the woman having the test. Some were just generally anxious; others had gone through brief periods of promiscuity and wanted to make certain they were healthy. A few had been involved with men they knew, or suspected, to be bisexual. One had been involved with a man who had been involved with an IV drug user.

We only spoke to a small handful of men who had been tested for the AIDS antibody, and in two cases the testing was incidental. One has an illness which necessitates having his blood checked on a regular basis; the other receives a complete job-related physical each year. Both requested the AIDS antibody test, just to be on the safe side.

Several of the women said that getting other types of sexually transmitted diseases and/or becoming pregnant had made them feel more vulnerable to AIDS. Their experiences with pregnancy gave many of them an increased sensitivity to the possibility that in one small moment something could change or affect their bodies.

Also, several women were aware of having slept with bisexual men or having had friends who slept with bisexual men. The possibility of having this happen without their knowing it made them nervous.

Many men and women under 25, as well as a good number of older ones, mentioned parental pressure. One young woman said, "My mother is like an AIDS clipping service. She sends me statistics, articles, brochures, etc. It's her way of telling me to be careful."

A 32-year-old man said, "My mother calls me at least once a month to make sure I'm practicing safe sex. . . . She would actually like to see me married to one perfectly antiseptic woman. It's amazing that she isn't embarrassed to call like this, but she's not."

In one way or another, just about every single mentioned the AIDS crisis and how it was or wasn't affecting their sexuality. Most said that it had made people less casual because it has made them stop and think. Many specifically mentioned that they have given up the bar scene; they say that they would never again pick up a stranger and take him or her home *that* evening.

However, giving up nondiscerning casual sex does not mean giving up sex. And while most of these people do express concern on some level, most also admit to behavior which, after the fact, they themselves questioned.

For example, several men and women said that they had recently become involved in new sexual relationships. At the beginning—that is, the first four or five times they had sex—they practiced safe sex and used a condom. As the relationship progressed and they found themselves more involved, they dispensed with the condom and the safe-sex restrictions. Many said that they were just using their judgment about the person—that he or she "didn't look like someone who would have AIDS," although they all also said they knew that this perception was ridiculous and had no basis in reality.

One woman said, "I lied at first. I told him I had no form of birth control, even though I am on the pill, and asked him to use a condom. After I got to know him, I decided that he was safe. So I told him that I got birth control and he could stop using the condom."

One man said, "I usually use a condom at the beginning. But I have found that after the first two or three times I start getting lazy, particularly if the woman has another method."

What about women carrying condoms? We spoke to a lot of young women, under 25, who were doing just that. Were they asking their partners to use them? Not always. Some were embarrassed, much as the older women were embarrassed about pulling out their diaphragms. One 24-year-old woman said, "Many of my friends are carrying condoms, but I don't know of anyone who has actually asked a man to use one. I think we are being careful instead. I would like to think that if I were about to go to bed with someone, I would be able to ask them to use it, but I don't know whether or not I would be able to pull it out of my pocket. I think I would feel extremely forward. I think it would make them think I was tremendously promiscuous. I don't think men would think, 'Isn't she smart and cautious?' I think they would think, 'Wow, she must really get around.' "

We spoke to one woman who had just had the AIDS antibody test and was therefore carrying the package of condoms, given to her at the test center. She said that she thought she would ask the next man to use condoms, but she didn't think she would be able to reveal that she had them in her purse.

Of course, some singles have said that they plan to ask their next intended lover to have the AIDS antibody test and that they will not have sex with anyone until that happens. But they are very rare. We also spoke to a few couples who met and began seeing each other within the last years who did have a serious AIDS talk before sex. In two of the cases the men had tests because the women requested it.

What does all this mean? It is apparent that AIDS has affected the singles we spoke to, but not so much that it has *drastically* altered individual life-styles. In most cases they have modified their behavior to a slight degree. Some people are still fairly careless, but they are less careless than they were two years ago; others are very careful, but they are only a little more careful than they were two years ago.

ONE-NIGHT STANDS AND OTHER PROMISCUOUS PATTERNS

Among the people we spoke to, many men and women, particularly those who were under 40, said that they had gone through a period or stage during which they engaged in behavior that might be described as promiscuous. Some of them were distressed that they had ever been involved in casual sex; others regarded it as an important part of their sexual and human development and felt they had learned a lot from it. Although these men and women all had a slightly different view of promiscuity, they tended to define it in approximately the same way; i.e., as a pattern of behavior that includes one or more of the following: multiple ongoing sexual relationships; one-night stands; casual sex with no intention or desire for any further contact.

However, with a few notable exceptions, these people stressed that for them promiscuity did not turn into a permanent life-style. Although some were more judgmental when it came to the behavior of others, for themselves they saw their sexual experimentations as being limited to a particular life phase or time period. Men and women pointed out that it is a familiar pattern for some recent college graduates and other young people who want to "play the field" before settling down. Those who had been divorced commented that it is an easy pattern to fall into right after a marriage has broken up, particularly if one is feeling rejected and uncertain about relationships. Seasonal promiscuity was also mentioned as a form of behavior for those men and women who "act out" sexually only during summers at beach resorts or when they are on vacation.

Although some singles, particularly men in their twenties, said that they went through a few years during which they had numerous one-night stands and other episodes of casual sex, we spoke to very few people who let this pattern continue for much longer than that.

YOUNG, SINGLE, AND SEXUALLY ACTIVE

A fair number of young singles, particularly men, said that they were enjoying themselves sexually and were not thinking about forming relationships until they were ready or until something special happened. These were people who were electing to have sex with multiple partners because they want the sex, but not the commitment.

Although there are certainly still some women who are having a lot of casual sex, we spoke to very few of them. Very young women, in their late teens and early twenties, told us that there is still a certain amount of casual sex among adolescents and college students but that they are becoming more careful as they get older. One young woman said, "My friends are still sleeping around a lot. Maybe we just don't see AIDS as a part of our world. It's something that happens to adults and drug users and, of course, homosexuals. We're having sex with guys we know, guys in our classes. It seems pretty safe to me."

However, several other young women stressed that changing times and life-threatening illnesses have reduced the popularity of this kind of behavior. As a matter of fact, in all our interviewing, we did not come across one single woman over the age of 22 who admitted to *currently* engaging in promiscuous behavior. This does not mean that these women don't exist; we just didn't speak to them. But many said that they had gone through a period of promiscuity in the past. Louise, 26 and recently married, was one. She said, ". . . for a few years there, right after college, all my friends were like bunny rabbits. It was just a lot of fun, and I don't think anybody wanted to get serious about anybody. I'm really grateful that I had this sense of freedom for a couple of years. I was very comfortable with it, and I experienced all kinds of different lovers. I think most of my friends feel the same way. Now that I'm married, I know that I will never regret not having had certain experiences because I have had them.

Of course, in the last year or two, AIDS has made a difference, and most of my friends have settled down."

We did, however, encounter a fair number of men who were currently having one-night stands or sex with numerous partners.

Dennis

Most people would think that Dennis, a 29-year-old man who lives in the Southwest, is still fairly active sexually, but he says he has definitely slowed down.

"When I was in my early twenties, I think I wanted to prove that I was attractive to women, and I went after a lot of them.

"Up until even a year ago I would often be working five or seven women simultaneously. It was difficult because I would have to maintain, and wanted to maintain, relationships with all these women, whose company I genuinely enjoyed. I would go out with them, go to places, court them. It was just like any other situation, but the thing is that there was no exclusivity."

Dennis says that he did not find it difficult to have sex with several women in the same time frame.

"But the dating. That was a hassle. Coincidentally, two of them lived in the same apartment complex, and I would sometimes forget and head for the wrong apartment. I lost track of my schedule and what I had said to whom. I wasn't pretending exclusivity, and I had no hidden agendas; everybody knew what everybody else was doing, but it still seemed stupid to not remember what I had said or told someone.

"But the sex was no problem. That was the easy part. I made it clear to all of them that I was seeing others, and it was very natural. No hang-ups whatsoever. Whoever I was with, I was with because I wanted to be there at the time. If I didn't feel like being there, I didn't call.

"I've only made love to one woman, and having sex when

I was in love was very different. But I've wanted to please all of the women I've been with. I get as much of a turn-on from watching them get pleasure as from being pleased myself. It's partially ego, because you want to think you can satisfy somebody. But it's also fun to give pleasure. When I get sexually involved with someone, they get the full range of treatment . . . the full range of emotion. I don't particularly disqualify people simply because they haven't achieved a certain level of time with me. I'm a big believer in that. Hey, if you want to go to bed with a woman, she deserves the entire pantry, not just the first shelf."

However, despite these feelings, Dennis says he is aware that he is usually holding back emotionally.

"I try not to let it come across, but I'm sure it does. You know, a few times I've had a woman start sobbing in the middle of sex, and I wonder whether it's because they might be giving more than me emotionally and they sense some distance. I never asked them why because I didn't want to hear that they felt the absence of emotional involvement. During sex I try not to let it come across to my partner that I'm not as committed as possible. And remember, at the time you *think* you're involved. Sometimes it's not until later that you sit back and say, 'Gee, I wasn't fully involved.'

"Right now I'm sleeping with two, maybe three women. In the past year I would say I've slept with maybe five women, but that's because I've consciously tried to slow down. I've been trying to gear myself away from the short-term stuff and more toward the long-term.

"You know, there's a question I would like to ask other guys. Do they feel as stupid as I do when they realize they're about to go to bed with somebody for the first time? There you are, and it's an incredibly intimate experience—yet you're supposed to be cool and act like you've been doing it with her for years. Very sophisticated, you know. Sometimes I wonder if the woman is worried about Mr. Goodbar. How does she know I'm harmless?

Sometimes I get nervous about her. There was a scene on *St. Elsewhere* a couple of years ago where one of the characters was attacked by a woman he was making love to—she had a razor coming out of her mouth. Sometimes I find myself remembering that, and I think to myself, 'Oh, God, that's all I need.' "

Craig

Craig, 27, says that he is enjoying his single status and wants it to continue for at least a few more years.

"My relationships have all broken up for pretty much the same reason—pressure on me to get serious. I can't blame the women; after six months or so, they want a commitment. Nobody's mentioned marriage—just pre-engaged to get engaged, something like that. I guess it's called going steady. I'm not ready for it.

"I had a relationship last year that lasted for about ten months, and I was monogamous at the beginning, but the pressure got too much—she would hint around about friends who were getting engaged and stuff.

"Right now I just go out with whoever I want to, and I sleep with whoever I'm attracted to who also wants to be with me. My friends say I can no longer keep track of them, and maybe they are right. I've had my fair share of one-night stands.

"This weekend I'll be with the same woman I was with last Saturday and Sunday—she's a real sweet girl. We're going skiing, but Friday night I was with a totally different person, and tomorrow night, who knows? I like women a lot. Three quarters of my friends are women, and most of these women I've slept with at some point or another.

"I've met a lot of women in clubs and bars—often at resorts, you know, on the beach or skiing. Most of the women I've been with have been on the pill. Sometimes I've used a rubber, but the thing is that often you use it the first time you have sex, but if you go for a second time that night, chances are you'll both want to forget about it.

"I haven't thought that much about AIDS. I guess I trust

my judgment, and I trust what the women say. Since I'm so active, I guess I should be more cautious than I have been. It's certainly something to think about. It's a little scary, but if you think of the woman as being a nice person, you don't think in your mind that she could have it. You think, 'Listen, she's a nice person, she comes from a nice family, she probably doesn't have anything' . . . but who knows?

"I would say sex is very important in my life. I've been in love a couple of times, but I don't think sex is all that much different as long as I'm attracted. There have been a couple of times where I've brought someone home and realized I wasn't at all interested. I've said to myself, 'Hey, wait a second.' That doesn't happen so much anymore, because I try not to let it happen.

"There's just about nothing I won't do to satisfy a woman because I figure she'll do the same for me. I usually start with oral sex—both ways—because I like that, and then we go from there. I was with one woman who didn't like oral sex for a while. She didn't mind being the recipient, but she said doing it made her gag. I said, 'Okay, I can understand that for a little while'—then the little while ran out. But that wasn't the only reason for the breakup. She really wasn't my personality type.

"I had some 'preemie' problems in college when I was very excited, but I trained myself out of that. Now I can last fairly long, particularly the second time when I actually sometimes have trouble coming—but I guess that happens to most men.

"I have most of my sex on weekends; I'm pretty beat during the week. I guess I've tried most things . . . oral sex, anal sex. But I've never done anything really unusual. I drink some. I certainly don't use drugs for sex.

"I've also been having an on-again, off-again relationship with a woman who is married. That's been very interesting. My sex life is pretty normal. Nothing unusual. I'm fairly quiet in bed. I like it warm and sexy and friendly. I try to satisfy the women I'm with, and I'm pretty affectionate. You know, a lot of cuddling and hugging."

RECENTLY DIVORCED

The newly divorced seem to be particularly prone to casual sexual experiences. Typically they connected their behavior to confused feelings after a marital breakup. This was particularly true if they felt that their mate had sexually rejected them. Many said that they left marriages that had been sexless for a period of time, and they needed to reaffirm their sexual identities. Several women stated that they felt they had ended up in bed with strangers because they had forgotten how to date.

Nancy, in her mid-thirties, talked about this: "It took me about a year of going out with men and going to bed with them before I learned how to date. I was so accustomed to the marital pattern of going out and going home to bed that I became a pushover. Most of the time I wasn't even that interested in the sex, I just didn't know how to say no. Also, I had totally forgotten about a man acting passionate. I had been married for years to a man who acted like he had no interest in me whatsoever, so when a man started panting and pawing, I took him seriously. I thought, 'Gee this guy must really like me. I had better be nice to him.' I forgot that men try to get you into bed just because that's something they do. That's not something husbands do."

Newly divorced men also said that they tended to act out for six months to a year after a divorce, but sometimes for different reasons. Bud, 45, describes his experiences. "It's the old candy-store mentality. I went a little crazy right after we separated. It's too bad because I met some nice women during those first few months, but I couldn't stop long enough to let anyone affect me, and I slept with everybody. I think part of my doing this was that I had been married for so long. I felt as though I had lost a lot of time, and I wanted to prove that women still found me attractive. I have to admit that I learned a lot about sex during those months. I started experimenting in ways that I never did with my wife. It was so much easier with no strings attached. Of course, it's never that easy because women started to call me up and ask why

I hadn't called them back. Also, I started to get tired. After a few months I realized that I was too old to keep this kind of behavior up—no pun intended—indefinitely. Nothing is as simple as it appears."

UNFORTUNATELY UNFORGETTABLE EXPERIENCES

Men and women said that their excursions into casual sex provided episodes that would be comedic if viewed from a distance, but that when one engages in totally out-of-character behavior, one's sense of humor tends to evaporate.

A 33-year-old divorced mother said:

"I never thought that I could be involved in meaningless sex. I was a good Catholic girl who married my first lover. When my friends went to bed with a lot of different men, I was shocked; I even delivered lectures on the subject. Then my husband took up with somebody else. The next thing you know, I'm going to bars with some of these same friends and picking up strangers. I think I was actually looking for a new relationship, but I didn't have the brains to figure out that this wasn't how to find one. I remember one of the last guys I picked up. It was at the Phoenix airport. We were both stranded between flights—there were tornadoes or something like that in Houston. Anyway, I'm always scared of flying, so I was drinking bourbon. I think he was drinking Scotch, and the next thing you know, I'm waking up in the airport hotel, and there are these strange feet sticking out at the end of the bed. I looked over at the chair, and there were a pair of men's red suspenders hanging there. It was like a scene in a movie, and I'm thinking, 'What is he, anyway, some kind of fireman?' It was pretty awful.

"When I think back on that period of my life, I could die from embarrassment. I'm always terrified that I'll run into one of those men and they'll recognize me."

Danielle, 37, remembers that after her husband left her:

"I wanted to marry every schnook I went out with. I didn't know how to be single, and I didn't know how to not sleep with a man, so I ended up in a lot of odd circumstances.

"The worse experience was probably this man who was married, with five children, but I didn't know it at the time. He sent me candy and flowers; I was so naïve that I didn't even put it together that he was after me sexually. He was in his fifties, almost twice my age, and he brought me to this apartment he had with nine rooms; I was very impressed. I just never figured that a married man would take me to his *home* to seduce me. He fed me wine and food and brandy, and I was just too stupid to say 'Take me home.'

"Anyway, he was very tall, a big athletic-looking guy, and he thought I was real cute and tiny, and he had this thing about being 'used.' When he got me into bed, he stationed me on top of him, and he started pushing me up and down, saying, 'Use me, baby, use me . . . that's it, use me.' That kind of stuff.

"His hips kept going up and down, up and down, and it was like flying up into the air and smashing down. Then he'd roll me over and bang away at me, roll me back, and start up with the 'use-me' stuff. I was seriously afraid I was going to land on the ceiling. He had this mustache, and he kept kissing me and banging his teeth into mine. I thought, 'If I live through this, I will never sleep with another man so long as I live.'

"Now I've come to the conclusion that I have absolutely no interest in casual sex. There is no man so handsome or so sexy that I want him for just one night. And I don't think AIDS has anything to do with this feeling."

Doug, a 25-year-old dental student, remembers a six-month "vacation" he took from his studies, thinking he was going to be able to have "sex with no strings attached."

"I had just finished college, and I was very conscious that I was going to have to buckle down for a lot more years, so I took six months off and got a job in the Caribbean working for a yacht chartering company. I figured this would be my first and last chance to be *wild*! My second night there, I went out with some guys to the local pub and, throwing caution to the wind, picked up this woman who was there on vacation. I went back to her room and we had sex. It was pure sex, nothing else. But afterward I wanted to be a gentleman, not a jerk. So I said, 'If you ever come back this way, come out with me on one of my charters,' figuring it was a safe thing to say. Two weeks later I look up at the dock and there she is. 'Surprise,' she says. What could I do?—I did invite her. That night some friends were giving a party, so I took her with me. She shows up wearing this low-cut, tight, totally revealing blouse. Everywhere I went, she was there, grabbing at me and touching me. It was embarrassing. That night she comes to bed wearing this skimpy little outfit—it was real apparent that she hadn't come to the Caribbean for the piña coladas, but I didn't like her style. I managed to have sex with her because it was expected of me, but I was really not interested.

"The next day we dropped anchor in this incredibly beautiful crystal-blue bay. The minute we get into the water, this woman starts grabbing my prick. I mean, I think the entire Coast Guard could have watched from their outpost. We're not talking murky pond, we're talking about clear Caribbean water with a hundred foot visibility, and I'm trying to keep her from pulling my bathing trunks off because she wants to fool around in the water. I got totally turned off and angry, and she got all huffy and upset.

"That's when I discovered that it's not all that easy being promiscuous and casual. You have to have the temperament for it. I decided I didn't."

A few men discussed the emotional difficulties involved in being promiscuous in terms of dealing with the women you meet. One man said, "It's all fine and well to talk about one-night stands, but it never works out the way you want it to. First of all, if you go to a singles bar, for example, chances are that the women you're interested in sleeping with are either not going to be interested in you, or interested in a permanent relationship. Also, the women you're not interested in are interested in a permanent relationship. So either way, if you take somebody home, thinking it's going to be casual, she's probably thinking about something else. Being casual sometimes means that you have to be able to handle rejecting a woman you've just been intimate with. It's not all it's cracked up to be, believe me."

7

What Really Happens in Bed:
Sexual Fantasies
and Experimentation:
Some Variations, Combinations,
and Permutations

Fantasy sex is not always limited to the imagination, and it's not always what one imagines. Some of our interviewees told us that on one or more occasions they had acted on some of their more nontraditional sexual impulses in attempting to bring the figments of their imagination to life. Most of them confided that they discovered that what works in the mind, or, for that matter, on the pages of "adult" magazines doesn't always play out in the real world of sex.

Stuart, 45, one of the first men we spoke to, said that throughout his marriage he had always imagined sex with a totally unrepressed woman, a creature straight off the pages of a girlie magazine. . . .

"After my wife and I divorced, when I met somebody who was like this, I discovered hot sex is not always what you want. This woman was the classic blonde bombshell. Everything about her spelled s-e-x. You can't believe the toys she had. She had oils and vibrators and bras without nipples. She owned undergarments that came off in a single pop, and high-heeled slippers and garters. Her bedroom was lined with mirrors. Even the ceiling was mirrored. I thought she was great fun at first, the answer to a sexually starved man's prayers. Then I spent the night with her.

"We had sex twice before we went to sleep, and then she woke me up three times during the night to try to give me blow jobs. Three times! Each time I was sound asleep, and suddenly she would be making a lunge for me and putting on the lights so we could watch. 'Look up,' she kept saying. 'Watch. See. Look. Watch.' By the third time I couldn't wake up. She is still down there rummaging around with her little vibrator and telling me to watch. I couldn't even open my eyes, let alone look!"

SEX WITH TWO OR MORE WOMEN— THE CLASSIC MALE FANTASY

What heterosexual man hasn't thought about it at least once? Several of our interviewees did more than think about it. They tried it. One 34-year-old man recalled:

"It was always something I wanted to do. Then one night, right after my wife and I separated, I was with these two women in a bar, and we started talking. We were drinking some, and one thing led to another. I found them both attractive, so I said so. I said right out that I wanted to take both of them home with me, and one of them said, 'So why don't you?'

"That's what I did. I'm not saying it was terrible, but it wasn't what I imagined.

"Two women are two women! It's different than one woman! It was sort of like trying to drive two cars to California, simultaneously. There was a lot of stopping and starting, running back and forth between the two of them, and running out of gas.

"You try to be fair, so you don't want to give either one more than her share, but the minute one starts getting warmed up, you look over and you can see the other one is feeling left out. Satisfying two women is not an easy thing to do. Both my knees ended up with a really bad rug burn.

"I'm glad I did it just so I can say I did it—and I can put it out of my mind as something special, if you know what I mean; it isn't something I would want to do again."

A 28-year-old man told this story.

"I had sex with four women. I still don't really believe it. I had read this story once in a magazine about a guy playing strip poker with all these women—so that's what I did. I was with these five women that I knew pretty well. I had never slept with any of them before, and it didn't start out like it was going to be sex.

"They were all friends, and I dropped by to visit the one I knew best. We were listening to music, and what happened is that I went into the kitchen and made everybody a really stiff drink. We were drinking vodka and orange juice. One of the women rolled a joint, and I said, 'Let's play strip poker.' There was a lot of joking and stuff, and I proceeded to find out that they didn't know how to play poker. Jack of clubs, ace of hearts—it was all the same to them; they didn't know the difference. So I said, 'Okay, we'll do one more hand, and whoever wins gets to choose what happens next.' Just between you and me, I cheated. I stacked the deck.

"So we all got on the floor and we had some fun. It was fine until I got to the fourth woman, because then, frankly, 'Pete' said, 'Sorry, I've had enough.' The women all said nothing like that had ever happened to them before. You got to understand, we were all very stoned by the time we got on the floor.

"If I were to tell another man about it, I would say, 'It's fun once, but it's not like you think it's going to be. It takes a tremendous amount of stamina, willpower, and physical energy. Also, it can be very confusing. You can't remember what you did to who, and you don't want to leave anybody out.' I don't think it's ever going to happen again, but if it did, I would wear knee pads. My knees were destroyed."

One of the things that amused us most while collecting information for this book were the number of men who commented on rug burn as being one of the most memorable aspects of their forays into the world of sex with multiple partners. They all said that the limitations on bed space send most people to the floor.

WOMEN AND MULTIPLE PARTNERS

Although we talked to several women who said they had been one of two or more women in a group sexual experience, no woman told us about being with two or more men.

One 38-year-old woman told us the following story.

"This is the weirdest thing I ever did. I was at a party, and I guess I'd been drinking pretty heavily. I doubt if I would have done it except that I'd been drinking. Anyway, I was standing there, and this woman I knew, but not well, came up to me and said, 'Listen, I want to give my husband a present. You have tits, and he's never going to get tits with me. Come home with us, please.'

"When she went into the bathroom, her husband came up to me and asked me what his wife said. So I told him. 'She gave you that old tits routine,' he said. 'Not true. She just wants to get you home for herself.' Anyway, I went home with both of them. I would never, ever repeat it. But the next day they both called me and asked me to meet them somewhere alone."

Another woman told us the following story about an incident in her sexual history. . . .

"This happened about ten years ago, when I was 30 and much more active sexually. It was at a summer resort community. I had a date with this guy, and we went to a bar where we ran into this woman who was part of the group who was sharing his house. I knew this other woman vaguely, but not well. Anyway, her name was Norma, and I ran into her in a bar with Mack, who was also a friend of mine. Mack and Norma were just friends.

"The sex sort of happened spontaneously. The four of us returned from the bar together, and we went back to the house my date and Norma shared. My date went into his room and passed out, and the three of us stayed up. We smoked some grass, had some more booze, and the three of us just started having sex. Norma and I were very much the recipients. We didn't really do anything to each other. It all revolved around Mack, who was doing 99% of the action.

"I remember we worried that my date would wake up, but he didn't. All the dope had made Mack harder and more potent, and he couldn't have an orgasm. It was an incredible performance. He couldn't come, but he kept going back and forth between the two of us. By the time he stopped, it was daybreak. He looked exhausted. I thought it was very good sex, though."

ALCOHOL, DRUGS, AND ATYPICAL SEXUAL BEHAVIOR

Of course, not everyone who drinks or uses drugs automatically becomes involved in nontraditional sexual behavior. But it does seem to lower inhibitions and help some men and women step into another sexual world.

Almost all the men and women who had participated in nontraditional sex, or sex with multiple partners, told us that the behavior was totally out of character. It was interesting to us that in each of these isolated episodes that reflected an extremely unusual or once-in-a-lifetime departure from a usual pattern of sexual behavior, the participant said that he or she was drinking or doing drugs.

We also spoke to a handful of men and women who said they had regularly engaged in nontraditional sexual behavior during a period of several years while they were habitual users of either alcohol or drugs.

Hugo, 56, said:

"I'm an alcoholic. I detoxed four years ago. The truth is that alcohol never affected me sexually, except to make my desire more intense. I've heard that liquor makes some men less interested in sex, but it never happened to me.

"I also did drugs. I don't even remember half the stuff I took. The contents of my stomach read like the *Physician's Desk Reference*. And I lived with a woman who was even crazier than me. We did everything, from underwear swapping to mild bondage. Alcohol definitely made me get rid of my hang-ups. Sexuality is not as good since I detoxed. For me there was nothing like a drunken fuck. Unfortunately the stuff was also killing me."

Another man told us a story in which he said drugs were a major facilitator in his sexual behavior. . . .

"I met this couple at a party. And they knew me, and knew that I was doing drugs at the time. The man suggested that I come over to their apartment because he had some great coke. I did that a few times. Then one night the man told me what he wanted. He wanted me to have sex with his girlfriend while he watched. He had done so many drugs that he had trouble getting aroused. This was the only thing that excited him.

"So that's what we did. We would do a lot of coke, and he would concoct these elaborate fantasies, and I went along. I guess you could say we had an affair that lasted maybe six months. Then I started to get sick from the cocaine. I had to stop using the drug, and I just couldn't perform in this capacity without drugs. I couldn't do it."

But Most Say Liquor, Drugs, and Sex Don't Mix

Although some men said that alcohol and/or drugs reduced their inhibitions to the point where they behaved in an un-characteristic way, many more men and women confirmed that alcohol can have a disastrous effect on sex. Several who had tried it also pointed out that for them, long-term cocaine use reduced their capacity to enjoy sex and/or reach orgasm.

A 30-year-old man said, "When I was younger, it seemed that alcohol and drugs didn't quite affect me as much, but now it's definitely the old 'drunken-dick syndrome.' If I've had a little too much to drink, I'm worth shit."

This opinion was echoed by dozens of men, particularly those who were not accustomed to drinking. They agreed with Len, 26, who said, "After a few drinks I'm ready for sleep. Forget about sex. That's why if I'm planning a heavy night with a woman, I have no more than one glass of wine. Then

I'm strictly a Pepsi man. I save my boozing for nights out with the guys."

We talked to other recovering alcoholics who told us that alcohol definitely had an adverse affect on sexuality. One 48-year-old attorney remembers that his sex drive was beginning to disappear as a result of heavy drinking: "I honestly thought I was done for. I either had no erection, or I couldn't come. It was pretty gruesome. But then I dried out, and within a few months I was almost as good as new, taking my age into consideration. I actually think sex is better now."

We talked to many women who had been involved with heavy drinkers or alcoholics, and they seemed to report the same sort of mixed picture.

Jo, 50, remembers her first husband: "Our marriage broke up because of his drinking, but it didn't really affect his erection. He couldn't speak, but he could still have sex. I just didn't want to because he was so disgusting."

But most women told us stories similar to this one: "He would start out wanting to have sex, but he couldn't do it. I knew it was from all the liquor, but he didn't want to hear it."

Another woman, who divorced her heavy-drinking husband, said, "He had no interest in sex. I think he used liquor as a chance to pass out so that I wouldn't expect sex."

A LIFELONG PATTERN
OF SEXUAL EXPERIMENTATION

We talked to a handful of men and women who said they had always been primarily interested in nontraditional sexual behavior, and did not need alcohol, drugs, or anything else to encourage them to lower their inhibitions. One said:

"My entire life I've always been fantasy-prone. When I go to bed with a woman, I bring with me a lifetime of fantasy. I've been to orgies, had sex with multiple partners, and generally tried to act on many of my more off-the-wall fantasies. It's very difficult because very few women are as sexually adventurous as I am. I love the woman I'm with now, but she's definitely not capable of what I call 'dangerous sex.' Sex with her, and with all of the women I've loved, has been more mundane. I somehow manage with a woman I love to keep fantasy to a minimum. In my experience women don't like fantasy. They like a man to be in the here and now.

"I've always dreamed of meeting a woman as totally wild as me, a creature without a superego, but the few times I've met such a woman, she's had complicated emotional problems and been on the edge in other ways as well. Women may be more civilized, more socialized than men. Perhaps they just have fewer fantasies.

"A few times I've pushed a woman to her limit, and when I have I've always regretted it. I remember one woman I took with me to this little planned orgy at one of those places where two couples switch. It was something that I wanted to do. She as much as told me that she would do it for me but that it totally went against her grain. I thought she would change her mind and begin to enjoy it. I thought the sex would take hold of her, as it always does with me.

"We all did the preliminaries, which included some oral sex and some fairly explicit language. But when the other man went to penetrate her, she looked at me and said, 'Please, I want to go home.' She got scared. The other man got angry, but the woman with him said, 'Let her go. Just let her go.'

"I felt terrible. I called her, but she said she never wanted to talk to me again."

S_____ is a man who refused to give us his name. He is the only person we interviewed whom we specifically solicited because of his point of view. He is a member of an organization designed as a meeting place for men and women who prefer a dominant/submissive sexual pattern and who organize fantasies around that theme. He said:

"Fantasy has always been a part of my sexual life. But one does not always try to integrate fantasy into the real world. Even within the organization, there are more lookers than partakers. Some things are easier to do than others. Putting on a dog collar and leash and being led around by your dominatrix is one thing—it's fairly easy to do. Hanging from the rafters while somebody whips you—that's a little tougher. A lot of these fantasies are not real workable. Even though we are members of a group that revolves around fantasy, most of us understand that it's illusion. Some of this stuff appears rough, but *appears* is the word that counts here.

"I started to have sexual fantasies of being tied up when I was very young. And although I have a normal family life, I have a need to think about these things—which is why I joined this group. My family knows nothing about this. I think they would be shocked. Certainly my wife would be, and my behavior at home is not tied to fantasy. I don't know how my wife would react if I told her, but for me it's not worth the gamble.

"I know others who feel differently. If you go up to your partner and say, 'I want you to put on a lace outfit and I'm going to put on a dog collar, and you can lead me around by a leash,' they are apt to get freaked. But some people get into it. You can work someone in gradually. Start with small things like, 'You look pretty hot in this pair of lace panties.'

"Some of the people who engage in dominant/submissive patterns integrate it into the rest of their lives; others do not. The s/m scene is very easy to keep in the closet. If you are playing behind closed doors, it's easy to hide.

"We believe in the concept of consenting adults, and how far anything is going to go in terms of fantasy is decided ahead of time. I think even among those who are whipped, they are not into the pain so much as the fantasy. I think very few are truly into pain.

"I think creativity is a big part of an ongoing sexual relationship. Sex without fantasy gets very boring after a while. So you fantasize. Then, after a while you want to do more than fantasize, you want to incorporate some fantasies into your sexuality.

"I've found that very few of our members use alcohol or drugs for sex. I've always been almost a teetotaler myself.

"We have a wide range of discussion groups, and often we talk about health concerns. AIDS, of course, is a big topic right now, and we encourage safe sex. In all my years as a member, I don't ever recall a discussion about birth control.

"But typically a submissive man doesn't have sex with his dominatrix. For dominant women I think sex is a very small part of all this. But if you are a dominant man, sex is a very big part of it. Sex is where it's at. A dominant woman will rarely have sex with her slave; and very few men can get off by being whipped. Friction is still a big part of a man's climax. The dominatrix might make her slave do it for himself, or she might touch him with her foot. A few women might touch the man, but it really isn't typical.

"Currently there are a couple of hundred members of this chapter. Frankly I don't think we're that different than many of the average people you see on the street. Sure, everyone looks fairly normal sexually, but if you put them under a microscope, who knows?"

LONG-TERM PROMISCUOUS PATTERNS AND LIVING ON THE SEXUAL EDGE

A very few women and a larger number of men described a lifetime pattern of seeking out sexual adventure, including a continuous search for new and more exciting partners.

Penny, a 46-year-old woman who says that she has had more than a hundred lovers, described her pattern:

"When I do a genuine analysis, I have to admit that although I had a lot of sexual activity, I wasn't happy sexually. In all the years I was sexual, I used sex as a way of not communicating rather than as a way of communicating. Sex for me was something I didn't think about seriously. It was like fast food. I was specifically looking for sex, not a relationship.

"Over the years I've had many one-night stands, and there has been some very good sex. But there has also been some very bad sex. I like casual sex, sex that I would call adventurous, but I also like lots of hugging, touching, and foreplay. It's difficult to integrate the two.

"I like the idea of sex that is cheap-novel good, but much of the sex that I've had has been bad to mediocre—maybe one out of every hundred experiences is satisfactory. There have been very few fireworks. I've faked orgasms a lot. A lot. I know when I've had a good meal and when I've had a bad meal, and I'm not sure what would be on the menu for something to qualify as a terrific sexual experience. Now I can't fake anything, and I feel that I need the intimacy of a loving relationship. I've changed."

One 53-year-old man said, "I've had thousands of sexual fantasies, and I would go out looking for fantasies and looking for women. Maybe fifty thousand fantasies, but I've never met a woman who was on my sexual wavelength. I look like, and I am, a respectable man. I think that's one of the reasons why I've had so much success with women. I don't look frightening or scary. I remember going out and picking up wild women, wild beauties on the street. They would get back to my house, and they would see that I was respectable, and they would immediately turn into wives. The sex would become respectable, boring marital sex."

People with this long-term pattern of casual sex seemed to indicate that they weren't certain where they wanted their intense sexuality to lead them, except that they were searching for an elusive fantasy, pursuing adventure as well as good sex. These men and women, some of whom described lifetime patterns of love with exciting strangers, told us that they were often sexually disappointed and were rarely, if ever, able to fulfill their fantasy of truly "wild" sex, saying that the sex they found was usually no more or less fulfilling than sex with a steady lover. However, for the most part, these men and women were very clear about saying that they were looking for good sex and adventure, not for love.

8

What Really Happens in Bed: Marriage and Sex

If there is one generalization that can be made about marriage, it is that one can make very few generalizations about any aspect of marriage, including the ways in which husbands and wives relate sexually. Simply put, there are too many variables. Human beings, in and of themselves, are incredibly different, and each of us has his or her own personality, background, body type, experiences, sexual needs, preferences, expectations, inhibitions, repressions and fantasies. People marry for a multitude of reasons, and once married, a wide range of outside factors, including children, in-laws, money, work, health, etc., can touch on and affect one's sexual behavior. Therefore, it shouldn't be surprising that when you combine two unique individuals and add in all of their unique circumstances, the character of their combined sexuality is that much more special.

Yet in spite of this individuality, this uniqueness, we did notice some differences, as well as similarities, in what people told us. Not surprisingly, what impacted upon us most was what has struck many other observers of human interaction in marriage: Although there is a remarkable dissimilarity between those marriages that are happy and those that are not, happy marriages tend to have much in common. Tolstoy may have said it best in the first lines of *Anna Karenina:* "Happy families are all alike, but an unhappy family is unhappy after its own fashion."

In other words, although the troubled marriage is troubled for a wide variety of reasons, it seemed very apparent to us that the seemingly simplistic common denominator in the so-called happy marriage is that both participants are deeply committed to making it work. Not surprisingly, this commitment to "making it work" includes working out a satisfactory sexual relationship.

We interviewed people who were happily married, people who were unhappily married, and people who had been divorced. What did we learn? We learned that sex, like everything else in this world, is not always easy. But when men and women are committed to each other, they tend to make sexual compromises and adjustments. Even if the sexual relationship is far less than perfect, they usually choose not to walk away from partners they love. On the other hand, when the marriage is lacking in commitment and/or love, people told us that they can—and sometimes did—turn their backs on highly charged and passionate sexual relationships.

WORKING IT OUT THROUGH THE YEARS

The "Honeymoon" Period and Beyond—Some Generational Differences

Even solid working marriages are in some ways dissimilar. One essential point of contrast is the decade in which the couple married. The year of the marriage tells us a great deal about the sexual behavior and expectations of the couple because the bride and groom typically reflect the attitudes of their era. Men and women who were married before the sexual revolution were understandably far less experienced and much more inhibited than those who met and married in the sixties, seventies, or eighties. These men and women often specifically commented on how uninformed they were sexually, telling us that their sexual expectations were based on imagination and fantasy. Most specifically stated that they had no realistic sense of what they could expect from their partners, or what their partners expected from them.

Many couples have to make some form of sexual adjustment. As one might assume, the couple's level of experience and sexual sophistication is frequently an indicator of how well or badly the couple adjusts sexually, and how easily they are able to communicate and resolve sexual problems.

Most husbands and wives remember the attraction and desire they felt when they first started having sex with each other, when they couldn't stop thinking about each other or keep their hands off each other. They remember the heightened anticipation, the sleepless nights, the stomachaches, the longing, and the lust.

Experts on marital sex tell us that sexual passion and interest is likely to be most intense and frenzied at the beginning of a sexual relationship, during the so-called "honeymoon phase." The marrieds we spoke to agreed that when they started sleeping together, sexuality was clearly the focus of the relationship. But there were enormous generational differences.

Among the group who married before the sexual revolution, sexual experimentation—if it existed before marriage—was usually limited by time and place. Remember that premarital sex was frowned upon, and "nice" girls lived at home and didn't go to hotels or motels. Many "nice" young men also often lived with their parents. For these couples, finding a place to be alone was an almost insurmountable problem. Our interviewees reminded us that, in those years, being able to have sex was a major incentive for getting married. Those who had experimented with each other said that these attempts were restricted by circumstances as well as by feelings. For most of these men and women, the actual honeymoon was often the first true introduction to real sex with their marital partners.

Although some of these men and women told us that these first sexual experiences with their partners were pleasurable, many more said that while their sexual feelings were intense, they were extremely disappointed and frustrated by the initial sexual experience—by the act itself, as well as by their partners' attitudes. They felt that reality in no way matched their expectations. And a fair number said that not only were they disappointed, but also they were traumatized by physical problems such as pain and/or sexual fit. Those who described themselves as happily married frequently commented on the high level of sensitivity and patience their partners showed in the face of trying circumstances. Those who said they were unhappily married, or who later divorced, remembered exactly the opposite and often described episodes that were emotionally scarring, as well as physically difficult.

Among the older marrieds, the other glaring similarity was a greater degree of shyness or discomfort when it came to discussing anything sexual. Those who were fortunate enough to make a good adjustment were not that seriously affected by these inhibitions. But in those marriages where there were initial frustrations and actual difficulties with physical adjustment, the inability to speak about them compounded and exacerbated the problem.

On the other hand, the couples who married after the sexual revolution were frequently sexually active before they met each other and had completely different experiences, reflecting not only a changing attitude toward sex per se, but also a more enlightened sense of female sexuality. Most of these couples began having sex together long before they were married, and many actually had lived together before marriage. For these men and women, the honeymoon period of sexuality usually took place during one of the stages of the dating relationship. By the time the marriage took place, these couples had few unrealistic sexual expectations. Many times the couple had already settled into an even pattern.

The following two stories point out these glaring differences and illustrate typical generational approaches to dealing with a sexual relationship.

Lloyd, 62, has been married for almost forty years. When he and his wife married, he had many expectations of what marital sex would be like—none of them based on reality. Nothing that he had ever experienced prepared him for the problems of physical adjustment he and his wife confronted, and he had no one to go to for advice or information. He says that when he and his wife met . . .

". . . we were both quite inexperienced. I had been with several women, mainly call-girl types. There weren't that many women who were sexual then, and starting when I was 15, I had a series of isolated one-night experiences but no ongoing relationships until I met Arlene, my wife. She really had no experience except some necking with neighborhood boys.

"Before marriage, we sort of fooled around—we touched each other and stuff like that, but we never had intercourse, and I had a lot of expectations about "real" sex, which is what I thought was going to happen once we were married.

"Anyway, finally we were married, and on our honeymoon I found sex very disappointing. Later on it got better, but at first it was impossible because of my size and her size. I was big, she was small. I couldn't even get complete penetration. It's interesting because there were several couples honeymooning at the same hotel, and some of the guys and I got friendly, and I discovered it was a common problem. Arlene also told me that other women told her the same thing. I remember one couple in particular: the woman wouldn't go to bed with her husband, and he came to the pool and asked everyone, men and women, what he should do.

"Somehow Arlene and I found out about lubrication; that made it easier, but even so, it was not what I expected. We had to work at it and work it out. With it all, it was months before we worked up to real intercourse. I was very frustrated, not at Arlene, because she was a very willing mate and very patient, patient with me and very understanding, but frustrated because it just wasn't working right.

"Don't forget also that the only form of birth control available to us at that time was rubbers. There was nothing else that anybody used, and they were dry, too. So the combination gave us sexual problems from day one.

"My wife and I didn't talk about sex much; we weren't too communicative. It just didn't feel comfortable talking. We always loved each other, but at first sex wasn't such a happy thing . . . not for her, and not for me.

"Then we had just sort of worked the penetration problem out when we had another problem as well. We were having sex very infrequently. Sometimes twice a week. Usually once a week, and maybe even less on occasion because Arlene didn't want to have sex. She had a desire problem. Because

I couldn't understand it, I felt very frustrated and angry. She knew I was unhappy, but I don't think she knew *how* unhappy. There were times when I was so angry, I would go out and leave the house in the evenings—go outside because I felt frustrated because she was going to bed early to avoid me. She would say she was tired. That's the only time in the marriage when I thought seriously about sleeping with someone else. I didn't do it, but I did flirt with other women. It was not a pleasant sexual relationship between us in the beginning, and we couldn't talk about it.

"I had expected a lot more out of sex than we got at first. I never expected sex every night, but a couple of times a week, and sometimes a little more, and I would have been happy. It turned out that Arlene was having trouble with something else that I just didn't figure. I was working a physical job at the time, and I would come home and I wouldn't always shower. Arlene later confessed to me that lots of times I really smelled bad, but she couldn't tell me about it, and it was a turnoff for her. Now, of course, I'm meticulously careful. Also then, you know, hot water was more of a problem. We were living in this old house and had a hot-water heater that didn't hold much water. It seems odd now, but it was much more of a problem forty years ago than it is today.

"I got another job, and I guess I didn't perspire as much, and then Arlene started concentrating on getting pregnant. She had this little menstruation calendar, and she was always calculating. She had a great desire to get pregnant, and when she had a purpose, she *almost* wanted sex. It was great for me because we could forget about condoms.

"Anyway, things got better sexually after the kids were born. I remember a real turning point when we went off on a vacation by ourselves. We had been married maybe ten years. The kids were still small, but her folks took care of them and we were alone in a vacation setting, and it was good sex. We started to talk together more . . . about our dissatisfactions in the relationship and about how much we meant to each other. We started to get more direct and honest with each other.

"When we were first married, neither of us knew anything. I was always a little too quick . . . always too quick. I always had to slow down, stop, start again. Otherwise I'd come too soon. Other people tell me that they can climax and then get another erection. I was never able to do that, so I always had to try to slow down, or else do something else. I always tried to make sure that Arlene had an orgasm, but I think she faked it a lot of the time. I tried to read articles on sex . . . no dirty magazines, just articles that had information. And as we got older and times changed, there was more information available. So I would read stuff and try to learn. We started using oral sex, me performing it, about twenty some odd years ago. We've never done anything really kinky. A couple of times we tried whipped cream, kidding around, but basically our sex life is based on our feelings.

"You've got to understand that there's always been a lot of love between me and my wife. When the sex got good, it became very good, and there was a lot of love attached to it. From the time we were in our early thirties on, I would say we've had a very good sex life. When the kids were grown, of course, we got to be together a lot more.

"I never thought about other women all that much. I didn't have much experience before marriage, so you always wonder—it's the old forbidden-fruit thing. But while I sometimes wondered about what other women were like, I always knew it wasn't real. Arlene and I have a healthy, loving relationship. No question about it. And once the original problems went away, we had a good sex life for a lot of years. We had sex maybe twice a week when we were in our thirties and early forties. Then it slowed down to once a week. But it was good sex, and there was a lot of love and affection between us all the time."

Kevin and Jennifer are a couple whose marriage took place after the sexual revolution. Both were sexually experienced when they met, and they lived together for two years before deciding to marry. Kevin says that Jennifer was strongly influenced by the sexual revolution and the women's movement. Their biggest sexual adjustment took place when they were first dating; it revolved around his being able to accept the fact that she was not only sexually experienced but had a different and more informed sense than he did of what she required in order to reach orgasm. In short, his fantasy of himself performing in the great-lover tradition, bringing his wife to orgasm through his efforts alone, was not going to be fulfilled in the real world.

"I'd started having sex in college, but most of my relationships were short-lived, typically lasting three or four months. There had been only one other long-term romance.

"Jennifer and I started sleeping together on the second date, and as much experience as I had, I still didn't know that much about giving a woman pleasure. In other words, the female anatomy was still somewhat of a mystery to me. I'm a reader, so I had read lots of stuff on women's orgasms, but I wasn't sure of myself as far as they were concerned.

"Even though Jennifer was only 22 when we met, she had been in at least one other long-term sexual relationship. Early on she sort of let me know that I wasn't satisfying her. How? She was very specific—she would take my hand and show me what to do. I asked her questions, and she told me.

"We've been married four years, so now we've been together more than six years. Everyone told me that it would cool down, but the sex itself has only gotten better. And it steadily gets better yet. On the sexual downside, I had a lot of expectations that were just wrong. I imagined myself as the great lover, giving women orgasms. But with Jennifer it doesn't work that way. For example, I like giving oral sex, but she can't have an orgasm that way. And she definitely can't have an orgasm from missionary-position sex. For warmups, any position goes, but for actually putting her across, she has to be on top, and it has to be with her own assistance. I can't do it myself, which is kind of disappointing for me. I achieved a lot of satisfaction in the past from that, from my involvement in giving pleasure.

"What I've had to do is realize that I'm not going to get everything I want. She can't force her body to respond the way I want it to respond. There was a little anger on my part about this at first. We talked about it. We had to talk about it, but I came to the conclusion that it didn't matter what road you took as long as you got there . . . and we kept getting there, and that was the most important thing. Most of our sexual adjustments were worked out in the first year we were together, and I think we have a happy sex life.

"We do have some frequency disagreements. I had at least three times a week in mind, and that's something we had to adjust because she's happiest and most turned on with sex once a week. So we compromise on twice a week most of the time. In between, if I really feel the urge, I masturbate. I didn't tell her about this for a long time, but now she knows. She says that she's impressed by my sexuality—but she doesn't have as strong a drive as I do. She doesn't ask what I think about, and it's a good thing, too, because it's not always about her. It could be about anything. It could be about subway trains. Sometimes it's about her, but usually it's about someone else. It's kind of like playing around with no damage.

"We have a rule to talk everything through when we are upset, and never to go to sleep angry, and that includes with sex, because there are times when the sexual act can just fall apart. With two sensitive people it's a vulnerable experience; if one of you blows it, the other's going to be mad, and you have to talk that through before you go to sleep. It doesn't matter if it takes till two or three in the morning.

"The sex we have is very, very affectionate. It really is an expression of love. A lot of times it will turn into a robust, lusty experience—the lust is definitely there, and that's the fun part, but it's not the dominant theme. I'm not thinking, 'Let's get laid,' I'm thinking, 'Let's make love,' and that makes it a lot better than any casual sex could be, even the best casual sex. I guess during sex, at least 90% of the time, I'm thinking about how much I love her."

Thinking About Sex the Married Way—
After the Honeymoon, a Change in Priorities

The majority of married people express a perspective on sex that is quite different from the single perspective. And most experts seem to agree that once a couple goes through its honeymoon phase, where sex is the focus of the relationship, something happens to sexual intensity with a concomitant drop in sexual frequency. But the marriage process doesn't automatically trigger a Jekyll/Hyde transformation; one doesn't go from being a hyperhormonal single to a sexually unmotivated lump in the bed overnight. What really happens to sex after marriage?

The marrieds we spoke to said that it would be a mistake to think that they are less interested in sex than they were when they were single, but they do think about it differently. It has a very different priority in their lives. What many of them stressed was that the presence of a steady partner had freed them emotionally to put more thought and energy into other things, such as work, the laundry, or the Mets game. This was particularly true of those men and women who considered themselves happily married. Several felt very strongly that having a sexual relationship that could be counted on left them with more energy that could be devoted to other things.

Brett, 34, has been married for six years. He told us, "Look, sex is no longer the main focus of our relationship. When we were going out together, we would get together so we could go to bed. That doesn't happen now. Now, most of the time we're together for other reasons. But that doesn't mean that I like sex less or like my wife less. It's just different."

Jackie, 36, says that she is shocked at the change marriage has brought about in her sexual attitude: "When I was still single, I remember reading articles on how people became less interested in sex after marriage, and I couldn't imagine that ever happening to me. By the time I got married, I was 33, and for most of my adult years I had been without a regular sexual partner. I'm not saying I was voracious—just sex-starved. When I met Dave and we started sleeping together, I was so turned on that I would practically swoon every time he touched me. I think he was almost as hungry as me, because we spent the first five months of our relationship in bed. My idea of a perfect date was an evening spent exploring each other's bodies; if he suggested going to a movie or doing something else, I was always disappointed. Now we've been married a little over two years, and I'm not saying I don't like sleeping with Dave. I like it a lot. But I don't want to do it all the time. I certainly don't want to do it to the exclusion of everything else, and sometimes I don't want to do it at all. I don't know what happened. Sometimes I'm tired; sometimes I'd rather watch *Nightline;* sometimes I don't want to have to think about birth control; sometimes I don't want to interrupt what I'm thinking about. I'm sure, though, that if, God forbid, Dave would disappear, I would be exactly the way I was before, and I would hate it. Knowing that I have a regular sex life gives me the luxury of not always wanting sex. It's great."

A 31-year-old new mother quipped, "Sex is not high on the list of things I want to do right now. It's maybe number nine, right after cleaning the broiler."

And a 38-year-old man was one of the many who cited fatigue as being responsible for the sexual shift in his marriage: "I still think about sex almost as much as I always did, but that doesn't mean that I can always do something about it, or that I even want to. I'm too tired a lot of the time. I used to think that maybe if my wife was more aggressive and initiated sex more often, I would be more interested—but the few times my wife has gotten cute and sexy when I'm doing something else . . . to be honest, I've acted annoyed. Later I feel bad about this. Maybe that's just the way we're supposed to be. If we continued having sex like we did at the beginning, we would both be dead."

A good many men and women said that they did not resent having less energy for sex. In fact, they were grateful that they felt secure enough to be able to focus on other things. Several young and recently married men particularly stressed being happy they could spend less time thinking about sex. They said that it was their impression that in many young marriages both partners are concentrating more on making money, acquiring property, and ensuring financial security for the marital unit before having children.

However, if both partners fail to agree on this and are not on the same wavelength in terms of marital priorities, problems can' emerge around the issues of emotional and sexual intensity.

To be honest, just about every married we spoke to indicated that there was always some slight difference in how the partners viewed the role that sex should play within the relationship.

One couple we interviewed together gave this insight into their sexual relationship.

Interviewer: "How do you decide on sexual frequency? Is it spontaneous? Do you negotiate? What really happens?"

Wife: "He says he would really prefer to have sex more often. But I'm not thinking about sex that much."

Husband: "I figure that if we could go to bed and start making love, we'll both start thinking about sex. That's what usually happens, doesn't it?"

Interviewer: "It doesn't work that way?"

Wife: "I'm too tired to find out. I'm too tired to start thinking about thinking about it."

Interviewer: "When did this change take place?"

Husband: "Soon after we got married."

Wife: "That's not true. Remember when we were still living together and you took on that new building? Come on, you were worse than me then."

Husband: "I think she's right. I was very involved in something for about six months right before the wedding. It took most of my thought and energy."

Interviewer: "So *when* did this change take place? Take me through the time period."

Wife: "When we first started to go out, we had sex day and night for about six months. Then we moved in together, and it slowed down to about three times a week."

Husband: "Then you took that vacation alone, and when you came back, that's when we decided to get married."

Wife: "And that's when it really slowed down to about twice a week, sometimes once a week, sometimes not even."

Husband: "It's true. Maybe there is some connection with deciding to get married and less sex."

Wife: "I don't think so, I think we're more tired, that's all."

Husband: "But we were never too tired before."

Wife: "That's because we weren't married."

Interviewer: "Do you think it's a problem with desire?"

Husband: "No, I don't think so. I think it's just natural."

Wife: "Yeah. How can we feel sexy? We're both busy. If I were to say to him right now, 'Okay, come on,' what do you think he'd say?"

Interviewer: "What?"

Husband: "I have to go work on my books."

Wife: "See? We both do it."

This couple assured us that they had strong feelings for each other, and their ability to talk about sex with each other in front of a relative stranger seemed to indicate an open communication. They said they did not think they had a sexual problem; however, one or both of them was often involved in a variety of projects that took much of his or her energy. But other couples in similar situations see it differently and define it as a problem revolving around desire.

DESIRE, THE SEXUAL "CATCHWORD" OF THE EIGHTIES

Within the last ten years we've seen more and more emphasis in the media on the role that sexual desire plays within a relationship, and many sex therapists are now saying that the most common complaint among couples seeking counseling is a discrepancy between partners in terms of desire.

Many people revealed that there was often a disagreement in their relationships about the frequency of sex or, for that matter, the duration of the act itself. It would appear that sexual drives are rarely perfectly matched, and no two people feel exactly the same way about the how and when of sex. Happily married people told us that they managed to negotiate a compromise. Unhappy couples never seem to get it together and often end up quarreling about sex.

Fatigue—A Prime Culprit in Diminishing Sexual Frequency

"I don't think I should feel this way at my age, but a lot of time I'm too exhausted to have sex except on weekends, after I've had a chance to recover. Work wipes me out."

Eric, 29, married two years

"At night sometimes my wife wants to fool around, and I'll say, 'Give me a break.' I know it's job-related stress, but I think I can go two weeks without thinking about sex. I never thought I'd see the day where I'd pass it up."

Kirk, 27, married ten months

Young marrieds frequently attributed one partner's diminished sex drive to a general sense of fatigue. Those who were attempting to work it out and find a compromise within their marriages said that they felt the most crucial element was that both partners understand that the drop in desire did not reflect a loss of interest between the partners or dissatisfaction with the marriage in general. One 30-year-old woman who has been married four years discussed the sense of rejection and loneliness she initially felt when sexual frequency changed in her marriage. To her, sexuality was an important element in intimacy and the bonding process. She says that both she and her husband have learned to find other ways of expressing intimacy and that her attitude has changed accordingly. . . .

"When we met, we were both working at the same company, and after we'd been going out a year we got engaged and took an apartment together ten blocks from where we worked. Because we saw each other all the time, we had a lot to share and talk about. At the end of another two years we got married. Through all this time there was no real drop in sexual frequency or in our closeness. We both got home at a reasonable hour, we'd go out for dinner, visit friends, hang out. It was very relaxed.

"Then after we'd been married two years, Nick got a job offer that was 'too good to refuse' in another city, and we bought a house near his office. In the meantime I received a promotion, so we decided I would continue working at my old job. What this means practically is that now I commute almost three hours every day, and I'm exhausted when I get home. In the meantime Nick has all the pressures of a very demanding new job, and he's totally wiped out.

"We're both so tired some of the time that even if we're interested in each other, we can't do anything about it. At first I think the drop in sexuality definitely affected the bond between us. But it wasn't just the sex; fatigue was making us relate differently. Face it, fatigue makes you grouchy.

"We began to fight more, and our fights took on more significance. When we fight, we have different styles. I become emotional and sob; Nick stonewalls.

"When you add all this up and include the drop in sexuality, you can see that we had a rough time for a while. Nick was tired, preoccupied with work, and less sexual. I became convinced that I had done something wrong or that something was wrong with the relationship. Nick is a very caring person, but I'm probably more affectionate. Physical closeness is important to me, and I see it as an expression of love. I don't think my husband always feels that way.

"We really had to work at it to try to understand the other person's point of view. I would ask him what was wrong, and he would say, 'Can I just get some sleep? We'll talk about it tomorrow.' I find that men often prefer not to address an issue and hope that it will go away. I had to learn to get my sense of hurt across without hurting him. It's gotten better because we're both feeling less stressed and less tired right now. But I also learned to convey my feelings. I managed to get him to understand that I could live without a sexual expression of love, but I really needed to have him hold me and tell me that he loved me even when we weren't having sex. I needed to have him listen to me and relate to me in nonsexual ways.

He's learned how to do that. We've both changed. I've become less volatile and angry, and he's become more sensitive to my emotional needs.

"I think our problem is a common one. I've been at parties with other couples and sometimes, you know, we all talk about it. Everybody's tired.

"Now that I'm sure it's not a sign of rejection, I don't think less sex is all that important. I feel totally comfortable with my husband; I feel I can tell him anything. We've learned to know each other better. I don't think this new phase in our marriage makes our relationship better or worse. It's just different. As a matter of fact, I love him more now than I ever did."

Children: Their Effect on Desire and Frequency

Many marrieds clearly felt that having children was responsible for diminished frequency, and that the major sexual shift took place not after the honeymoon but after the birth of the first child.

We all know that children bring a sense of reality into any marriage. Within most relationships certain little romantic moments automatically fall by the wayside.

One happily married woman with two small children said, "We were together for several years without children, so we had a lot of little rituals that had to be discarded. We would light candles for dinner and take showers together. An example of what we can't do now: We used to make love on the living-room floor. If I tried that today, I'd end up with a piece of Lego stuck to my rear. It's not the same, but it's part of having a family. And I definitely wanted children. Sometimes my husband gets wistful, but most of the time we're both grateful for what we have and accept that we're in a different place right now."

Most of the contented marrieds we spoke to said much the same thing. The reality of being a parent means less sex and less romance, but there are, of course, many compensations.

Ron, 33, has been married to Margo for ten years. . . .

"When we first started going out, we were both living with our parents, but we would have sex whenever we could get a minute alone. We moved in together a few months before we were married and had sex constantly. The pattern really didn't slow down that much until the kids were born. The kids changed everything. There are just things you can't do when you have kids around. I can't grab my wife and take her upstairs in the middle of the afternoon. But I don't mind, because I love my kids, and it really doesn't stress the relationship—it just changed it.

"At the beginning it was all heated passion. I remember weekends when we had so much sex we were both sore and could barely move. Then it was a reaction to not having had that much freedom or that much sex when I was single. Now I have Margo all the time, and that changes things. I know she's there, so other things become important—like if I want to read the newspaper or watch television.

"Margo and I have never had a fight so big that we stopped being affectionate. I've never had stress against Margo . . . I've only had stress with her. Like when the kids were born, they were both premature, so we both felt a lot of stress. But Margo never gives me stress. Stress is caused by work or by other things not going right. Sure we have fights. Everyone has fights and disagreements, but never big, giant blow-out fights like some friends I know. We just get it off our chests and that's it. It certainly doesn't affect us sexually.

"What affects our sexual pattern? Kids and colds. When the kids have colds, we get colds, and then we have this giant cold going around the house. She'll get it, I'll get it. Then we'll decide not to kiss so we can stop giving it to each other. Then two weeks have gone by, and we look at each other and say, 'Oh, God, do you remember how to kiss?' Sex drops off because you're dominated by other factors. Think about it. When you have two kids coughing in the next room, it's hard to get sexy. A cold lasts an average of ten days. Then one of us gets it . . . plus my wife gets her period.

"I'm never so tired from work that I can't think about sex, but other things happen. Sometimes I'll look at Margo and realize that she's had a long day, and I figure I can live without sex. Most weeks we have sex a couple of times but . . . not always.

"No, I never long for the good old days. I love my life. I love my kids. I love my wife. I would certainly never cheat. I've had opportunities; sometimes you see a beautiful girl and you think about it for a second, but not really. It's not my way—my family and my wife are too important to me.

"We have most of our sex at night. If I woke Margo up in the morning, she'd probably chop my arm off."

Like Ron, almost all parents told us that sexual spontaneity was a fantasy as long as there were young children around. They said it just wasn't a realistic goal.

Life's Ebb and Flow Dictates a Natural Fluctuation in Frequency

Some marrieds we talked to acknowledged that there is a shift in sexuality but said they don't feel that reflects a loss of desire. They accept a certain fluctuation or reduction of sex as part and parcel of a long-term bond.

One 39-year-old man who has been married for fourteen years said:

"I don't really think that it is a loss of sexual interest or desire so much as a preoccupation with other things; there's a change in emphasis. I think you only have so much energy and your body can only cope with so much at one time.

"I think over time you start to see that sex is *part* of your relationship, and not an issue. It's not something you have to do; it's just part of what you are as a couple. When you first marry and start out, you don't have 'one life' as a couple, so at the beginning sex is a large part of what's bonding you together—but later on you have so many other things together, and you've shared so much, all those other things bond you just as much. I think there's an unconscious shift. But if people are focusing on sex as the thing that bonds them together, I think they are missing a lot of other things. And if a couple is focusing on a lack of sex, there's probably some-thing else that's missing.

"In our life together, sometimes we have more sex; some-times we have less; it depends on what's going on. I think our sex lasts longer now than it did at the beginning. It's just as pleasurable, if not more so. I still have as much desire—I may not act on it as often. Other things have priority. It's just different than when we were single."

"Not Better, Not Worse—Just Different"

Almost identical words were used by many men and women to describe the way in which a sexual relationship changes over the years.

Newlyweds say that sex after marriage is different than it was when they were dating; parents of young children say that it is different once the children are born; older parents say that once the children are grown and have left, sex again changes and becomes different, frequently regaining spon-taneity; older marrieds say lovemaking is different as one gets older—not better, not worse—just different.

It seemed to us that this ability to accept the pleasures of each new different stage without regretting what has been altered is one of the more remarkable similarities among hap-pily married couples. These men and women appear able not only to change personally but also to reinvent the marriage so that it, too, adapts and fulfills their needs through all the various life stages.

DISTINGUISHING BETWEEN SEXUAL DESIRE AND EMOTIONAL INTIMACY AND ROMANCE

Many of the more happily marrieds pointed out to us that less sexual desire does not mean less romance or less affection or less intimacy. Both men and women were very clear in telling us that there were different kinds of emotional intensity that could be shared with a partner without having sex.

One 36-year-old man who had been married for five years said, "I used to look at my wife with this . . . I guess you could call it an intense stare. She knew that meant that I wanted to fool around. Now I still look at her that way, and I still feel that way about her, but it doesn't always mean I want to hit the sack. Sometimes it means I think she's cute. Sometimes it's my way of telling her that I love her. But I'm with her all the time. I don't want to have sex all the time. There are other feelings."

A 38-year-old woman who has been married for three years said, "We used to make love every time we saw each other when we were dating. After we moved in together, I realized we couldn't make love every night. He would still try almost every night, but it didn't work. I figured out that it wasn't that he wanted to have sex. He wanted to show me that he loved me. He wanted the closeness; so did I. But I started discouraging sex, indicating that I would rather just cuddle and hug and kiss sometimes. It works much better. We still feel intensely. Or at least I know I do, but it doesn't have to lead to sex. If that means less desire, then we have less desire. But we have more feelings. I love him more now than I did when we first got married."

Do Desire and Frequency Drop Off for Everyone?

We talked to a small handful of marrieds who said that sexual frequency had dropped off very little, if at all. Most of these men and women felt that they had a lot of sexual energy and were married to partners who felt the same way. None of the men and women in these highly sexual marriages had young children living at home, and they all had life-styles that allowed them a great deal of free and leisure time.

Jesse, 40, and his wife, Jane, 36, have been married ten years. They are both free-lance commercial artists who work at home. About three years ago they bought a large house that they share as both home and studio. Although Jesse states that he has a very strong sexual drive to begin with, he is certain that his love for his wife is what continues to engage his interest. . . .

"By the time I met my wife, I had slept with so many women that I had sort of lost count. There was one woman with whom I was obsessed sexually because she was so wild, but otherwise, until I met my wife, I had never been in love before. I guess you could say I was a real sleaze; I just didn't care about anybody that I slept with. I had several long-term girlfriends, but I was never faithful to any one of them. It's strange that I should have changed so much, but it's true.

"Then one night I was in a bar with a friend of mine who was married, and he sort of looked around and pointed to this woman and said, 'That's the girl for you.' So I started talking to her, and the more we talked, the more I thought, 'This girl is great.' It was literally almost a love-at-first-sight type of thing. I kept waiting to find the flaws, but now it's ten years later and I still haven't found them.

"I took her home with me that night, and she spent the weekend. When we'd been together a week, I basically said to her, 'Listen, I've fallen in love with you; you're going to fall in love with me, and we're going to get married.' She said, 'Oh . . . right.' She sort of didn't believe me at first, but now she does.

"I can't put my finger on why I feel so strongly about her, but she's just the only girl I've felt this way for. Everything worked out. Looking at her today, she's the best-looking girl in the world. Now objectively I know that's not true . . . objectively Loni Anderson's prettier. But to me she isn't. To me, even on that superficial level, Jane is the most attractive woman in the world.

"When I was younger, I was definitely from the wham-bam school. I didn't care about giving pleasure, but I care a lot about Jane, so I try to control myself. Usually before and after making love I'm thinking about how much I love my wife. When we're making love, the only thing I'm thinking about is the pleasure at hand, for me and for her. Jane is on the pill, which makes birth control easy. I don't know if we want children, but we still have a little time to think about it.

"Do we talk about sex? Some. But it's embarrassing to this day. For example, I still find it hard to come right out and say, 'Do you want to make love?' So I usually joke about it. We have a lot of communication in the relationship as a whole, and do just about everything together. Sex is just one of them. Even so, sexual communication is still a little limited. I always ask Jane if there is something else I can do. She says, 'It's wonderful' or 'It's fine.' But neither of us are that specific.

"For me the best sex I've ever had I'm having right now because of the emotional feeling I have for my wife. I can live without ever having had certain other sexual experiences because I don't feel I'm missing anything.

"I very rarely have any sexual problems, although sometimes stress will affect me. If I've held back because my wife hasn't climaxed and I'm under stress about something else, then I may not be able to have an orgasm. The few times it has happened, Jane has a tendency to think it's somehow her fault. In all honesty I reassure her that it has nothing to do with her except for the fact that I held back . . . that it is just physiological.

"Jane and I have a lot of the same tastes in everything, including sex. Neither one of us is that much into oral sex, for example, and we both like to make love in the light. If I feel Jane is getting very excited about it, then I love it. But if it seems that she's climaxed and is just waiting for me to, then I just want to get it over with. It would be nice to say that I'm totally egalitarian, but it's more because I would never want to have her say, 'I love you very much, but my sex life is dissatisfying.' As I said, we discuss sex, but we don't discuss it in depth. We both smile a lot after sex and joke. We're pretty happy together.

"I would say right now we make love about seven times a week because we're both here all the time. Some days we make love in the morning and at night. When she had a job in an office, we weren't making love as often . . . maybe only three or four times a week. Other men have told me that they have trouble making love when they're tired, but I don't; I can do it when I'm beat tired. But it's different for Jane. When she's tired, she's tired."

NEGOTIATING WHEN TO HAVE SEX—THE CONTEMPORARY COUPLE

The happier contemporary couples seemed to us to be very successful in working out a relationship that acknowledges different sexual appetites and needs, much in the same way as they acknowledge other differences in tastes and interests.

Preston describes his eight-year marriage to Doreen as very close and satisfying. Yet they have different sexual needs. Preston says that . . .

". . . if I had my way, we'd have sex four or five times a week. Doreen is a once-or-twice-a-week lady. We try to find a compromise position that satisfies both of us.

"I could tell when we were first together that lots of times she would go through the motions just to please me. I would suggest sex, and she would sigh before saying okay. A real sigh attack, you know. So I said, 'Hey, look . . . if you don't want to have sex so often, just say so. Say you're tired, say you have a headache. Just don't sigh and say, "Okay." ' I figure that there is no sense in pressuring her—if I really feel that much sexual tension, I can always masturbate in the shower.

"And the truth is that she is much more turned on and a much better lover when there are a few days between encounters. However, I think it's important to have sex at least once a week. If a week goes by and we're too busy with other things and nothing happens, then we talk about it, and we both start rearranging schedules. If it's been a week, I think the body wants it even if the mind isn't turned on. Sometimes I don't feel like it, and we'll start, anyway, and I discover I'm very turned on. My wife is the same way.

"We usually decide together when we are going to have sex. We're both busy, so we make dates. Like we had made a date to have sex last Friday. We had a wonderful dinner and ended up holding hands in front of the fire. It was really romantic, but we started talking, and we don't always get that much of a chance to talk together, either. We didn't want to stop, and eventually it was late, and we didn't want to have sex when we were exhausted. So we agreed to wait until the morning. We had sex after breakfast. It was great. A real turn-on, very comfortable, nonpressured. We were both up for it and had good energy."

MARRIAGE AND THE MYTH OF SPONTANEITY

Many of the sex manuals encourage spontaneity as a good thing. Sexual spontaneity is supposed to be a goal, something we all want to achieve . . . but do we?

Many women point out that all too often spontaneity within a marriage means that the husband has carte blanche to initiate sex at just about any time. Take a look at some of these women's least favorite times:

"Two minutes before the alarm is about to go off, and I can already hear the kids waking up. The dog is prowling outside the bedroom door trying to get my attention, so I will let him outside, and I'm still semiconscious and getting anxious thinking about all the things I have to do that day."

"In the shower when I am worried about the baby waking up, and we won't be able to hear her."

"My husband has a way of grabbing me every time I am about to go out the door for something important. Sometimes I think it's because he's insecure and doesn't want me to have a life apart from him."

"Anytime I'm asleep. I hate it when he wakes me up for a poke."

"Halftime at the football game. I'm not a commercial. I tell him that my idea of romantic music is not John Philip Sousa. Who needs a three-band hump?"

Spontaneity doesn't always work for a man, either, if the woman is doing the initiating.

"Unfortunately my wife always decides to get sexy just when I'm falling asleep."

"I wish that I could respond on command whenever she's interested, but I can't. If I'm thinking about something else, I'm thinking about something else."

One pattern we noticed among happy couples is that when both partners work, spontaneity is rarely attempted. Instead, they tend to have certain set times. For all of them spontaneity is something they can rarely afford. For years many of us laughed at the old couple who regularly had sex every Saturday night at ten o'clock. But many of the younger couples say that knowing when to expect sex is reassuring.

Sex that is planned is also more efficient for those couples who use a diaphragm or a condom as a means of birth control. As we said before, spontaneous sex and unplanned pregnancy are an oft-mentioned combination.

Jeanne and Sam have been married a little over a year. When they first met, about three years ago, there was an immediate, intense attraction, and by the third date they were having a sexual relationship. Jeanne says:

"When we first met, we would have sex every time we went out, three or four times a week, and sometimes twice in one evening. That lasted until we moved in together, and then the pattern changed—rather quickly, as a matter of fact. I would say that within a few weeks sex had slowed down to three times a week, and within a couple of months it was where it is now, which is sex once or twice a week, usually on the weekend.

"I would prefer more sex, but Sam says that his job is very demanding, he is too tired, and he needs to pace himself. When we first started living together, this was hard for me to understand. I'm a few years older than Sam—he's only 27, and I thought he would want sex more often. I was accustomed to dating relationships and affairs. With all the other men I'd known, whenever we got together, sex was a big part of it. The man I went out with before Sam was in his forties, and he was always interested in sex. It was the same with Sam when we were dating; I don't understand why sex changed after he moved in, but it did. It's funny, because I have a few friends who tease me about marrying a younger man. They're sure he's 'hot to trot' all the time, but no way.

"Now I have come to expect sex once or twice a week, almost always on the weekend. Fortunately Sam is a very affectionate man. In other relationships hugging and kissing were mainly only a prelude to sex. Sam is very romantic and very loving all the time. He can take me out for a romantic dinner, buy me presents, hold my hand, cover me with kisses, and then pass out in bed, without sex. It was hard for me to adjust to this and understand his attitude. But now that I have, I realize that I would rather have what I have. Last week was fairly representative of our relationship.

"Monday night: When I came home from work, Sam was making dinner. He likes to cook, and he listens to classical music while he's doing it. He chops and stirs and races around the kitchen, and the stereo blares. It's cute. Before and after dinner he was very affectionate and grabby. There was a movie on television that we both wanted to see, and we watched it in bed. We had not had sex that weekend because we both had colds, so I sort of thought he might start, but nobody initiated anything except some cuddling, and we both went to sleep. By the way, although Sam is always touchy-feely with me, he doesn't like me to get forward with him sexually. He does all the initiating, and I don't think he likes it when I do.

"Tuesday: I went to a business cocktail party, so I came home from work late, and I had already eaten. Sam was working at his desk and was all preoccupied. I think he secretly resents my having work-related social activities, but he would never admit it. Nonetheless, he is always a little less affectionate when this happens. In any event, during the evening I had a couple of glasses of wine, which always makes me sleepy. When I came home, I just collapsed. I vaguely remember Sam coming to bed and cuddling around me for a few minutes, which he does every night. Sam is always affectionate before falling asleep. In the morning, however, he is only affectionate as a prelude to sex.

"Wednesday: We went out to dinner with friends and had a really nice time. On the way home he was very romantic and held my hand. I thought it was going to lead to sex because it had been almost two weeks, but it didn't. Sam got in bed before me when we got home, and by the time I finished brushing my teeth and got into bed, he was half asleep. When

I leaned down to kiss him good night, he pulled me over, gave me lots of kisses and close hugs, curled around me, and fell sound asleep. He was half snoring within seconds. The next morning I teased him about it and told him that I had thought I was going to get lucky.

"Thursday: I got home first and started dinner. Sam likes it when I'm there first and jump up and down and make a fuss when he gets home. We had a fun dinner. There was a lot of petting and hugging and telling each other how gorgeous we are. Remember, we've only been married a short time and there's still a lot of fooling around. We have pet names for each other and stuff like that. We're really disgusting to be around. But nothing happened in the sex department that night. I don't think either of us was in the mood.

"Friday: We ordered dinner in, watched rented movies on the VCR, and fought over who got to lie down on the couch. When we first lived together, we would share it, even though it was uncomfortable. Now sometimes we share it; sometimes we fight over it. We were both exhausted and fell asleep as soon as we got to bed.

"Saturday: When I woke up, Sam was leaning over me, staring at my face. He had this real adorable fresh look, and he said he was 'about to get lucky.' So we both got lucky. This was pretty typical sex, with Sam being the most active partner because that's the way he prefers it. He takes his time and makes love to me. The whole thing took about forty-five minutes; it was very nice. It always tends to be more loving after we've had sex, and today was no exception. We get pretty mushy with each other. We did chores during the day and went out to dinner and a movie at night.

"Sunday: Sam and I woke up together, and sex just sort of happened, but this time he was really half asleep, so we had this dreamy sort of sleepy sex. It was faster, and he wasn't doing anything fancy. I wasn't having an orgasm that quickly, so we got my vibrator to join us, and I came very quickly. So did he. Sometimes he likes the vibrator, and sometimes I think he resents it. Anyway, I let him be the one to suggest using it. Sometimes we use this position where we put the vibrator over my clitoris—while he is still in me. That way we can both feel the vibration. I don't have orgasms that easily, but this always brings me to orgasm very quickly and takes the pressure off him to maintain an erection.

"On vacations our pattern goes back to the way it was when we were dating. He's always interested, and it's spontaneous and fun."

Different Body Clocks—Finding Time, and Finding the Right Time

"At ten P.M. she's feeling sexy. That's the way I feel at six A.M. She's dead in the morning. We usually agree on Saturday or Sunday afternoon."

—30-year-old husband

"When I was younger, it didn't matter so much. I could have sex at any time. Now I really perform best in the morning."

—52-year-old husband

"My body doesn't start responding until the middle of the morning. It's not that I don't like morning sex, it's that I'm numb and can't feel anything."

—34-year-old wife

Almost all the married men and women we spoke to said that they had preferred times for sex. Many men, particularly those over 45 or those who felt drained by job stress, said that they were too tired in the evening to really enjoy making love. They preferred weekend mornings.

A great many of the couples we spoke to said that they set aside a special time each week. This time was often during the day, when both husband and wife were less tired. Couples with very young children said that Sunday afternoon while toddlers and babies napped was a favorite time.

Those with school-age children often commented on how difficult it was to find time during the day and pointed to this as one of the reasons why sexual frequency dropped.

Those whose children were grown commented on how pleasurable it was to be able to get back in bed on the weekends
for some leisurely lovemaking.

Everybody said sexual frequency picked up on vacations
and holidays that were taken without the children because
then spontaneity became a genuine possibility. On an every-
day basis, those who had given up spontaneity in favor of
sexual "dates" did not feel that their relationship suffered.
In fact, they said that they preferred knowing when they
were going to be having sex because it gave them something
to look forward to; they could prepare themselves emotionally
and physically so they were more totally into the act and
less likely to be focused on outside distractions.

THE DESIRE QUESTION AND THE
PERFORMANCE PROBLEM

We spoke to a fair number of marrieds who were having
more serious problems around the issues of desire and/or
performance.

Those who were trying to work through the sexual problems said that it was counterproductive to look for someone
to blame; they stressed the importance of not assigning blame
to their partners or assuming blame themselves. Several
women mentioned that they had to learn that a partner's
sexual difficulties did not automatically mean that they were
being rejected, or that they were somehow less attractive.
Both men and women said that on some level they always
worry about being rejected or being judged inadequate if
they exhibit any sexual weakness.

Some of these men and women see the sexual problems
in their relationship as being purely mechanical or temporary,
and feel they can be worked through or accommodated within
the marital structure.

Marilyn, 35, is deeply committed to making her marriage
work and is hopeful that the sexual void in her marriage is
only temporary. . . .

"My husband and I haven't had sex for over a year. When
we first met, we had great sex. Wonderful, natural, loving,

and uninhibited. We would have sex every night and then wake up in the morning and make love again. We just kept getting closer and closer, and then we moved in together and got married. By the end of the first year our pattern had slowed down, and we were having sex three or four times a week. Then I became pregnant, and we had sex a little less frequently, particularly toward the end.

"After our daughter was born, I was having a lot of pain from sex. I didn't realize it at the time, but when hormone levels change after pregnancy, it can make a woman feel exceptionally dry and cause pain. It is not all that uncommon. But I went to the doctor, and they didn't really explain it to me. Because of the pain, we got into a pattern of having sex about once every two weeks. My husband was very sensitive about the pain, but I think it bothered him. He took much longer to get aroused. I think he felt rejected by my reluctance to have sex, and then, when he was less insistent, even when the pain went away, I began to feel rejected too. I like it when the guy acts like he is going to die unless he gets his hands on you. I like that feeling. But I felt it much less from him.

"I was beginning to get very upset about the change in our sexual pattern, but then we decided to take a vacation, and the whole sex problem went away. It was really good again. When we came back, I discovered that I had gotten pregnant. This time after the baby was born, there was no pain. But my husband definitely felt little, if any, desire. He became depressed.

"I think it was a combination of things. For one, he was having work problems. He had a job he hated, and no chance of changing it because we needed the money. Then also, I think he was having trouble adjusting to being the head of a family. First it was just me and him. Then him and me and the baby. Then him and me and two babies. It was very stressful for him, and I didn't think I could help him.

"He had less and less libido. A few times he initiated sex, or I initiated sex, but he was having an increasingly difficult time becoming aroused and getting an erection. It was very painful for both of us. We just stopped sleeping together. He's very apologetic about it. He's hurt too.

"I used to masturbate more, particularly when I had insomnia. I would get into another bed to fall asleep. But my libido is low, too, right now. I don't think my husband masturbates, or at least not very often. I asked him, and he said not very often. I genuinely think he simply doesn't feel sexual any longer.

"For a while I was very upset, and I began to consider separating, but then sort of a small miracle happened. This man at work began to pay attention to me. I could tell that this man was really attracted to me. I didn't act on it. I mean, nothing happened, but it made me feel that I was still attractive, so it was good for me. It made me better able to deal with the situation with my husband.

"This problem with my husband has been going on now for almost two years. If I thought our sexual relationship wasn't going to return, I would probably get a divorce. But I don't feel that way. I think it's on the back burner, and that when the time is right, it will flower again. I still feel very attracted to him. And I know he loves me. I know he'll go the distance for me. We still have the commitment and we have each other.

"It has actually changed for the better. Last year I had serious doubts about staying together because not only was he not giving to me sexually, he had withdrawn emotionally. He wasn't giving, he wasn't talking, he wasn't telling me what was wrong. But that's changed. Now we can talk about it, and I don't feel that he's withdrawn or running away from me emotionally. Now he's affectionate. A year ago he wasn't, and I couldn't handle that. I let him know, and he tried for me. It's made a difference. Just hugging and kissing and warmth makes a big difference. At least we have physical comfort together."

A variety of problems—health, age, psychological stress —can change a sexual relationship temporarily or permanently. Among the long-standing healthy marriages we've come across, this seems to have very little effect on the stability of the relationship and the marriage bond.

Nate, who is in his early sixties, says that he and his wife have always had a reasonably active sex life, but now he is complaining about a problem that he has been told is not unusual for a man of his age or older. . . .

"For the last year now, I don't get a full erection. This has never happened before. Maybe a few times, when we were making love, my wife might make a joke or say something kidding around, and I would immediately lose the whole magic of it, and my erection was finished. But now it's not like that. Now, no matter what I do, or what she does, it never gets rock-hard, and if I finally get it hard enough to get inside her, it gets soft in a very short time. I don't think it's psychological, because there's nothing really wrong. And it's not an absence of desire. We're not kids, but the desire has always been there, and it's there now.

"We try to have sex, but it's difficult, and it makes me anxious. My wife is still a willing partner, and until this started happening, we were both enjoying our sex life. I don't know what to do or what is causing this.

"I'm frustrated by it. I don't feel emasculated or anything, but I don't think this should be happening to me. I'm in good shape; I'm healthy, and I'm just wondering why. I have friends who talk. One guy I know in his mid-seventies says he has sex once a week . . . who the hell knows if he's telling the truth, but the guy I play golf with is in his late seventies and he tells me that he's still sexually active . . . and I think he's telling the truth.

"I think my wife wants me to go for help. I saw one doctor who says there is nothing unusual with this, but I don't know. I think something should be able to be done. I can still ejaculate, but a semi-hard erection isn't good enough to have sex with. It's difficult to enter and stay there. I don't know what doctors can offer someone like me; one told me about a surgical procedure, which I don't really want to do, but I've got to do something, that's for sure. It certainly hasn't affected the marriage in any way. I don't think my wife is frustrated, but we always enjoyed our sexual relationship, and I think we're too young to give up entirely."

Cheryl, 42, says that for a brief time her husband's sexual difficulties made her insecure, but she has come to realize that it's not her, and it's not the marriage. . . .

"We've been married four years; I don't have any experience with long-term relationships. My first marriage ended in divorce, and we hated each other so much, I can't even remember the sex. Ted and I have what I think of as a very loving sexual relationship, but sometimes we start making love, and he doesn't get an erection. When it first started happening, I became concerned that maybe he was no longer attracted to me. It's very anxiety-provoking to go to bed with a man who is trying to get erect and can't. You want to do what you can, but it's not easy to get accustomed to it. I was raised to believe that if a man was interested in you, he had an erection. After the third time it happened, I called a friend, who is very sensitive to these kinds of problems. I think she has experienced just about every one of them firsthand. She said that we should have sex only in the morning because as men get older they sometimes take longer to get erect or can't get erect as often, particularly in the evening.

"My husband is 46, and every couple of months or so, he will go through a cycle where nothing works. My inclination is to forget about it and go off and do something else, but he usually wants to keep trying. My problem is that I feel as though I can't relax. When he gets an erection, I want him to have an orgasm quickly, so I don't have to worry about his losing it in the middle. It's a real nuisance. But I'm afraid that it may mean he is no longer interested in me. It scared me for a while, and whenever it happens, it still does. That's what bothers me the most. I think my insecurity is my problem and not his. He's very, very loving. He always hugs and kisses me and tells me that he loves me. He's pretty romantic, too, which I really appreciate. He pays attention to what I do, what I wear, what I'm interested in. Little things, like remembering to order the wine that I like and my favorite music. I feel as though I am lucky in most things in this marriage.

"My husband said he went to the doctor about his sexual problems, and they found nothing wrong, so I guess it bothered him too. But he seems to indicate that it's his problem, not mine, and the marriage is very even and loving. Also, I think my friend is right because the problem doesn't seem to be as much of a problem in the morning."

Some men and women said that their partners were simply not that sexually oriented but that they had come to accept it because they were getting the rest of their emotional needs fulfilled.

Renee, 34, says that her husband has what she perceives as a very low level of sexual energy, but she accepts it as just being the way he is. . . .

"I had a good deal of experience before we got married, and Jules and I started sleeping together on the third date, so there were no surprises for me about his sexual interest. I don't think it's so much that he doesn't have sexual drive. I think his drive goes into his work and into other things. When we started going out, he was busy setting up a career, and he worked all the time. After marriage, not that much has changed.

"We have two small children, and I know he loves me and loves the children. It's interesting, but as the marriage has grown, I think he's become more passionate, not less. Something about the fact that I'm his wife, these are his children, and we are his family—this seems to have brought out more emotion.

"He's a good man and he's a thoughtful man and he's a kind man; he's not a very sexy man. But you can't have everything, and I went out with a lot of sexy men when I was single, but they weren't very good or very kind. I appreciate my husband.

"We have sex usually when the children are napping, or sometimes we get a sitter to take them to the park. Our favorite time is probably Sunday afternoon. It's sort of a small ritual with us. There are some weeks, however, when we don't have sex. I think after the children were born, both times we went months. I wasn't interested, and he didn't push it. I think I'm definitely more sexually oriented than he is. I like oral sex, for example, and he goes along with it, I'm sure mostly to please me. Sometimes he's a very mechanical lover, but as I said, with time, he's gotten more passionate and interested, not less. The sex has definitely improved as the marriage has grown more secure.

"We have a very routinized married life. We do a lot with the children; we have a baby-sitter a couple of nights a week and go out together, alone or with friends. Even though I had a career and most of my friends are working, I decided to stay home with the children, at least for a while. We're affectionate and loving and very normal."

Unstable and in Trouble

Other men and women who talked to us are more uncertain that their sexual differences and problems can be worked out. Within these marriages, one or both partners are unable to adjust or compromise, and friction or overriding unhappiness over sexual incompatabilities is threatening the relationship itself.

Gil is 31 and his wife, Kim, is 23. They have been married for less than a year, but Gil says they are having serious problems around the issue of frequency of sex. He feels his wife has unrealistic expectations that he cannot fulfill. . . .

"When we first met, the attraction was instant. I had dated hundreds of women and typically had little interest in seeing them more than a few times. With Kim it was different; I wanted to see her every night. We had a lot of sex—basically we had sex every time we got together.

"Our problems started after marriage—on our honeymoon, to be exact. Kim's mother told her that newlyweds should have sex at least once a day on the honeymoon, and preferably two or three times a day. We were in Europe. It was my first trip, and I wanted to see something other than hotel beds. Sex we can always have. For my budget, Europe was a once-every-ten-year opportunity.

told her that I liked oral sex. I did like it, but I'm just
too angry at her right now to want to please her. When I
started out, all I cared about was pleasing her. Now I'm
just angry."

Gerald is 39. He has been married for more than twelve
years; he and his wife have three children. He says they rarely
have sex. . . .

"My wife doesn't want to sleep with me. I don't think she
hates me. I think she just hates sex, but I don't know what
to do about it, and it's not getting any better.
"When we were married, I always knew she was a little
funny about sex. You know, she didn't like to do certain things.
For example, she wouldn't have oral sex—either way. She
never liked sex to last very long. For a while I thought I was
lucky. After all, I was in a relationship where I never had to
worry about prolonging my erection.
"Actually I don't know whether we would have gotten
married, but she got pregnant, and neither one of us believes
in abortion. What this meant practically is that for the first
six years she was always pregnant, or there was a young
baby who was tiring her out. In other words, she had lots
of excuses for not having sex. If I tried at night, she said
she needed her sleep. So I tried in the morning, and then
she was too tired. She would promise that we would make
love that night. Then when the evening came around, she
would say something happened, like she slipped during
the day and her back hurt. Or she would go in to put the
kids to sleep and fall asleep in one of their beds. And I
couldn't wake her.
"We would end up having a quickie maybe once every
two weeks. It's kind of amazing that she got pregnant that
way, but she did. Twice.
"I kept thinking things would get better, but they
didn't. They got worse. In the meantime, I love my wife;
I love my kids; I like our life, our home. It's important
to me. My parents were separated, and I don't want to
do that to my kids. Also, my wife is a good person; she

"That's when it started. She began to complain. She said, 'If you were really attracted to me, you would make love to me all the time.' It was constantly, 'What's wrong with you?' At first I would try to make love at least every night, but she could tell when I wasn't as enthusiastic.

"By the time we got home, sex was an issue. To be perfectly honest with you, sex is not such a priority in my life right now. It was when I was single, when I was running around dating dozens of women. But now that I'm settled down, my priorities are on making money, having friends, starting a family . . . but she doesn't see it that way.

"She wants me home at seven, seven-thirty, every night. She wants me around all the time. For her, she wants sex more than anything. That's her comfort. She works, but she would probably quit tomorrow if she could, and she doesn't relate to my other needs. She watches these TV shows and it's kissy-kissy, lovey-lovey all the time, with guys tearing women's clothes off. She thinks this is real life. She says I don't lust for her because I'm not trying to attack her. She wants to have to fight me off all the time. She says to me, 'Don't you have human male needs?'

"We've split up a couple of times already. I love her, but I don't think I can live like this. It's too emasculating.

"I do everything I can to make her happy, other than have sex with her all the time. I'm affectionate. I massage her back. I rub her head. I make her breakfast. She says that I'm just trying to buy her off and take her mind off what she really needs.

"I've tried talking to her, but how do you have conversations with somebody who says it's all your fault? I've gone with her to a counselor—because I really want this to work. And she sits there blaming me. She yells in the counselor's office. She yells at home. She tells me I'm a 'closet case.' She says I'm a selfish lover. And lately she's started to complain that I'm not successful enough. Frankly, I've had enough of her attacks.

"Now I have to admit that I've started to punish her. She can only have climaxes through oral sex, and I've stopped having oral sex with her. She says that I lied to her when I has a good heart. She's kind to everybody. Everybody but me.

"I suggested counseling and finally forced her to see somebody with me. She said she thought I would start wanting sex less often. She also said that her father tried to touch her when she was little, and that's why she doesn't like sex. I tell you the truth, I don't believe her. I think she's exaggerating some small incident to find a good excuse for not going to bed with me. You know, something to make me feel like an unsympathetic brute if I try to force the issue.

"Lately I've really started fighting with her. Her attitude is beginning to make me resent everything. If she spends money, I think about it and get angry because my needs aren't being met. So I'll fight with her. I know that if I weren't angry about the sex, I wouldn't get so angry about the money. Same thing when she lets things go in the house. You know, like she ran out of toilet paper. She does all the shopping. Instead of just grabbing a box of tissues, I got furious. I was thinking, 'You don't have time to sleep with me, you don't have time to shop, what exactly do you have time for?'

"I've stormed out of the house a couple of times. The thing is—and this is really funny—she's very, very jealous. If she thinks I so much as talk to another woman, she starts getting nervous. I know I can get her into bed by pretending to flirt with someone in a store or by mentioning another woman. It's not right, but I do it sometimes. Then I'm furious at both of us.

"I really don't know what I'm going to do. I've tried to be gentle. I've tried to be understanding. I think she's sick as far as sex is concerned. Some days I think I'll have an affair. Other days I think I'll get a divorce. The therapist didn't really help, because my wife promised to try, but she doesn't. She promises me that it will get better tomorrow or next week. In the meantime she stays downstairs until she thinks I'm asleep, or she goes to bed before me and pretends to be asleep herself. We're having sex about once every ten days to two weeks, but it's not just the frequency, it's the attitude. She acts like she hates it. When I ask her what I can do to make it better for her, she says, 'Just take care of yourself.' "

Sharon, 27, has been married to her husband, 32, for two years. She says that he is so disinterested in sex with her that she is currently considering an affair with a man at work and is thinking about asking for a divorce. . . .

"This is not what I had in mind for a marriage. Chip shows no interest in me whatsoever. When we have sex, which is about once a week, it is perfunctory and unsatisfying. I guess I wanted something more romantic and more emotional in my marriage. My parents weren't happy together, and I never wanted to repeat my mother's pattern, but it looks as though I have.

"Chip rarely kisses me, never tells me that he loves me, and ignores me a lot of the time. He does buy me presents, I've got to say that—but they are never things I would have chosen for myself. It's almost as though I don't exist, except as some figment of his imagination.

"The first few months we had sex more often and he was a little more affectionate, but he soon started to stay out late and just be generally cool to me. I've tried everything: I've cried, I've pleaded, I've warned him that I'm going to have to leave, but he doesn't seem to believe me. When I cried, he got angry and walked out of the house.

"Believe me, I've tried all the normal ways to get his sexual interest. I spent a couple of hundred dollars on fancy underwear, and I do everything short of grabbing at him. One of my friends went to one of these parties that sells toys and stuff, and she got me all these lotions and creams. I suggested to Chip that I cover him with stuff and lick it off . . . or he could do it to me. He laughed. He says that I'm cute, but I could never learn to be sexy.

"One weekend I took him away to a hotel in the country as a birthday surprise for him. They had cable TV, and when we got there, all he did was watch ball games. For sex, I think he masturbates. He always subscribes to *Playboy, Penthouse*, and all that stuff. He watches pornographic movies after I go to sleep. He's right—I'm very straight, but if he wanted somebody who acted like a *Playboy* centerfold, why did he choose me?

"I think the only reason he married me is that his family wanted him to. All his friends and relatives told me that he wasn't very feeling or emotional, but I thought he would change once we were married. He has changed. He's become even less feeling and less emotional. He has no interest in anything I do or say. He looks at other women, and he's attracted to women who don't look anything like me.

"A man at work is coming on to me, and I think I may follow through, even though he's probably not right for me, either. I know it's because my ego is bruised and I feel rejected. I could live this way if I knew it would end, but I'm afraid this is the way it will always be if I stay with him.

"I have an appointment with a therapist because I want some counseling about what to do. I want to be happy— this is not happy."

EMOTIONALLY SHUT OFF

Several women told us that they felt that their mates were emotionally totally detached or "shut off" and that this in turn affected sexual intimacy.

Leigh, 29, has been married to her 30-year-old husband for five years. She says, "I had really looked forward to the closeness of marriage and was anticipating a sensual as well as sexual relationship. Because my husband and I are both very religious, we had not slept together before marriage. I had some experiences when I was still in my teens before I became fully committed to my religion, but I had been celibate for four years before marriage.

"I was tremendously hurt and disappointed by my husband's attitude. He's very mechanical sexually, and although one can't fault his performance, it's totally lacking in passion or enthusiasm. He is totally mechanical and absolutely refuses to be sensual with me. He doesn't understand, for example, that I can't have an orgasm through intercourse, and he resents doing anything else. We saw a therapist who explained that my needs were reasonable, so he started trying, but his disinterest is so obvious that it is a total turnoff. Once he turned on the TV news while he was stimulating me with his hands, and he couldn't understand why I got upset. He adamantly refuses to compliment me or tell me that he finds me attractive or desirable. In fact, if anything, he makes me feel bad about the way I look. Most people tell me that I am very pretty, and lots of guys are always trying to pick me up and talk to me. But not my husband. I think he's essentially very stubborn, and as a matter of principle, he refuses to give anything that I want. I don't understand it. I've tried to present my needs in a non-manipulative, non-threatening way. I've planned romantic weekends; I've tried seductive techniques. I've done everything I can think of, but it doesn't work. He's sexually cold. I used to cry about it more often than I do now. We have a lovely child, a nice life. And my religious feeling is against divorce, but this is very hurtful to me."

Miriam, 38, said that her ex-husband was very skilled as a lover, but that he was totally turned off emotionally. . . .

"He was like a machine. Nothing affected him. We had sex every day of our marriage, sometimes twice a day, up until the day we separated. Nothing I said, nothing I did, nothing that happened altered his sexual performance. He was the total performer, but he didn't understand intimacy. I don't think he ever kissed me intimately or said my name. He was like a machine. I didn't know how to mention it to him because it seemed rude to point out such a serious emotional flaw. When I was married, I was much more insecure than I am now. I went through the entire marriage without orgasms because I didn't know how to tell my husband what to do.

"I think he was also sleeping with other women because sometimes he wouldn't come home. He always denied it, of course. He finally left me.

"I now know that you are who you are, and sex is a part of that. The problems I had with my husband had everything to do with who we were and nothing to do with sex."

MARRIAGE AND THE COMMUNICATION PROBLEM

Underlying many sexual problems in marriage is a basic failure to communicate both before and after marriage. Men and women of all ages and all generations marry without ever verbally articulating their sexual expectations. People tend to wear blindfolds at the beginning of a relationship. Some are aware that they don't always agree with their partners' sexual attitudes and that there are underlying areas of disagreement. But they often believe that once the relationship stabilizes, the partner will change—or somehow, miraculously, they will be able to talk about the problem. We all know that it is never easy to communicate about sex. Even those men and women who told us that they had very close relationships in which they had made a conscious effort to discuss sexual differences, needs, and misunderstandings confirmed that they were never 100% successful.

We saw this failure to communicate in virtually every interview, but perhaps one of the most disturbing stories we heard, reflecting an utter failure of communication, was told to us by a 52-year-old woman who was describing her first marriage. . . .

"I refer to my son as the immaculate conception because sex with my husband was almost nonexistent.

"The honeymoon sex was very difficult. At first he didn't really try, which I took as an indication of his concern and a reluctance to inflict himself on me. I had absolutely no experience. We had necked and petted some before marriage, and he always seemed eager. He indicated that he was sophisticated and experienced because he had been in the Army. I assumed he knew more than he did. In retrospect, I realize he was probably as naïve as me. Finally we did try to have sex, but he couldn't penetrate. We decided to get me drunk, and that's what we ultimately did. It was mildly traumatic for me—I don't know what it was for him, and it didn't occur to me to ask.

"We had very little sex for the first eight years; it was very, very infrequent even at the beginning, gradually becoming nonexistent. For the last seventeen years, from the time I was 30 on, there was absolutely no sex. My husband was only a few years older than me. I was very frustrated for a big part of our marriage. It made me question my femininity. I tried to discuss it, but he always took it as an attack on him, and he indicated that it would somehow get better. So we never discussed what was wrong, and he never told me what was bothering him. Within the first year I realized that he saw physical affection as demanding. If I tried to touch him, he would stiffen. He just drew this psychological circle around himself over which I couldn't cross. I didn't. My pride came into play here, because I didn't want to be rejected anymore.

"It was a strange marriage, but it wasn't a bad marriage. It just wasn't a physical marriage. Our one child was conceived with a thermometer. I knew exactly when I ovulated and my husband went along with my desire to become pregnant. We threw ourselves into the community and into our lives. We both loved animals, and we ended up with a houseful of dogs and cats. We were busy.

"He was also a good friend to me. He was proud of me, and very concerned with how I looked. He substituted money for affection, and he would go on buying sprees for me. I think a part of that was wanting a wife who looked as good as anybody else's.

"He was supportive in everything I wanted; he encouraged me to go on with my education and get a career. I wasn't miserable, I was just dissatisfied. For sex, I masturbated.

"I have a picture of the two of us sitting in the living room. I'm sitting in a chair, and it looks as though his arm is around me. If you look closely, you can see his arm is around the chair, not around me. That's the way it was. I don't think anybody would have noticed the core of unhappiness in the marriage. I tried to tell my older sister about it once, but she stopped me. She said I shouldn't talk about these things. I didn't tell anyone else until after he died suddenly when we were in our mid-forties. I still have no idea why we had so little sex. I think perhaps he was ill and didn't talk about it. In retrospect, I cannot imagine what it could have been.

At the time I thought maybe he was having affairs, but now that I've given it more thought, I honestly don't think that was the case.

"After he died, my life changed drastically. It all seems very far away and very distant. But I can talk about it now, something I couldn't do at the time, not to anyone."

An Uncommunicative Male

In this age of sexual openness, it's always surprising to talk to someone who has the inhibitions and repressed attitudes of an earlier generation. Although Zack is only 28, he impressed us as being a classic example of the uncommunicative male. He and his wife have been married less than six months. Zack acknowledges his attitude problem, but he doesn't seem prepared to do anything about it.

"How long does sex typically last?" (interviewer)

"Who knows?"

"Twenty minutes? Ten minutes?" (interviewer)

"Maybe ten. I'm a quick gun, man."

"Do you try to slow down?" (interviewer)

"Not really. It's 'Thanks . . . bye . . . I'm going to sleep. Go talk to the cat.' "

"Is that okay with her?" (interviewer)

"I think she would like more."

"Do you try to compensate?" (interviewer)

"You mean, like putting on numbing cream?"

"No. Oral sex? Or manipulation?" (interviewer)

"Not me. I admit I'm a male chauvinist pig in that department."

"Tell me something. Does she climax during sex?" (interviewer)

"Yeah, sometimes. It's not like she never has with me."

"But you don't stimulate her any other way? Do you use your hands?" (interviewer)

"No, not really. I may play with her breast or something."

"How much do you actually talk about sex with your wife?" (interviewer)

"Talk about sex? Not much."

"How much have you ever talked about sex together?" (interviewer)

"We never talk about sex a lot."

"In other words, you've never had specific conversations, such as, 'This is what I like, what do you like?' " (interviewer)

"No."

"Never?" (interviewer)

"Once when I was down there, fingering her, whatever, she said, 'That's not where I like it. Move it over here.' "

"And you think you've only had this discussion once?" (interviewer)

"Yeah, that was it."

"Is there a lot of affection in your marriage?" (interviewer)

"From her. I'm a cold-type person. I know that. I can be pretty distant."

"But she doesn't complain?" (interviewer)

"Maybe once or twice she said, 'I wish you'd give me a hug.' "

"What do you do?" (interviewer)

"Sometimes I do, but sometimes I don't. Some of the times she likes to cuddle, I find inconvenient. Put it that way. I don't want to sound too cold."

"Do you love her?" (interviewer)

"Oh, yeah. I love her."

"Are you satisfied in your relationship?" (interviewer)

"Oh, yeah. My perception is that she's not."

"But you've never talked about it." (interviewer)

"Nope."

Can We Talk?

On the other end of the spectrum, we talked to many men and women who said that they are desperate to communicate with their mates and are always looking for openings. One such example is Evan, a 24-year-old newlywed who was fairly inexperienced before meeting his wife. He says that he wants to be able to have sex more often and develop a more relaxed attitude in his marriage. . . .

"But it's amazing how tired we both are a lot of the time. Like last night. Absolutely nothing happened. I was studying in the living room. Suzie was watching *Dynasty* on our new stereo television in the bedroom. I didn't hear another word from her. I walked into the bedroom at about eleven, and she had crashed. I woke her so she could change, and went out to brush my teeth. When I came back, she was still in the same position. So I shut the light and went to sleep.

"We rarely have morning sex because I'm just not easily aroused in the morning. Until I've had my shower and my coffee, I'm not together enough.

"Right now my wife is getting over the flu, and I don't like her to get sick. When she runs around, she gets sick —I wouldn't let her out of the house this weekend. You know, its oranges and vitamin C and shit, and sometimes she gets sick again.

"This weekend we made love for the first time in about a week and a half. She initiated it. I remember saying to her, 'I don't think we should do this because you need your strength.' Then I definitely broke down. But it was quick, about ten minutes.

"I think she may initiate sex more than me—you know, just by body language. I tend to go to sleep later than she does, so my way of initiating is just to get into bed with her at eleven instead of one. We really need to find another way to get our needs across to each other, and that's something that should happen when we're together longer.

"We sleep curled up around each other. Suzie's cat, who has become my cat, sleeps with us . . . usually on my side of the bed. I'm sort of tucked between two women.

"Before we were married, when we made love, we would usually do it twice in an evening, but maybe it's true what they say about after you get married—the pressure of doing something more than once isn't there . . . it's not there for us. I think I come too quickly. I try to ask her if it's too fast. Sometimes she says something like she wishes I had the ability to stay longer. When we were doing it more than once, I was definitely spending more time making love to her.

"I still remember our honeymoon because we would take a nap and make love in the afternoon, then go out for dinner and come back and make love again.

"I don't know about whether or not she has climaxes every time. I ask her, and she says things like, 'Can't you tell?' I wish she'd tell me directly. How am I supposed to tell? Sometimes we talk about it, and she talks about books she's read about how women have orgasms from special stuff. I've asked her if she wants me to do anything else or more, and she doesn't indicate that she does. I don't think she's feeling unfulfilled or unsatisfied, but neither one of us is that experienced, and there are more things we should know. I was her first lover, and she still hasn't really tried to learn about oral sex. We haven't been together that long. Here we are in our new apartment, with our new bedroom set and our new television. These things take time. I don't know how many women don't want to perform oral sex or do this or that—I figure it will play itself out. You know, I don't want to say anything like, 'This is what I want,' so I hint at it. I guess in due time it will happen.

"In the meantime sometimes we try different positions, a few different variations. We experiment slightly, very slightly. Sometimes things you don't expect happen. Like right after we got back from our honeymoon, she developed a urinary-tract infection which she said she thought was from certain positions. Another time she took an antibiotic, and she got a yeast infection, which made sex difficult.

"I've suggested bringing home a video, but I can tell from the expression on her face that she finds it repellent. We also have some 'blue' channels on the television, but she doesn't want to watch them. Maybe eventually we'll get some books, some sex manuals. I mean, why not?

"We haven't even settled on a form of birth control. Right now we use condoms because neither one of us likes the diaphragm, 'cause it's messy and interrupts things. I don't think I want her messing around with her body by taking the pill.

"When I was a kid fantasizing about how it would be, I would sometimes go to a porn movie and think, 'Geez, can you believe those two? That's incredible!' But it's different when you love somebody. My wife is my wife . . . she's not really a sex object. She's somebody I love, and I'm going to be with her for the rest of my life. Sex is going to have to work itself out. I'd like to try new things, but when it happens, it happens. I want to be able to talk to her about these things, but it takes time."

ANGER, THE GREAT SEXUAL TURNOFF

Everyone agrees—anger is not an aphrodisiac. Anger that is allowed to fester and become angry resentment can ultimately destroy the most torrid sexual relationship.

Gina, 37, said: "When we were first married, we would have terrible fights. It was sort of like something in the movies. You know, then we would make up and we'd make love. I remember that our fights used to hurt me because it would make me feel so distant from Howie, so removed that I couldn't wait to snuggle up to him and feel close again. Over the years the fighting has never stopped. But I don't care that much about making up. I'm too mad now, and it takes us longer and longer. Sometimes we go weeks without really speaking, and without sex."

Robin, 40, very explicitly described a marital fight that she says was a turning point in her marriage. She and her husband ultimately were divorced. . . .

"I would cook every Sunday and wrap everything in freezer paper, label it for the day of the week, and store it in the refrigerator. All you had to do was open the refrigerator or freezer door and you could see what needed to be defrosted or put on the stove or in the oven. A child could have started dinner.

"I agreed to move to be near his job, to a community I disliked, and every day I would commute one and a half hours each way. He worked five minutes from the house. Each day I left the house at 7 A.M to catch the 7:38 train. I returned on the 8:17 train. And when I walked through the door, every night he said the same thing to me. 'What's for dinner?' After three years of this, one night I broke every dish in the house, starting with the desert plates and ending up with the large serving bowls. 'That's for dinner!' I said.

"I wouldn't sleep with him for two weeks after that."

And then, of course, there are those men and women in marriages where the stress has been so destructive that the couple no longer have sex.

Glen, 44, says that he thinks he will eventually get a divorce once his daughter is grown. In the meantime he has stopped sleeping with his wife. . . .

"The sex never went bad. The marriage went bad. We have totally different interests, and she has no respect for what I am trying to do with my life. About five years ago I decided to change careers. I had been miserable for years, so I went back to school. You can't imagine anyone being less supportive. All she did was make fun of me. She totally disapproved. Maybe she felt scared because I was making good money doing what I was doing, and she didn't want me to throw it overboard. We had a lot of fights over that, and with each fight, there was more distance, more space between us.

"We always had good sex, but I would get so angry, I didn't want to sleep with her—and I don't think she felt any different. There had been a lot of other arguments over the years, so our arguing was nothing new. But the fights got more serious, and we made up less often. We became accustomed to living this way, like roommates. Actually we may get along better this way. We haven't had sex in close to three years."

Sophie, 58, married thirty-five years, says that she stopped having sex with her 63-year-old husband about seven years ago. Until then they were having sex about twice a week, sometimes more. . . .

"We have a very bad relationship, and we fight a great deal. About everything. I think Gus is just determined to disagree with me. If I say black, he says white. If I buy a steak for dinner, he says, 'Why didn't you get chicken?' If I take an umbrella, he fights with me and tells me it isn't going to rain. It's been like this for years. Also, he doesn't want to do anything with me. If I say I want to go to a movie, he says no. If I suggest a play, he says no. He has his own interests, but he doesn't share them with me. There is a great deal of anger between us, and I can't surmount it enough to have sex with him. I just can't. I think he resents it—actually, I know he resents it. We've never really discussed it, but I've made it clear that I want no part of him sexually. I just told him that unless he changes, there will be no sex. He as much as told me he has no intention of changing. He wants me to change. We still share the same bed. And we still cuddle some, particularly on cold nights. I don't know what that means.

"We're both going to retire in a few years. When we're stuck together in the same house all day, I don't know what's going to happen. I've never really told my friends that we don't have sex anymore, but I think everyone has seen us fighting so much that they would be shocked if we *were* having sex.

"I don't think about sex anymore; I'm just getting older. I never really masturbated, so I'm not about to start now. I guess I've just accepted that this is the way it's going to be. I made a bad choice for a husband, but it's too late to do anything about it now. I don't think he would ever leave me. He's afraid I might get the house. He tells me I should leave. I know he's not having affairs because he's always home fighting with me.

"A couple of years ago we were on a vacation and Gus

got romantic, and I thought, 'Why not?' For a moment I thought it might be a new start. So I agreed, and we had sex. We were no sooner finished than he started a fight over something I had said to the waiter in the dining room that morning. I decided that was the last time."

Lili, 52, says that she has not had sex with her 56-year-old husband in more than twelve years. . . .

"For years sex was what tied us together. My husband gave me very little else in the way of attention or affection and there was little companionship, but we had sex about five times a week, and it was very important to me.

"He always had a very detached personality, sort of cool and removed, but he changed when we had sex. During sex he was very intimate, and I had more of a sense of him as a person. Otherwise he was never much of a family man and left all the responsibility of the children to me. He was distant from all of us and still is. Sometimes I would complain about the lack of affection and connectedness, but most of the time I would try harder at the marriage. I thought that someday if I tried hard enough, he would appreciate me and become closer and more emotionally giving. I thought that the good sex we had was the basis on which we could build a better relationship and a more rounded existence. Now I realize that was a long shot.

"Considering everything else, our sexual life was too good to be true. I was never tired, never had a headache, never said, 'Not now.' I always wanted that bonding with him. I wanted it to work not just for me, but for the kids. Maybe I was too interested, too eager. Then about twelve years ago he began to leave signs around the house—clues that he was having affairs. He also began to have sex with me less often. There were always explanations and excuses for his behavior.

"I thought about it. I thought about a divorce and decided against it. But I can't have sex with him again. At first I couldn't do it because I was too hurt and angry. Now I'm scared about AIDS. Who knows who he's with? If he's foolish enough to risk his life and his health, that's his problem. We still sleep in the same bed, and we still cuddle. We've been together a long time, and it's a partnership even without the sex."

WHEN SEX IS PART OF THE BREAKUP

Obviously all couples do not live happily ever after, and we spoke to numerous men and women who went through the divorce process. Sexual incompatability or difficulties were often cited as significant contributors to the rift in the marriage.

Too Much/Too Often/Too Controlling

A disproportionately large number of women told us that they had left marriages and/or long-term cohabiting relationships because of what they perceived as their partners' sexual demands.

Dana, a 41-year-old stockbroker, said that during the marriage she simply didn't understand what was happening, but that she became totally turned off by the intensity of her second husband's sexual needs. . . .

"In the last year I've read articles about people who are sex addicts, and I think that's probably what he was. When I think about it, I realize that the whole relationship was bad, but the sexual aspects were a nightmare. It was just awful.

"My first husband barely slept with me, and he left me for another women, so when I met Howard, my ego was pretty bruised. Howard seemed so sexually intense and so attracted to me that at first it made me secure even though we seemed to be having a little too much sex, even for a new relationship. However, I thought it would become less frequent once we got used to each other. It didn't. If anything, his sexual demands increased, and he became irrationally demanding about everything else as well. I think he was on good behavior until after we got married.

"He was incredibly controlling out of bed, and he had an insatiable sexual appetite in it. He was like a bad child—he didn't want me to do anything but pay attention to him, and he wanted everything done his way. He had rules about everything, from how the container of milk should be opened to the way the clothes should be hung in the closet. He even stopped me from reading the newspaper because he didn't like the order in which I read the sections. Even though we both worked, he expected me to make a four-course dinner every night, which he would complain about. He was impossible.

"Well, take that level of control and multiply it in the bedroom. Not only did he always want to have sex—usually every night and for hours; he was also a frustrated choreographer and stage manager. He wanted to try every position ever thought of. He would insist that I get my body into these contortions, and then stay there while he carried on like he was a great lover. He also bought all these ridiculous sex toys that he wanted to try. I assumed that if I went along with some of his more outlandish postures, they would turn him on enough so that he would reach orgasm faster. But no such luck. He would hold back for hours. I think he was pleased that he had so much control. But I just wanted him to stop. If he thought I wasn't enjoying myself, he would concoct fantasies that he wanted me to have so that I would get more turned on—you know, like imagine being gang-banged by a group of cowboys and tell him about it. Now isn't that a turn-on?

"Although I was humiliated and embarrassed by his sexual attitude, I said very little. I tried to reason with him about all the nonsexual ways in which he tried to run my life, but I never said anything to him about the sex. I guess I didn't want him to feel rejected, and I didn't want to hurt him sexually. I didn't know how to tell him how repulsed I felt and how sick I thought he was. The marriage lasted a year and a half. I moved in with my sister, and I'm filing for divorce."

Michele, a young mother, is another woman who said her husband never stopped thinking about sex. . . .

"I was very young, and although we were sleeping together before marriage, we were both living at home, so it was complicated. I knew something was a little off sexually before marriage, but I guess having a husband was more important to me than being married. Besides, I thought we would work everything out after the wedding.

"Well, after we were married, I discovered he had incessant sexual desire. I couldn't do anything. He would try to have sex with me while I was cooking or talking on the phone. Have you ever tried to have a phone conversation with your mother or father while some man is pushing at you from behind? He thought it was funny and a turn-on. I thought it was disgusting and annoying. On an average weekend, he would want sex seven or eight times.

"I remember once I was doing dishes, and he was as usual crawling around on the floor on his hands and knees trying to reach up under my skirt. This time I was so angry that when he made a lunge for my crotch, I pretended that I was totally startled and dropped a pot of hot water on his head 'accidentally.' He got much more careful after that.

"I would do everything I could to avoid him. I would stay up late and pretend to fall asleep in front of the TV. I would crawl into the baby's crib and spend the night there. I found places to fall asleep in that house that you couldn't imagine.

"When we were first married, I went along with him because I thought it was my role as his wife. I loved him, and I thought if I didn't sleep with him, he would find somebody else who would. When I told him I thought we were having too much sex, he would imply that there was something wrong with me.

"Our last night together we had a knockdown physical fight. He told me that I was his wife and that I had to sleep with him. I couldn't do it anymore. He knocked me down and tore my sweater. I finally went to bed with him to get him to stop ranting. When he fell asleep, I took the baby and left. I moved to another state and I didn't talk to him again—except through our lawyers—until after the divorce papers were signed."

There must certainly be women who would like to be married to men with insatiable appetites. Yet the women we spoke to said they hated it and described feelings of rage and fury, particularly during the sex itself. One woman said, "I would lie there with him on top of me, and feel totally pinned down and completely furious. I would bite at my arm to keep from hitting him or screaming. I didn't know what to do to make him go away, and yet I thought I had to go to bed with him. Otherwise the marriage would dissolve, and I wasn't sure if I wanted that. Also, I hoped he would change. I thought maybe if he were more secure, he would become more normal, but that never happened."

These women also stressed that what they resented most was feeling like an object. Several expressed almost identical feelings about having a sense that their husbands didn't care who they were having sex with. One said, "I don't honestly think it would have mattered if it were me or the parakeet. I just think he was so obsessed with his own needs that I became a fantasy sexual object . . . just an orifice with no feelings whatsoever."

Interestingly, these women all said that they had orgasms regularly, yet they spoke about the mechanical aspects of it. One woman said, "I had orgasms because he pressed the right button the right number of times. But I didn't care. I just hated him. I hated the sex, and I wanted him to go away."

Too Little Sex

At the other extreme were the men and women who said that their partners became totally disinterested in sex to the point of being actively rejective.

Maggie, 42, says that she is absolutely convinced that the lack of sex is what ended her second marriage. . . .

"When I married Bart, I was 29, and he was 50. Despite the difference in our ages, the marriage had a strong sexual base—for me, at least. And I think it did for him too.

"The first time I was married, I was very young, and there was nothing sensible or intelligent in how I chose my first husband. By the time I was 25, I was divorced with two schoolage children. My daughter and son were very much involved in my wanting to marry Bart. He seemed perfect because he was settled, and secure professionally. He had grown children from his first marriage and, unlike younger men, certainly didn't want to start another family. Yet he was very understanding and kind to my children. I felt that he would be willing to help support them and give them a strong male parental image, something they didn't get from their natural father. I thought we would be a family. I wanted this for both me and the children.

"I think Bart liked me because I looked young and glamorous to him. When we first met, he was very into me, and very into my body. For my part, I liked him, respected him, and was very attracted to him. We also had a lot in common. We're both very opinionated, but we were opinionated in the same way. We liked the same people and we liked the same things. His friends were older, but they became my friends, too, and my friends were younger, but he fit in well with them. The age was not a problem in terms of interests. I did expect that eventually it might make a difference sexually, but I thought there would be a good ten years before that happened, and then I thought there would be a gradual tapering off. I was prepared to adjust to that.

"I've had stupendous sex, and the sex with Bart was never stupendous, but it was good sex, and at the beginning I felt I could take it for granted because we made love almost every night. I liked the constancy of it, and if he wasn't particularly inventive, his caring and commitment more than compensated for originality.

"The first year was a good one; we bought a house and decorated it, and that got a lot of the focus in the relationship. My children were delighted with the new neighborhood and the new school. His son had a baby and I became a step-grandmom.

"The only problem—and I will admit that it was there from the very first—was that although he was very politically and socially current, he was very much an old-fashioned macho male in terms of how he regarded himself. My friends would tell me that I catered to him too much. I did wait on him a lot, but I enjoyed it, and so did he. And he liked to be deferred to, which I did. It wasn't difficult to do because I basically agreed with him about most things.

"We were married a little more than two years when, for the first time in his life, Bart had a work problem. His law firm was implicated in some dealings that were not totally straightforward, and even though he was not responsible, he took the heat. That's when our problems started. He became irritable and annoyed with me, and more important, his sex drive started diminishing. At first he dropped down to sex once a week; then it was once every two weeks, etc. It was a drastic change, and it made me feel very uneasy. When I asked him, he said he didn't feel that sexual anymore.

"He decided to leave his firm, and start out again on his own. And then, even though his work situation improved, we stopped having sex altogether. I tried to be understanding, and I was for a long time, but after about a year of it, I started to confront him about it.

"I think this is where his being an old-style male is important. Bart was very focused on erections and intercourse. He was accustomed to always having an erection; intercourse was the only way he knew to make love, and he didn't want to try anything else. He wasn't somebody who would just start fooling around with me to see what might happen. If nothing happened, it seemed to make him feel worse about it. I think he was embarrassed about his lack of desire, so he was also less affectionate. It was as though every time I touched him, it reminded him of what we weren't doing, and he became annoyed. So affection disappeared along with the sex. He was just withdrawn from me.

"I begged him to see a doctor, and he actually did go have

some physical tests, which showed nothing wrong. But he didn't want to discuss it or deal with it. And he was so adamant that I began to feel like I was always nagging him about sex, which in a way I was. I think the problem fed on itself, and became even larger in his head than it really was, but he didn't see my attitude as trying to be helpful; he thought I was finding fault with him, and his ego couldn't handle my attitude any more than it could handle his reluctant erections. He didn't want to try making love, because I think as far as he was concerned, unless he had a perfect erection immediately, he felt foolish. He was accustomed to being the strong male, and he didn't know how to be anything else. I fought with him about the sex because I desperately wanted the marriage to last, and I knew I couldn't live indefinitely without a physical relationship.

"He actually told me I should have an affair, but I didn't want to do that. I wanted it all in one place—love, sex, family, marriage—all with one man.

"We went on like this for at least five more years, but the whole relationship disintegrated around the issue of sex. We really couldn't communicate about it because he saw my attempts to communicate as faultfinding. He, in turn, began to find fault with me for other things, and we just stopped being a happy unit and became, instead, two people pretending to be together. We even stopped sleeping in the same bed. I don't think any of our friends knew what was happening. I certainly didn't let on. Eventually there was one fight too many, and the marriage collapsed from it."

Glenda, a 33-year-old divorced mother, said:

"I think the main reason I divorced my husband was that he didn't want to sleep with me. It started soon after we were married. But it got really bad after our first child was born, and then by the time we had the second, it was all over. I was 24 at the time, and he was 30.

"I fought with him about it, a lot. I thought I was going to die without ever having a real sex life. Besides, he made me feel so rejected by never wanting me. I think he couldn't get the wife-mother thing together. He had a history of a lot of women before we were married, and I was a virgin when we met, and he wanted to marry a virgin. It was nuts, but I think that's what happened. Then after he married me, I think he figured I wasn't his type. I know he masturbated because I discovered him doing it a couple of times. And he had some affairs. Now, I think they didn't amount to more than a couple of short flings, but at the time I thought they were really a big deal. I really cried a lot. But truthfully, I wasn't that crazy about him sexually either.

"He was also totally ungiving and withdrawn. He never acted like he loved me. I would think that maybe I was being too romantic or wanting something that was unrealistic, but then we would go out with friends, and I would see other men hugging their wives and stuff, and I felt terrible.

"The other thing that was really strange about it is that after we separated and I started to date other guys, he got really nuts. Then he began to ask me out. Once when he brought the kids back, he made excuses until after I put them to bed and then he chased me around the living room. I couldn't believe it. We were married six years, and the last two years we'd had no sex whatsoever. I would get baby-sitters, put on fancy dresses, negligees, the whole thing. Nothing. He wanted no part of me. Then all I had to do was say 'Good bye, Charlie' and start going out with other guys, and suddenly he's chasing me around the living room. Now you tell me—is that normal?"

On-and-off Sexuality

A few men and women said that they had very turbulent marriages in which sexual activity peaked and waned in response to variety of factors, including jealousy.

Keith, divorced, says that when he stopped sleeping with his wife and began to have a series of affairs, she reciprocated with her own infidelity. The on-and-off nature of their sex life was a precipitating factor in their divorce. . . .

"I think the sex thing had to get to her after a while, but don't get me wrong, the marriage had many problems as well. We got married too young. I wasn't prepared for marriage or for sex, and she got pregnant right away. When she was pregnant, it felt very strange to me. And then afterward, she had stretch marks. I remember thinking I was too young to be with someone with stretch marks. They were a real turnoff to me. I was very young.

"We were only married a few years when I started noticing other women. My wife didn't help because she kept gaining weight. Twenty pounds on, ten pounds off, thirty pounds on, five pounds off. That kind of thing, like a yo-yo. At one point she was really fat. A total turnoff. I never told her that it bothered me, but it bothered me. I'd come home and find her eating a pizza and watching TV, and I wanted to say, 'Can't you just have a salad?'

"I started having affairs, and I started avoiding sex with her. I had more hobbies and activities than anyone could imagine. I became active in local politics. I pulled away from her in every way I could. Every night I had another meeting, and then I had a job with long hours. And girlfriends. With it all, I was never home—I was always away.

"Sometimes my wife would say things like, 'We never have any time together,' or 'We haven't had sex in two weeks.' I sort of always shrugged it off and said, 'Well, I'm busy. It's nothing personal. I'm just working hard.' I guess I did a lot of stuff rather than confront the issues with her. When I talk to her now, I still act that way. Even now. A part of me wishes she had been able to cut through my wall of avoidance. Let's put it this way: We had a problem, and I didn't want to discuss it. I didn't want to bring it out in the open. I had concluded that it was useless. Somewhere in the back of my mind I felt that the pain of dealing with it was worse than whatever the payoff might be.

"You've got to understand, it was a very stormy marriage because she would fight with me a lot. Then she had an affair, and I was shocked. Stunned. I couldn't comprehend that she had an attraction and a need for another man. I thought she was doing it to punish me for my stuff. I told her about somebody I was with. I think we both felt very threatened by what was going on, and surprisingly our sex life picked up for a while. Jealousy always perked the relationship up, but we would always slip back into the old pattern. Once things got calm, I would notice the stuff that turned me off. We fought a lot. I came home later and later, and the last two years we didn't have sex at all. You realize I'm compressing seven years of marriage here."

GOOD RELATIONSHIP/GOOD MARRIAGE/ GOOD SEX

Not all marriages have such unpleasant underlying dynamics. Many couples are lucky enough to have found love, intimacy, stability, and satisfactory sex. From the people we talked to, there are some definite patterns that do emerge. There are, for example, few conflicts about when and how to have sex. Frequency and time evolve through compromise and consideration. In these relationships, sexual spontaneity does not seem to be as important as spontaneity of affection. In fact, some of these couples seem to have learned how to not have sex.

Happily marrieds assured us that everything is not always perfect in their unions. Like other marrieds, they have had to learn to adjust and compromise on a wide variety of issues, including differences in sexual needs and expectations. Some of these marriages have survived and thrived, despite ongoing sexual problems.

LOVE, NOT LUST, THE PREDOMINANT THEME IN HAPPY MARRIAGES

At the core of the happy marriage there seems to be something quite special: love.

It sounds corny, we admit it, but we were impressed, and often inspired, by the way in which so many happily married men and women voluntarily expressed the strength and quality of love they feel for their partners.

In the light of so many books and articles that focus on male insensitivity, we also think it's worth commenting upon how many of our male interviewees talked so unabashedly about the level of love they felt for their wives, as well as the critical role this love played in their lives.

But among the people who considered their marriages successful, both men and women were consistent in telling us that love, and not lust, is the glue that keeps a relationship together; love, not lust, is what motivates couples to work on their problems and accept or overlook those things that cannot be changed. Love, not lust, is what creates stability, productivity, and marital longevity. Even some of our interviewees appeared self-conscious about sounding corny, but love clearly is the bottom line in these relationships. It has the greatest effect on what really happens in a relationship, both in and out of bed.

Long-term Marriages/Long-term Love

Andy, who is in his mid-sixties, has been married almost forty-five years. He says that his love, as well as his romantic feelings for his wife have lasted through all forty-five years. . . .

"Of course, sex has become infrequent in recent years. But you have to separate romance from sex. When they come together, it's the best of all possible worlds. Romantically we haven't stopped. I still feel romantic toward her. We take vacations, walks; we travel. We hold hands. The sex has become infrequent, and it probably has changed the relationship. I would say that the transformation that takes place when you get older and have less sex is that you either become best friends, as we have, or you grow apart, which I've seen some of my friends do. Right now there's a lot of love between us; we're very close, and we're best friends.

"The beginning of our romance was idealized romantic love. I fell in love with her almost from the moment I saw her. We were both kids. We took long walks, we gazed deeply into each other's eyes, we wrote letters. I didn't ask her out for several months after we met. When I did, on the first date I proposed. She said she was too young. Then I went into the Army, and for months I wrote to her every day, no matter where I was or how tired I was. That summer she took a job in a Five and Ten, and I figured that the women she worked with were probably going to be a romantic bunch, so I had somebody go into the store and get all their names—it was easier to do in those days—and I wrote them all notes telling them to tell her to marry me.

"When we got married, I was 22 and she was 19. I was in the Army and stationed in Oklahoma, so we couldn't really have an active sexual life at the beginning because we were separated so much. I remember once she came down for the weekend, and we didn't go out of the hotel once. You always remember those weekends.

"Through it all, we wrote all the time. Now we use the phone if we're separated. I take a lot of business trips, sometimes to Europe. The phone bills cost me a fortune, but even in the jungle I'll find a phone to call Esther.

"At the beginning, after the war, we had sex all the time, evenings and mornings. It changed some when our oldest was born. We used to tease that the kid was hooked up to its mother's womb because the minute we started to make love, the child would cry. We had four children, and she was pregnant a lot. There was less frequency because there was less opportunity, but the desire was always there.

"Also, I loved having kids. We did everything with them, and I liked it. There was less sex because of them, but there was also a lot of joy that we both derived from being with them. It was a fair trade-off, even though the pregnancies weren't all planned. At least two of them were a direct result of condom failure.

"Then we had a couple of rocky periods when I was in my mid- to late thirties. I had a real career blow, and that affected my mood and my sexuality. Then my wife—I think trying to make our sex lives easier—went out and had her tubes tied without really consulting with me. I was a real jerk about it and took it very badly. I really disappointed my wife because she thought this was our time to have a relaxed sex life. But with the combination of a forced career blow, stress, and everything else, my sex drive declined. It was not a good time for us but we weathered it, and I think we emerged more affirmative in our love for each other, but there was a decline in passion. Age may have also played a part, so I don't know whether that decline was induced by outside factors or by the fact that I was hitting 40. Although there was less sex, I don't think it really affected our love for each other. We always talked to each other, so even when we were not getting along that well, which is what happened for a while, there was never any question about our love for each other. I don't think either of us considered a divorce; we both rode it out even though we were a little bit distant for a couple of years. I withdrew into work.

"When that period ended, our combination romantic/sexual interludes went back to almost where they had been. I say almost because I had become accustomed to less sex. I didn't want it as often.

"But from the time I was about 42 to 50, we had a terrific sex life. Then I started getting headaches, and I was put on this medication that got rid of the headaches, but it also made me impotent. I think my wife thought I was having an affair, which of course I wasn't. I just couldn't get it up, and nobody had told me that impotence was the dreadful side effect to the drug I was taking.

"Eventually I stopped taking the drug and our sex life picked up, but again, there was a decrease in frequency, I think because we had grown accustomed to less. And then in my mid-fifties, I had to start taking another drug for arthritis, and that really affected my ability to perform.

"It's interesting because the desire is still there; it's the inability to perform that's the problem. We cuddle, snuggle, feel, touch. But all these factors mean less sex. I should also mention weight. I used to be thin. I put on weight, and I think that it esthetically lowers desire. It's like when you watch Aida and you see the fat tenor and the fat soprano bumping up against each other, trying to make love, you want to break up. I'm not obese, but compared to what I used to be . . . Anyway, it makes you self-conscious, and it changes the way you make love.

"The arthritis and the headaches subsided some, and we had a respite from drugs for a couple of years; the sex got better. Then my blood pressure went up, and it meant more drugs. Last year I lost some weight and cut back on the drugs, and for a while we went back to having sex two or three times a week, and it was terrific. Then there was a new bout of medical problems. That's the way it goes.

"The business I'm in has afforded me many opportunities to start affairs, but I've never considered it. Over the years most of our friends have gotten divorced or had affairs. But I think Esther and I have been very lucky. People ask me how I am, and I say fine, even when all my medical problems are plaguing me at once, because I *am* fine. I think if you have settled on your feeling of love, there is a well-being at the core of your system that can't be touched. And I think Esther and I are very fortunate in achieving the kind of core relationship where Sturm und Drang, fatness, pills, illness, fatigue—all of these things become less relevant against the core of love. As twerpy as it may sound, I look forward to being with her; I think we're closer and tighter now. I think love segues into genuine friendship if it is a real good love, so that while the love remains, the romanticism remains, and the aura of sensuality that surrounded you remains, friendship does take over. Don't get me wrong, there's still a lot of desire and affection, and foreplay. There's just not as much sex."

Annie, who is almost 60, has been married thirty-nine years. She says that she and her husband have always had a close, loving marriage, with an easy, natural adjustment to each other from the very beginning. . . .

"We used to joke that we had been a couple on Noah's Ark. We had an intense bonding and connection from the very beginning. Because of this we had strong confidence that whatever we were going to experience would work. When we married, we did not have parental approval, and we had many barriers. My parents would have preferred to have me marry a doctor or a lawyer. My husband was a writer, and there was never any guarantee that we would be able to tough it out financially. Although he would have preferred to work on his own things, later he took a staff job with a publication.

"My husband has recently retired, and now we spend a great deal of time together. He is also free to work on his own material, and he spends much of the day in his office.

"My parents did not have a perfect marriage, and although there were strong loyalties, there was always a certain amount of arguing. Even as a child I knew that I wanted a good and happy marriage. I wanted a family and closeness, and I've been very fortunate in having that. Our children are grown and happy. And we have a very strong relationship. We really respect each other. My husband is truly my best friend, and I love to hang out with him. Soon he'll come down and he'll start cooking dinner—he is clearly the better cook. I'd rather do the cleaning up. We'll watch the evening news together, and maybe one or two other programs. Sometimes we'll work a little. We go to bed early usually, and we read in bed together.

"Many of my friends have had affairs or gotten divorced, and I feel badly about that. We really never had very many problems as a couple, but those we did have, we worked out. The biggest change in our marriage over the years is that we stopped trying to change each other. I tried to get him to be more talkative, less withdrawn; he tried to get me not to harp on him about his communication problems. Actually we both changed gradually—now he's more forthright, and I'm less likely to nag. But now we tend to just say, 'Oh, well, you're the way you are.'

"We've never had much money in our marriage. One of the things we agreed upon was that we weren't going to stress this, and this decision has freed both of us. He hasn't felt that he should take time away from his own work to look for a more lucrative occupation, and when many of my friends took jobs, I felt that I could continue to stay at home. Having less money meant being able to do less, but it also allowed me to do those things I enjoy and to be creative in my own way—I do ceramics for my own pleasure.

"In the early years of our marriage the world was a much more rigid place, and I was more rigid also. I had very strict ideas of what was acceptable for me to feel and what was normal or not normal. Now I think if it feels good, do it. If an individual sexual episode doesn't turn out well, I'm easier on myself. I realize that each sexual episode is not the last word in performance.

"Our sexual pattern hasn't really dropped off. In certain ways it has picked up. We started to have children right away, and for many years the children were our primary focus. We both have a lot of interests, so we were often busy. During those years sometimes there wasn't time or energy for sex. Now we feel that it is ours to enjoy morning, noon, or night. Sometimes it happens spontaneously, but often we plan for it. We'll decide that we're going to have sex later in the day or in the evening, and we'll plan for it specifically.

"Neither one of us is really conventionally romantic. We don't buy presents or make a big deal out of evenings out, but I feel my husband conveys his romantic feelings in other ways. For instance, he has always been enormously supportive of me. When he went to work, he would wake much earlier than me, and almost every day before he left, he would leave me a note on the pillow. It was always full of support and love. These notes meant a great deal to me, and I've kept them all. I've been very fortunate in marriage. I have a husband who listens to me; he thinks about me. We still enjoy being together—we're interested in each other."

2

What Really Happens in Bed: Extramarital Affairs

SOME COMMON REASONS FOR AFFAIRS

Although the men and women we interviewed told us that they had affairs for a variety of reasons that were unique to their own personal situations, these reasons typically fell into one of several fairly well-defined categories. The most common reason they cited:

The Marriage Was "Over" Long Before the Affair Began

We spoke to many people who had been divorced. In almost all instances, one or both partners was having an affair by the time the couple separated. In some cases, the affair was what ultimately precipitated the breakup. A fairly standard response among those we interviewed is that they had started affairs because they had come to the conclusion that the marriage was basically over, and there was no longer a reason to pretend. In some instances these men and women mentioned a partner who was sexually rejective or who was already having his or her own extramarital relationship. Some typical responses:

"The marriage was already dead and we both knew it, but I wasn't ready to let go. Sleeping with someone else made it possible for me to break the dependency."

"I knew I wasn't going to stay with her, but I didn't know how to tell her. I know now that fooling around with other women was just my way of letting her know."

"My husband hadn't made a sexual overture in over nine months. I think he had somebody else. I put up with it as long as I could, and then I called an ex-boyfriend."

Gary, a 36-year-old physicist, remembers:

"My first wife was the first woman I ever slept with, and I was brutally naïve—I had never even masturbated. I was a science major in college, so I knew on a molecular basis what to do, but in my own life I was very awkward, so when I met my wife, who had the same kind of repressed Catholic upbringing that I did, and we started to experiment with each other, I didn't know how to do anything besides get married. Not only was I inexperienced, I genuinely thought more about school than I did about sex.

"My first wife and I never had a good sex life, and it was always infrequent. It wasn't the sex that was boring; it was her. She was very passive and not too bright. It wasn't a total turnoff, but it didn't do much to turn me on. We shared very little except the child we had within the first year, and it was a marriage in name only. It was a dreadful relationship, and I withdrew more and more. I would stay in the lab a lot of nights rather than have to spend time with her. I never planned to have affairs, and I never 'lusted after women in my heart,' as Jimmy Carter would say. In truth, I never considered doing anything about it. What happened is that a woman I worked with propositioned me. She came up to me in an elevator and said, 'Let's go back to my place.'

"This was the first in a series of affairs, and I became very promiscuous. In the meantime I had become more and more disenchanted with my marriage and my wife, and the frequency and passion sort of died there. My feelings and behavior were symptomatic of the relationship as a whole. In retrospect, it's amazing that I didn't get a disease. But it wasn't just sex I was missing; it was also the emotional connection. Consequently I ended up having a couple of serious affairs, and it got messy. As for my wife, I was so desperately hoping to find some signs of life in her that I would have welcomed her having an affair.

"About six or seven years ago I met my second wife, and I knew that I couldn't continue in the charade of a marriage I was in. So I asked for, and got, a divorce. My second marriage has been very different from the start. This time I'm monogamous. But there's a lot more between us. I'm satisfied emotionally as well as sexually, and if we have any problems, they are the usual ones—like my wife and I both have demanding jobs, and we don't have enough time together."

Liza, a woman who had been married and faithful for ten years, said that at the end of her marriage she had one affair, which definitely helped her break her dependency on her husband. . . .

"My husband always had other women. I don't know how serious they were, but there was always something. Nonetheless I was guilty about leaving him, and I felt very tied to him and dependent on him emotionally. Going to bed with somebody was a very important step in breaking away from an impossible marriage. In a peculiar way it gave me strength and made me believe that it would be possible to have another relationship someday. The man I had an affair with was also married. But I really knew that I would be getting a divorce. I wanted a relationship, but I think he was just interested in extramarital sex. I picked him up in a coffee shop because he looked like a ball player. It turned out he was a college professor. So was his wife, but at first he said he wasn't married. Then, *after* we went to bed, he told me he was married but said that he didn't sleep with his wife. I don't know how much of anything he said was true.

"The affair was a classic affair. We could never meet in public because he was worried about his wife. He said he didn't like sleeping with his wife because she ate peanut butter all the time, and the taste of it was so strong that he couldn't stand to kiss her. He liked kissing me.

"He would have me wait for him on street corners, and he would drive up in his Volvo, and we would chug off. Usually we'd stop someplace and neck in the car, and the windows would get steamed up; I think we both felt like high-school kids. The excitement was great.

"However, I was no longer sleeping with my husband, and I knew we were splitting up; so did my husband. I felt as though I was making a statement to my husband and I really wasn't cheating on him because the marriage was over, but my lover was really cheating on his wife. We'd go to this motel on the highway. You know, I remember everything about him. The way he looked, smelled, tasted, talked. But I don't remember the sex. I think he had a strange-looking penis, sort of turned down, and when he moved, he didn't have any real rhythm and I would pretend that I was getting excited, but I wasn't. I'm Italian, and I think he believed that meant that I was automatically very passionate and a hot number, certainly a hotter number than his wife. I don't know where I got this idea, not from anything he said, just from what he didn't say. He acted as if I wouldn't understand anything he said, which was ridiculous. He traveled in a world where everyone had a graduate degree. I was looking for work as a secretary, and I think he thought that he was slumming with me. I don't know; maybe I'm wrong. But he was real worried about his wife finding out. He would say things like, 'What's going to become of us?' He never once did anything nice for me, and somehow, in the name of women's rights, I always got to pay for half of all our meals. And he had much more money than I did at the time. Anyway, I got bored and fed up with his wimpiness. I think with all his complaints about how his wife ate peanut butter, didn't like sex, and wouldn't suck his cock, he was happier where very little was expected of him in bed. I felt certain that he would end up his life with the same wife, and I felt sorry for her. I think her family helped them a lot financially. Anyway, I just got disgusted with him—with his whining and with his bent dick. It was too boring. It wasn't the sex; he had a shitty character."

A Chronic Inability to Sustain Monogamy

Several people, all men, told us that they always have affairs. They said they do this because they enjoy having them, and they don't like monogamy. In a couple of instances these affairs ultimately precipitated a divorce, but the men told us that although their affairs may have caused their wives to be unhappy, they themselves were perfectly content within their marriages. These men also clearly stated that it was not the sex per se that led them into extramarital relationships. They said a large part of the thrill and an additional enhancement was the sense of adventure and risk. The plotting and planning, along with the idea of getting caught, seemed to fan their desire. We did not speak to any women who described this pattern.

Randall, 50, told us that when married, he had numerous affairs. . . .

"My wife and I were married less than a year when I had my first affair. It was with a young woman who lived in the same town. I fell in love with her. She was quite wild, and so was I, because I also slept with two of the young woman's friends.

"The thing about my sexuality is that I always continued to make love to my wife. I'd make love to her even when I didn't want to make love. I'd make love even when *she* didn't want to make love. I thought that if I kept making love to my wife, she wouldn't be able to figure out that I had been out screwing around. As a matter of fact, she would complain about how frequently we were having sex.

"I was also a petulant ass in those days. And my wife, who sincerely loved me, wasn't having orgasms. I think I made her feel bad about it.

"I used to have a small drinking problem, which may explain some of my behavior, but my wife and I lived in this pretty suburb of Chicago, and we had all these friends with whom we socialized, and I kept having affairs with the other wives. Through it all I kept sleeping with my wife, and she kept getting pregnant. So we had all these children, which made it possible for me to not feel guilty about the affairs. I felt fantastic, as a matter of fact. I rationalized that I was working so hard to support the lot of them that I deserved a good sex life outside of marriage.

"Eventually what happened is that I fell in love with one of my wife's friends, and we had an incredibly torrid affair that went on for years. During the course of it my wife gave birth a couple of times, and so did the woman. Her husband was clearly the father of her children, because we used birth control, but nonetheless, it was strange.

"I remember the first time we made love. I was driving this woman home from the hospital where she had been visiting my wife, who had just had a baby. The heat between us had been brewing, and instead of taking her home, I just kept driving. Eventually we stopped the car. We ended up making love on the side of the road, in the bushes. It was an astonishing experience.

"I discovered how cruelly easy it is to fool people. My wife never found out. Neither did my friend's husband. He was totally unsuspecting even though we used his house quite often during the day.

"I suspect I had affairs because the guilt, shame, nervousness, etc., are an enhancement to sex. In fact, the thought that you may get caught makes it more exciting, and then because you don't see each other every day, there is also the anticipation. In this case the sex got steadily better to the point where it was hysterically good.

"Perhaps the most exciting sexual experience of my life is one that happened in the church on the day of her sister's wedding. We were sitting next to each other, and we were touching each other's legs and body during the service when nobody was watching. Then while everyone was congratulating the bride and groom, we ran off to the choir room and made love on the floor. It was stupendous!

"My wife eventually discovered another affair of mine, and

asked for a divorce. As amazing as it may seem, I felt quite hurt by her attitude. Eventually, I remarried and once again began having affairs. I think monogamy may not be my strong suit."

Several men told us that they have had affairs that have lasted longer than their marriages. Tom, one of these men, told us: "I've had an ongoing relationship with a married woman that has lasted through two of my marriages. We only get together once or twice a year, but we do it regularly. We have sex and we talk. It's incredible. We talk about everything. I don't think there is anything we haven't discussed. She's really into taking pictures—you know, photographs, and she's taken pictures of us in every possible pose. Pictures of us fucking, of her giving me a blow job, of me wearing her underwear, her wearing my underwear, her on the toilet, me taking a leak, anal intercourse—everything. We use vibrators and oils and jellies. She's got, like, this traveling suitcase full of the stuff. Sometimes we don't even have sex, we just take pictures and talk."

Harrison, 45, is an executive in the Pacific Northwest. He lives in an affluent community with his wife and his two school-age children.

"I started to have affairs within a few years of being married, and at first I thought there was something wrong with the marriage. But when I analyzed the marriage, I really couldn't find anything wrong. Then I realized that married or not, every so often you're going to meet people who you want to know better, and if you get sexually close to them, you're going to get to know them better than if you don't. It's interesting to me to live this way. I have never been unhappy in my marriage, but we've been married a long time, and over the years I have periodically become interested in other people. It's never been a one-night thing; it's always a genuine interest in the other person. But there's always sexual hunger, too, of course . . . I wouldn't be satisfied with these relationships if they were just friendship —sex is always a big part of it.

"I should tell you that my wife found out that I'd been seeing other women, and she did not respond well. I tried to explain to her that I'm less romantic than she is. She has this till-death-do-us-part mentality, and she's very idealistic about commitment and marriage. When she found out, she got into bed and she didn't come out for two whole weeks. I had to bring her meals. For a couple of months there, it was very rocky going. But I think we made some sort of adjustment.

"If I have to admit it, sex is probably better with my wife than with any of the women I've had affairs with. I've had maybe four or five affairs. The shortest was six months; the longest lasted close to six years.

"My sex doesn't read like a good novel; it's just pretty good normal clean fun. Nothing kinky. With all the women, the affairs, it has been a process, like I said, of getting to know them. So it's an adjustment like everything else—you know, finding the positions that work, or one set of things that one lady likes and another doesn't, and trying to vary it a little within the framework.

"One of the women I was with had trouble coming unless we were in this god-awful position where I manipulated her while I was in her, and that sort of limits your options on pleasure. Another one only had orgasms through oral sex, so I had to figure out how to do it so she could come. Another one couldn't get the birth-control thing right and kept getting pregnant.

"The sex is never so complicated that it's not worth it. It's always worth it because the harder you have to work at it, the more fun it is. It's the scheming and the planning that help make it interesting. Even the getting of hotels and going to her place. One woman I went out with was going with a bunch of married men at the same time. That got pretty complicated in terms of scheduling. I'm very open with everyone—I've never lied about being married or about the fact that I'm going to stay married, so I generally attract a certain kind of woman.

"When you're having an affair, and you're a married man having an affair, you get accustomed to a lot of lunch-hour sex. Sometimes I would pay for a hotel and tell my wife I had to go out of town. At the beginning of some of these affairs I would be 'going out of town' two and three times a week. Usually they'd slow down, though.

"Since the AIDS thing started, I've become more cautious. I carry a condom now when I go someplace. I have friends who say that you can tell whether or not a person is apt to have a disease, but I know enough to know that you can't tell shit. I don't usually attract wild people, but who knows? I know my wife is worried.

"I try not to let it get emotionally complicated. The women I've been with have been using me as much as I've been using them."

Mild Dissatisfaction and Intense Curiosity

We talked to several women who, from outward appearances, seemed to be very unlikely candidates for marital affairs. Although these women did not want to end their marriages, they all spoke of feelings of restlessness and vague dissatisfaction. A recurring theme was one that centered on "just wanting a few more experiences before I die."

Phyllis, a 43-year-old homemaker from California, said:

"Frankly I got married when I was very young, and I had almost no sexual experience. I watched all my friends getting divorces and dating, and I wanted to try it too. I wanted the experience, but I didn't want the divorce. I think a lot of this had to do with turning 40, because most of all I didn't want to grow old and lose my looks and look back with regrets about not having had more lovers. I wanted to hear bells. It may sound stupid, but that's the way I felt.

"I had a lot of sexual fantasies. When I tried it, I found it upsetting, not because I was guilty, because I really wasn't. What happened is that I met this young man and got totally hooked on the sex. He was very passionate and had a lot of endurance. It made me feel alive. But my young man got careless and started calling me. I told him that I didn't want my husband to find out. He behaved in a normal fashion and went out and met somebody else. After a few months he rejected me. I became depressed, and I got scared about the way I was threatening my home and my life, so I stopped. I don't think my husband noticed because he didn't want to notice—there were a couple of nights when I didn't come home until four A.M. I don't know what he thought, but he accepted my explanations."

Marianne, a 40-year-old college English teacher, said:

"Until I met Smitty, I was your typical uptight suburban housewife. Before I got married, I had a couple of brief sexual relationships in college, which is where I met my husband. We got engaged Christmas of my senior year, and we were married the following Labor Day weekend. At the beginning, I was in love, and I didn't notice all the little problems in the relationship. My husband is not a very giving or emotional man, and our sex reflected that. It was perfunctory, and although he was satisfied, I wanted something more. I started wondering about what I had given up, or what I would never know. At a certain point I found that I was looking at other men and flirting with them. I began to envy friends who seemed to have more fulfilling relationships than I did. With two kids and sixteen years of a boring marriage, I decided that the problem was that I had no outside interests and I needed a career. I went back to school. That's where I met Smitty. He was one of my professors. He was the exact opposite of my husband. My husband is very cold and witholding. Smitty was passionate and caring.

"Some of my friends think I was attracted to Smitty because he was so totally 'off-limits.' Not only was he married, he was also black and *very* politically radical. I honestly don't think it was any of that; I think it was just that he acted like he was totally attracted to me. He paid attention to me. He listened to what I said. We would go out for a drink sometimes after class, and he always remembered what I drank. He took a proprietary interest in me. At lunch he would watch me chew my tuna-fish sandwich and act like I was doing something sexy and desirable. He just made me feel special and loved and taken care of, and I adored the feeling.

"When I was first married, I remember sitting once in a playground with a group of women my age; they were talking about oral sex. I had never done it with my husband; I didn't want to. Our second time together, when we were in bed, Smitty pushed my head down. I wasn't even sure what to do. The interesting thing is that I wanted to go down on him. Unfortunately the relationship quickly deteriorated into only that. We had no place to be together, so . . .let's be blunt. I gave him blow jobs—in cars, in his office when no one was around. Once we even did it at a party in a separate room.

"I was totally turned on by him, but I also was very frustrated. We rarely got together to have real sex. Once I made hotel reservations, and he showed up an hour and a half late and said that he could only stay for a short time because one of his kids was sick. We had sex then, but it wasn't for long enough to satisfy me. In fact, once I was willing to meet him anywhere, anytime, anyplace, he began to avoid sexual contact. I walked around the entire year in a state of constant sexual arousal. He continued to see me, but he made excuses for not having sex. Eventually he ended it. I think once we started to sleep together, he had a lot of conflict about his wife.

"But the feeling I had with him, I kept trying to recapture with other men. I would go out to bars to look for men; I would go away weekends with single friends. I lied to my husband, I rarely came home. It was bizarre. I'm a middle-class suburban housewife and I would be hanging out in singles bars. I had a series of affairs, none of them satisfying, and eventually I went into therapy and stopped.

"If I had the courage, I would get divorced, since I know that I'll never be happy with my husband, but I feel as though I'm too old to start again."

A Personal or Marital Crisis or Problem Precipitates Uncharacteristic Behavior

We talked to several people who had isolated affairs in the middle of an ongoing marriage, usually in response to a personal or marital crisis.

George, a 52-two-year-old printer, remembers that he had

an affair twenty years ago: "I have a very happy marriage. I love my wife, and I've always loved my wife, but twenty years ago, when my wife decided to go back to work, I had an affair. It lasted about eight months. It was a very bad period for the marriage. I know it's ridiculous now, but at the time I felt very threatened by having her out of the home. I imagined her doing things with other men. Now I know I was totally nuts, but at the time it seemed plausible. First she made the decision to work without consulting me. She just came home one day and said that she had a job. I felt very left out. She had always been home, making dinner, taking care of the kids. When she went to work, it was a shock to my system. Suddenly she would come rushing home at the same time I did, tired like me, grumpy like me. She didn't pay as much attention to me; she was too tired for sex. So I did something I never did before. I began to look at other women. When you look, you get into trouble. Anyway, I had an affair, and I'm not particularly proud of it. She never found out, thank God."

Dora, 50, said that she had an affair more than fifteen years ago.

". . . I think my husband had one too. Danny and I got married young, and I got pregnant within the first month. I had three children by the time I was 23. We were lucky because Danny always made a good living, but I think the strain of an early marriage took its toll. We used to have a group of friends our age, all of whom got married about the same time we did. We're the only ones of that whole group who are still together. The sixties and seventies are what happened to us. When we were in our mid-thirties, all our friends started fooling around and getting divorced. It was a strange time, and I think both my husband and I started to get restless. Everybody we knew was running around smoking pot and acting like teenagers. Our oldest kid was already a teenager, and we were home feeling like Ma and Pa Kettle.

"I think both Danny and I had a mid-life crisis, and it sort of made us both resentful of each other. I felt as though I was always the responsible one, the one who took care of the kids and knew where everything was. I felt old and ugly and generally unloved. I think he was having his own problems, because his best friend had left his wife and was going from woman to woman like they were going out of style. I knew my husband was feeling jealous of him, and I resented it. We had several fights about it, and I would get nervous whenever they went out together. Before we had gone out as couples.

"Men don't often flirt with me, but in the past when they did, I would ignore it. But this time was different. My husband and I went to a PTA party, and another husband started talking to me. He called me in the middle of the next week and asked me if I could ever get away. I can't believe how naïve I was!

"Anyway, I started to go out with him. We would get together during the day—his wife thought he was at work. It was very sexual, a fabulous sexual experience. It was sex, pure and simple. I can't believe how uncomplicated it was. I wish I could tell you that the sex wasn't worth it—but that's not true. The sex was fabulous. This guy had obviously been fooling around for years, and he was a real Don Juan type. He knew what to do with a woman's body, let me tell you.

"I honestly think Danny started playing around at the same time. I don't know if it was one woman or several, but he began to make excuses about coming home. . . . I was so concerned about covering my tracks that I didn't pay as much attention as I might have. We were both acting very strange during this time. We would go to parties and flirt with other people—stuff like that. Somehow the marriage lasted through all of this. My friend went on, I'm sure, to another woman. I got a job, which took up a lot of my time. Eventually Danny's friend settled down again, and so did Danny. We never talk about it, really. I've asked him a couple of times, and he denies that he did anything. But when he's asked me, I deny it too.

"Now we really are like Ma and Pa Kettle. Our sex life is better than it's ever been, though. I think it's because we're both very relaxed. We've also learned over the years to allow each other a lot of freedom to do what interests us.

"There was never any question of us ending the marriage.

We had too much together—kids, family, house, summer house, joint bank accounts. Everything we own, we own jointly. . . . Besides, I would be lost without him."

The Revenge Motive

Several men and women said that they began extramarital affairs in response to a real or imagined infidelity on the part of their partner. In these instances hurt and revenge tended to blend together. Among the people we spoke to, some got divorced, and some stayed married after the affair.

Sally, 29, says:

"I wanted to get even with my husband. Lee was not very giving, and he had this girlfriend he wouldn't stop seeing. I was always attracted to Lee's best friend, Earl, and he was always attracted to me. We did a lot of things together, as couples. We took a couple of vacations and went out all the time. I was never that friendly with Earl's girlfriend, even though we spent so much time together. I think that made it all easier.

"Anyway, Lee and I were having a lot of problems, and so were Earl and his girlfriend. We all knew it. We went away for the weekend, and Lee and Earl's girlfriend both had too much to drink and went to bed. Earl and I stayed out on the porch together. We knew that if anyone looked out of the house, they could see the back of our heads, but that's about all. We had all been drinking wine, and Earl put his hand up my skirt and started playing with me. It was unbelievable. The only problem was that I was certain that he got so excited that he went back to his room and had sex with his girlfriend, but he denies it. Anyway, that was the beginning of the affair.

"It was so hot between us that you could steam asparagus. I don't know what we did to generate the heat. Every time we looked at each other, we ended up in bed. I felt like I could die from the level of desire I felt. I remember once we got into a cab and did the classic. We gave the driver fifty dollars and told him to keep driving through the park. We made love on the floor of the backseat. Oral sex—on my fur coat.

"The affair made it impossible for me to continue with Lee, so I split up. For some reason, that scared Earl, and he stopped seeing me. I think he was worried about Lee finding out someday.

"After Lee and I divorced, I kept expecting to hear from Earl—but I never did."

But Marriage and Fidelity Usually Go Together

Among most of the happily married people who talked to us, fidelity was viewed as an integral and vital part of the marital contract. In fact, many went out of their way to let us know that they couldn't imagine a sexual opportunity so appealing that it was worth putting their marriages in jeopardy. Yes, there were exceptions. But by and large these people gave and expected exclusivity along with love.

10

What Really Happens in Bed: What We Learned

EVERYONE'S SEXUAL REALITY IS DIFFERENT

Scientists tell us that for each of us there exists a unique and totally different genetic blueprint. Down to the smallest molecule of DNA, no two people are exactly the same. Until we did the research on this book, we assumed that this fact had nothing to do with sex; we assumed that we were all, more or less, pretty much the same sexually, and that everyone experienced sex in a similar fashion.

So many different ideas were expressed to us about what generates desire or makes the sexual act pleasurable that we came to the conclusion that it is extremely difficult, if not impossible, to make generalizations about men, women, and sex. Some people love oral sex; others hate it. Some people are turned on by fancy lingerie; others think it's stupid. Some people like anal sex; others cringe at the idea of *anything* coming near their behinds. Some people are turned on by pornography; others are repulsed by it. Some people want to make love at six in the morning; others want to sleep. Some people are completely fantasy driven; others don't have an imaginative erotic thought in their heads. And still others fall somewhere in between.

We're all different. Our motivations are different. Our physiology is different. The intensity of our sexual drive is different. We are chronologically different. Our sensitivities are different. We have different levels of arousal. We have different concepts of what is erotic. We have different insecurities. We are anatomically different. We have different levels of physical stamina. We are psychologically different. Our inhibitions are different.

No one has sex in a vacuum. Every time we engage in a sexual act, we bring with us our personalities, our bodies, our hopes, our hormones, our fears, our fantasies, our previous experiences, as well as our religious convictions. These are all different, and we are all different. And we cannot expect everyone, or for that matter, anyone, to like or want what we like or want, when we like it or want it.

Yet even though there are no generalizations we can comfortably make about individuals, there are some conclusions to be reached about sex in general and what really happens in bed.

WHAT REALLY HAPPENS IN BED
—40 SEXUAL REALITIES

1. Sexual statistics tell us very little about sexual reality.

Consider, for example, what may be the best known sexual statistic from the best known sexual scientist. Dr. Alfred C. Kinsey, who collected data from 12,000 men and women for his work on *Human Sexual Behavior*, tells us that the mean frequency of marital sex for the college educated male aged 26–30 is 2.6 times a week. What this statistic fails to tell us is how many people are having sex .5 times a week while wanting it 10 times a week, or how many are having it 20 times a week at their partner's insistence and wanting it once. It doesn't tell us whether anyone is enjoying it; it doesn't tell us whether both partners are in agreement about frequency. It doesn't tell us whether the sex is lasting for five minutes or five hours, and it doesn't tell us anything about the quality of the relationship, or, for that matter, the quality of the sex.

Perhaps no one was more acutely aware of the problems with statistical norms than Kinsey himself, who wrote: ". . . no mean nor median, nor any other sort of average, can be significant unless one keeps in mind the range of the individual variation and the distribution of these variants in the population as a whole. . . . Calculation will show that the difference between one ejaculation in thirty years and mean frequencies of, say, 30 ejaculations per week throughout the whole of thirty years, is a matter of 45,000 times. This is the order of the variation which may occur between two individuals who live in the same town and who are neighbors, meeting in the same place of business, and coming together in common social activities. These sexually extreme individuals may be considered as very similar sorts of persons by their close friends who do not know their sexual history. It has been notable throughout our field collections that a sample of as few as a hundred histories is likely to show a considerable portion of this full range of variation."

2. Sexual expectations are rarely based on anything real.

Movies, television, romance novels, erotic literature—all depict sexual activities in which everyone looks perfect, and everything works perfectly. Our concept of what sex should be is too often derived from these entertaining yet intrinsically unrealistic sources. In real life, genitals are not airbrushed by a photographer, and human lovers are not viewed through a gauze filter.

Even books such as *The Joy of Sex*, as helpful and liberating as they have been, have placed high performance standards on the typical couple. Among the people we spoke to, very few actually require or desire this level of variation. Sex is supposed to be exciting, but it also fulfills needs for comfort and bonding. Let's face it, it's sometimes hard to bond from opposite sides of the bed when the only parts that are making contact are your genitals. It's not always perfectly comfortable, either.

3. All men have sexual anxieties.

Young men are anxious that their inexperience will show; they are also typically anxious about premature ejaculation and whether they know enough about female anatomy. Middle-aged men are worried that their erections are not as firm, or quickly achieved, as they were when they were in their late teens and early twenties. Older men worry that erections are less frequent, less firm, and more temperamental.

From the men we spoke to, it would appear that the vast majority of men have many expectations of how they should behave and/or function, and that these expectations cause some level of anxiety for just about every man.

4. Most men have experienced performance failure.

Some of the most sexually active men we spoke to confided that no matter how many women they slept with, they regularly anticipated and experienced problems with their erections and/or orgasm control in the first few encounters with a new partner. Other men told us that it is most likely to happen when it is most important for it not to happen. In other words, whenever they are especially concerned about pleasing a partner, they are more likely to have problems. When we started these interviews, we thought, erroneously, that men who had been to bed with numerous women would by definition be very confident about their ability to reach and maintain an erection. What we learned is that this is not necessarily the case. What these men are confident about is a sense that their erection will eventually return, and that in the meantime they are still capable of enjoying a sensual experience and pleasing a woman, even without an erection.

There are a wide variety of other reasons for performance failure. Some men have gone through weeks or years of impotence in response to a job crisis, bereavement, illness, depression, or other personal crisis. Although sometimes this is a medical problem, and it always requires a medical opinion, we certainly heard many stories from men in which the condition was temporary and eventually disappeared.

We think it is extremely important for men and women to know this so that they don't give up just because everything didn't work right the first time, or for that matter the first dozen times. If desire is there, and the partners care, they can still find enjoyment in lovemaking despite the absence of an erection or, for that matter, in spite of any other performance-related problem.

Unfortunately some men are paralyzed by one or two failures and shy away from sex in response to the kind of performance difficulties that other men have learned to take in stride.

5. *The absence of an erection does not mean the absence of desire.*

Men brought this to our attention time and time again: A vast spectrum of factors can intercept or block desire and interfere with, or affect, an erection. Some of these factors are physiological and caused by illness or lowered hormone levels. Others are psychological. Anxiety and worry are the factors most commonly implicated.

Men frequently fail to make a distinction between desire and performance and are shocked to discover that they can be too exhausted to have sex, but not so exhausted that they can't want it. Men who are experiencing impotence, whether it is temporary or chronic, can still feel desire and be interested in a sexual experience, despite a penis that is less than fully erect.

6. *The absence of an erection does not automatically mean the inability to ejaculate.*

Women, and some men, told us that they were surprised to discover that even a limp or semierect penis can ejaculate. A perfect, or even imperfect, erection is not necessary in order to make love or to achieve satisfaction.

7. *Women have been misinformed about, and are frequently confused about, the nature of male performance problems; as a result they are often too harsh on either the men or themselves.*

Typically women told us that when a man has performance problems, they get scared and don't know what to do. Depending upon how she has been programmed, she may have one of two reactions: She "blames" the man; or she blames herself. Few women realize that many men who suffer from performance difficulties do so because of a physical rather than a psychological problem.

Women who "blame" the man buy into old mythology or misinformation, believing that problems such as the absence of an erection, or premature ejaculation, are always an indication of a deep-seated psychological problem or conflict regarding women, reflecting anger, resentment, oedipal conflicts, madonna/whore conflicts, etc., etc.

Many women don't see performance problems realistically; consequently they tend to lump them all together, failing to perceive a distinction between younger men who are anxious or older men who may need more stimulation or more time. A woman may be so conditioned that she can't consider the possibility that this is a very nice man who can be a very satisfactory, pleasing lover and intimate partner even if he has less than perfect control over his penis. Furthermore, depending upon the situation, a woman may not recognize that the problem is a temporary one.

Women who blame themselves told us they feel that they are totally responsible for a man's physiological reactions. They respond to male performance problems by thinking any one of the following: He must not find me attractive; something I'm doing is turning him off; I don't feel good to him; if he cared enough for me, he wouldn't have this problem.

Some women are made viscerally insecure by the absence of an erection. If they go to bed with a man and don't see physical proof of desire in the form of an erection, they panic. Nothing has prepared them for the possibility that a normal, healthy man who desires them can't perform like a *Playboy* stereotype.

8. *Ejaculatory control, or lack of it, is an issue for most men.*

The sexual revolution has put much focus on a man's ability to sustain an erection long enough to satisfy his partner. For many men what this has translated into is a sense of pressure. A fair number of the men we spoke to described themselves as always being "too quick." But "too quick" means different things to different men. For one man it is five thrusts, for another it's five minutes.

Men pointed out to us that orgasm control is never a simple issue. For many it's the frustration of not having any control; for others it is the frustration of being overcontrolled to the point of inhibiting their own natural sexual response. Many men told us that they could "hold back" orgasms, but if they do so for too long, they go into another phase during which they are unable to reach orgasm.

Some younger men said the only way they could count on an erection that lasted longer than a minute or two was to plan on having sex twice within a short period of time because they always lasted longer the second time.

It seems that control is always an issue, but that the specifics change depending upon age. How important control is within a relationship depends not only upon a man's capabilities but also upon his partner's expectations and requirements.

9. Men say they know how women reach orgasm; women say that despite all the books and articles available on the subject, men still don't know what to do.

The typical man we spoke to, particularly the sexually active single, appeared confident in his understanding of female physiology. But on closer questioning, the descriptions of the precise sexual activity combined with statements such as, "Hey, as soon as I pick up the pace and hammer at 'em for a few minutes, they all go over the top," makes one question the man's ability to judge. Further, most women told us that very few men had a clear concept of women's orgasms.

10. Women wish men would ask them specifically how they reach orgasm and how many orgasms they wish to have; they also wish men would believe their answers.

Women told us that few men ever ask them exactly how they reach orgasm, and that often when they try to explain their preferences, even if the men themselves initiate the conversations, the men don't fully integrate the information into their behavior.

The typical man doesn't clearly understand that every woman has a different way of reaching orgasm. Kinsey referred to this possibility; Masters and Johnson pointed it out; Shere Hite highlighted it. Yet, within most relationships, it's a fact that is ignored. The vast majority of men we spoke to, both young and old, are still under the mistaken impression that their technique, whatever it may be, works for every woman. And if it doesn't, it is the woman who has the problem. In short, few men ask, and fewer women speak up.

Men can be equally tuned out when it comes to the subject of how many orgasms a woman can have or wants to have. Single, sexually active women frequently complained that they felt that men who had been influenced by literature on the multi-orgasmic woman were now placing too much pressure on them to have orgasm after orgasm, whether or not they were capable or desirous.

11. Almost every woman has faked orgasm; but just because a woman fakes orgasms doesn't mean she's inorgasmic.

Most of the women we spoke to said that they had faked orgasms. Women told us that they fake orgasms for a variety of reasons. Sometimes it's to please the man by trying to make him feel like a better lover. Sometimes it is an attempt to get the man more excited. Sometimes it is to please themselves, i.e, to get it over with.

The primary problem with faking is, as several women told us: They may do it at the beginning of a relationship because they don't really feel comfortable enough with the man to tell him exactly how they do reach orgasm. Later, they have an established pattern that is hard to break. They say then it's embarrassing to admit that you weren't honest by telling him what type of stimulation *does* work.

12. For women, an absence of orgasm does not mean an absence of desire and/or pleasure; but that doesn't mean that women don't want orgasms, too.

The women we spoke to continued to draw a distinction between desire and orgasm. Most say that as long as they feel desire and are turned on by what's happening in their beds, they feel pleasure, even when they fail to reach orgasm. The whole sexual/sensual experience is pleasurable to them. However, typically when a woman says she doesn't care whether or not she is reaching orgasm during sex, it doesn't mean that she doesn't want an orgasm; it usually means that for some reason, she and her partner have not fully communicated about how she does reach orgasm, and she isn't receiving the specific stimulation she requires.

13. Everyone has a sexual secret.

No one is totally forthcoming about sex. Everyone is afraid of revealing something. Sometimes it is a harmless fantasy;

other times it is a big chunk of their sexual history; often it is a major sexual need that is not being met.

Within a relationship, most experts agree that some things are best kept secret, especially if they are clearly hurtful to the sensitivities of one of the partners, and thus detrimental to the relationship. But in some relationships, there are other kinds of secrets. These are the secrets that are the end product of inhibition and a fear of constructively expressing reasonable sexual needs and feelings within a trusting, intimate relationship. This kind of secret-keeping often blocks vital pathways of communication and can lead to sexual dissatisfaction or unhappiness for one or both partners.

14. Couples are now using oral sex to compensate for a wide variety of sexual incompatibilities and difficulties.

Many women cannot reach orgasm through sexual intercourse; many men cannot sustain prolonged intercourse. In steps oral sex to compensate.

Oral sex has long been a part of foreplay in many sexual relationships, but it seems to be playing more of a role these days. Some men and women told us that at times they just found it plain easier to depend upon oral sex to either bring partners to orgasm or closer to orgasm. Younger couples, particularly, don't seem to make as much of a distinction between intercourse and oral sex as older couples who grew up before oral sex was popularized. Because of this, younger couples appear to be relying upon oral sex to resolve difficulties or incompatabilities that might have become problems for an earlier generation.

Oral sex, however, doesn't work for everyone. Some people told us that they don't like it or are inhibited about introducing it into their lovemaking.

15. Almost everyone, married or single, masturbates.

Masturbation is still associated with desperation and loneliness. But in fact, among the people we spoke to, many said that when they were in brand new, highly charged sexual relationships they were masturbating more than when they had no one, because they were excited all the time by the stimulation of thinking about their new sex partner. Many marrieds also said they masturbated regularly, using it as a means of balancing different levels of sexual need within a good relationship. Older men and women masturbate, younger men and women masturbate; and those in between told us that they masturbate.

16. Acting out your sexual fantasy is likely to be disappointing.

By and large the people we interviewed confessed that whenever they tried to turn their sexual fantasies into realities they were less than thrilled with the results. A fantasy doesn't have to consider real mechanics, real body parts, real fatigue, and real feelings.

Fatigue and human stamina aside, people also told us that when another live human joined them in their fantasies, the other person usually had his or her own ideas about who should go where and what should take place. Another person's idea of how a fantasy should be acted out may not always coincide with yours.

17. Even the most sexually experienced men and women can be sexually misinformed.

Experience is no guarantee of sexual proficiency, especially if one has had limited communication with one's sexual partners. We talked to a fair number of men and women who were extremely experienced in terms of numbers of both long- and short-term sexual relationships. Yet, many of them articulated attitudes and beliefs that were surprisingly naïve and ill-informed as well as unrealistic.

18. One person's ideal lover is another's nightmare.

Sexual satisfaction has a tremendous amount to do with compatibility of expectations and requirements. We spoke to dozens of women who said that they had left or were considering leaving relationships with men who were great "performers" because the men didn't connect on an emotional or intimate level. But we also spoke to a fair number of women who wanted that kind of sexuality, saying, "Forget the romance, forget the intimacy, I like a man with a hard erection and steady thrusting."

On a purely physical basis, some people long for a partner who is into performing oral sex; others loathe having oral sex performed on them and always prefer straight intercourse. Some men pride themselves on being able to sustain an erection for an inordinately long period of time, and some women yearn for such a man; other women say that after the first ten minutes, the only thing they get is bored or sore.

Some people wish they could find a partner who enjoyed fantasy and sexual playacting as much as they do; others are actually turned off by fantasy. We talked to men and women who felt that they had an incredible amount of sexual stamina and wanted lovemaking to go on for hours; other men and women said, "No way."

19. Men with serious sexual problems are sometimes the most satisfying lovers.

A remarkable number of experienced women confirmed that men who can't sustain an erection or who have poor orgasm control have sometimes learned how to turn lovemaking into a more intense and erotic sensual experience by focusing less on intercourse per se and more on everything that surrounds intercourse.

20. Real sex involves real body parts.

Sexual fantasies rarely take into account the basic realities of human physiology and its limitations. There are a whole range of positions which are unattainable, and while others can be accomplished, one partner or the other is apt to be acutely uncomfortable.

In fact there are a wide variety of things that can create discomfort and/or actual pain. A fair number of men mentioned that performing oral sex for an extended period of time resulted in stiff necks, numb tongues and lips, and stiff jaws. Women complain of all of the above plus the gagging reflex.

For some women, past a certain point, hard thrusting is agony and has been known to trigger bladder infections.

Women also cited complicated positions that they are expected to hold for more than a few minutes as producing more pain than ecstasy.

Another real consideration: Real body parts don't always fit into real body parts the way we would like them to. Men and women can be too big or too small for ideal sex with a particular partner, without some physical compromises. Big or small doesn't apply only to genital measurements. It includes weight and height as well.

Men and women told us that they have walked away from prolonged lovemaking with chafed genitals and bruises on the pubic and pelvic bones, and that this sometimes only happened with specific partners. Every pairing brings with it a unique set of physical complications.

Other physical factors can interfere with sex. Women's menstrual cycles can affect sex; pregnancy affects sex; bad breath affects sex; bad hygiene affects sex; bad backs affect sex; muscle cramps affect sex; even colds affect sex.

21. The best sex is not necessarily spontaneous sex.

Sex manuals have placed a great deal of emphasis on spontaneous sex. Yet, most of the people we spoke to, particularly those in long-term happy unions, said that spontaneity was a myth, and not necessarily desirable.

People tend to remember the early phase of their sexual relationship as being more spontaneous, failing to remember that in the beginning, couples are often getting together to have sex. Sex is usually a part of the plan, whether it is an actual honeymoon, or early dating in a sexual relationship. Many women reminded us that when they were dating and always expecting sex, they wore a diaphragm at all times. Men said that they were always showered and shaved. Sex was totally on their minds, and they made preparations for it—it was not truly spontaneous.

Later on, in ongoing marriages when other things are happening or children are in the house, not only is spontaneity not possible, it's not preferred. Women specifically mentioned that they prefer having time to mentally get in the mood for sex as opposed to just being grabbed without warning. When women were the initiators, men were no more thrilled by having women start tearing their pants off when they were trying to watch the evening news.

What often happens when one partner spontaneously initiates sex is that the other goes along because he or she doesn't want to hurt the other's feelings or appear to be not as sexual.

In fact, many of the happier marrieds told us that they made dates for sex, on more or less the same schedule each week. They did not find it boring or routine. In fact they found that it gave them something to look forward to, and they were ready for it both physically and emotionally.

Obviously everyone enjoys some spontaneous sex, but as a regular thing, people told us that it's very hard to pull off successfully.

22. Sexual behavior, attitudes, and expectations differ significantly from generation to generation.

We all tend to view the world from our limited perspective, and it frequently doesn't occur to us that someone younger, or older, might have an entirely different set of expectations. Those who came of age before the sexual revolution suffered from a dearth of hard information and experience. Those who came of age after the sexual revolution often suffer from information overload.

Older men and women frequently said they would always wonder what they missed by not having more experience. Younger men and women sometimes voiced the opposite concern; many confided that they had had so many experiences by the time they were in their mid twenties that they felt burned out.

Because of the sexual revolution and media coverage, many couples of the older generation said that their sexual relationship experienced two phases: the first, uninformed phase, and the second, enlightened phase, which was triggered by the revolution in available sexual information. Many men in long marriages specifically mentioned making a real attempt to read articles and books in order to bring this information back into their bedrooms.

23. Aging affects sexual desire, sexual thoughts, and sexual performance, but it doesn't make them disappear.

You don't have to be 85 years old to experience changes in your sexual ability. Sex at 20 is different from sex at 30, which in turn is different from sex at 40, etc. Some people seem to panic when they first sense a change in their sexual responsiveness; some become so upset that they withdraw from sexuality. Sexually happy older men and women all indicated that sex is different as one gets older, but still extremely pleasurable. A few even felt it was more pleasurable because there was more time and fewer distractions. But as most people go through all of life's stages, they find they have to alter their expectations.

As men age, they frequently have more difficulty with erections, which can become unreliable or take longer to achieve. This doesn't mean that they can't enjoy sex or give their partners pleasure. Unfortunately some men have unrealistic expectations, and are afraid of appearing less sure of themselves in front of a partner. They sometimes decide erroneously that the smallest problem is an indicator that they are "washed up," and they give up on sexual feelings.

Women, too, have different physical reactions as they grow older. Experts say that while some of the physical changes that occur after menopause frequently require a gynecological visit, these changes usually can be treated and need not interfere with sexual pleasure. Sexually content women in their sixties and seventies told us that sex was very pleasurable and exciting.

24. Good sex cannot hold together a bad relationship.

There is a myth that some couples fight all day and have sex all night. When we started doing research, we specifically set out to find at least a few examples. We failed. Every time we thought we had such a couple, half of the story wasn't true. Either they weren't fighting, or they weren't having sex. We did speak to a handful of people who experienced this phenomenon for a short time in their relationships, but all of these relationships and/or marriages ultimately dissolved, or the fighting became so frenzied that the couple withdrew from each other in all ways, including sexually.

25. A good marriage can survive, and sometimes flourish, despite mediocre or even problematic sex.

Frankly we were surprised by how many happily married couples were dealing with ongoing sexual conflicts, disappointments, and outright problems. What this highlighted for us is that sexual perfection is not a necessary element in a good marriage. Many of these people pointed out that the presence of a problem does not mean the absence of desire or satisfaction. Two people who are satisfying each other emotionally can usually find a way to compromise or alter sexual behavior or the sexual act so that both partners can be pleased.

26. A sexual problem isn't a problem unless it's making someone unhappy.

We discovered that one has to be careful not to be judgmental in evaluating anyone else's sexual relationship. A physical relationship that might send some couples racing to the nearest sex therapist leaves other couples perfectly content.

We talked to many people who complained bitterly about the sexual conflicts or problems in a particular relationship; yet we talked to others who were experiencing much the same kind of problem, but they didn't perceive it as a serious problem.

In relationships where there is a sexual conflict, it is often one partner who maintains that the other's behavior is somehow flawed. But another person, in another relationship, might perceive the same behavior without feeling distressed. Some women, for example, state very firmly that they cannot handle the slightest difficulty when it comes to male sexual performance; others blithely say that they feel they can find a way to get sexual pleasure with any man to whom they feel emotionally connected as long as the man is flexible and interested in giving pleasure in ways other than intercourse. Some men say they have no tolerance for women who aren't always responsive to their sexual needs; others, married to women with much lower sex drives, say that they prefer to wait until both partners are feeling sexual.

27. Women who have erratic and infrequent sex lives are sometimes more likely to have an accidental pregnancy than those who are sexually active.

Among the women we spoke to, inexperience and/or infrequent sex was typically implicated as a factor in an unplanned pregnancy. Young women having their first sexual relationship don't truly believe they can get pregnant, so they are careless. Even if they have obtained a form of birth control, they sometimes don't know how to use it. Women who have infrequent sex often don't have a reliable method of contraception, or they are inexperienced in using it.

28. Men and women typically fail to discuss with each other all the ramifications of various birth-control methods, including proper use, limitations on spontaneity, and almost unavoidable physical discomforts; well over 50% of the men and women we spoke to had been involved with one or more unplanned pregnancies.

Among singles, men assume that women are "taking care of these things" unless they are informed otherwise, and women typically wait for a man to "say something." Marrieds are only slightly more communicative. Married men and women usually, but not always, have a regular form of birth control. However, unless they are using condoms, or withdrawal, the woman is completely responsible for all the details surrounding the method. Husbands rarely, if ever, consult with gynecologists about the pros and cons of various methods. Few couples ever fully discuss the ramifications or difficulties surrounding any of the methods. Women don't fully understand the problems associated with proper use of condoms and "trust" the man to put it on and remove it properly. Men don't understand why it can "take so long" to insert a diaphragm, or the discomforts involved in wearing one for "six hours" after sex. Women don't realize that men can often "feel" the diaphragm, etc., etc.

29. Sexually active singles—and unfaithful marrieds—are still incredibly careless about sexually transmitted diseases, including herpes and AIDS.

Condoms are being sold in vending machines in rest rooms, both male and female, and in college campuses across the country. Radio and television spots, print ads, billboards, and talk shows are all reminding us of safe sex. Nonetheless, the single men and women we spoke to still feel that they personally are not at risk because they "trust their partners." Consequently, although many said that they have cut back somewhat on extremely casual sex, few had drastically altered their life-styles. Typically, men and women said they were using condoms the first few times they were with somebody new, but ultimately discarded the practice once they felt they "knew" their partners.

30. Almost no married couple is in perfect accord about sexual frequency.

Jack would like to have sex four times a week; Jill is more than satisfied with twice. Because Jack and Jill, who are happily married, want to please each other, they compromise on three times. This kind of negotiation, spoken or unspoken, takes place in bedrooms across America. When enough things in the marriage are working, these compromises seem to work as well, and both partners may be truly satisfied even when their ideal sexual needs are not being met. But when there is trouble in the marriage, these differences in frequency needs seem to serve as additional friction points.

31. Physical affection should not be viewed only as a prelude to sex.

Many of the happily married men and women we spoke to stressed the importance of affection within their relationships. They said that while affection, in and of itself, couldn't replace sex, it was at least as satisfying. They described an ongoing pattern of hugging, holding, and kissing that was being done for the pleasure of these acts in and of themselves, not as a means of initiating sex.

Yet too many other people, both men and women, have an unreasonable view of affection. Both men and women complained about partners who couldn't be touched without a sexual follow-up. And many women complained that men were not affectionate except when they were sexually motivated.

Noted psychologist Dr. Bernie Zilbergeld, who discusses affection, particularly as it relates to men, in his thoughtful, realistic, and highly recommended book, *Male Sexuality*, perhaps says it best: "The myth that touching must lead to sex is harmful to everyone, but particularly to men since we have been most powerfully affected by it. It robs us of the joys of 'just' touching, it confuses us as to what we really want at any given time, and it puts pressure on us to be sexual whenever we touch or are touched."

32. Romantic moments, special times, and shared intimacy do not have to lead to sex.

We've all seen the same movies, and most of us have the same notions about romantic dinners leading to sex; special occasions such as birthdays or New Year's Eve leading to sex; or moments of closeness or feelings of intense love leading to sex. It doesn't have to happen that way. People in happy marriages told us that these moments or feelings can exist and be enjoyed for themselves without the expectation of a sexual follow-up. People can be romantic without being sexual; they can have a lovely birthday dinner and evening out and be too exhausted for sex; or they can feel intense love without a sexual follow-up.

33. Some of the most unhappy men and women are in relationships with extraordinary sex.

Sexual obsession is a common theme in great literature. From the people we spoke to, it would appear that it is a common theme in real life as well. When we asked people to tell us about their best sexual experiences, a large number of men and women told us about relationships that they characterized as obsessional. Unfortunately, obsessional sex doesn't ensure a great relationship. The only thing it ensures is obsession and all the sleepless nights that go along with it.

Interestingly, when we ask people to put the sex in these

relationships under a microscope and analyze what made it so unforgettable, they sometimes said that the actual sex itself was no better or no worse than the sex in other relationships. What made it so memorable was the quality of obsession and desire for fulfillment that accompanied it.

34. Unrealistic sexual expectations will ultimately take the joy out of sex.

Everyone has the right to expect a lot from his or her sexual relationship, but when "a lot" is an unrealistic fantasy, the most one can hope for is disappointment.

An insistence upon fulfilling one's fantasy expectation of what sex should be places constraints not only upon oneself, but also upon one's partner. Unrealistic expectations leave little room for exploration, experimentation, sharing, or a natural development process.

35. Love, not lust, is the glue that binds a happy marriage.

Scrutinize enough good marriages, and one has to conclude that the special something that is keeping both partners happy in good times and bad times is love, commitment, and an ever-present desire to make things work. Sure, sex has a role, but it is love that is the more powerful motivator.

36. Sexual thoughts increase in direct proportion to the unavailabity of a desirable partner.

This is another variation on the old theme of "We all want what we don't have," and it's turbo-charged by hormonal intervention. Granted our sexual needs are great, but they are probably not as great as they seem to a sexually deprived single whose needs are not being met at all. Time and again, it was confirmed to us that men and women who are fortunate enough to be able to take their sexual lives for granted didn't think about sex with anywhere near the same level of intensity as those who have no sense of sexual security.

37. Most sexually satisfied couples have discarded the myth of simultaneous orgasm.

Sex therapists and marriage counselors regularly point out

that simultaneous orgasm is an unrealistic goal and more likely to occur through accident than through careful planning. Nonetheless, to our surprise, a few men and women are still searching for the elusive simultaneous orgasm.

But, these few people aside, more sexually savvy types say that while simultaneous orgasm looks quite beautiful when choreographed by Hollywood movie moguls, it is more fun to watch than it is to attempt.

38. *Sexual choices help shape our lives.*

Sex is the great motivator. For good or for bad, most people have found themselves making minor and sometimes major life decisions, i.e., choice of schools, choice of careers, choice of neighborhood, because of a sexual involvement. People have been known to abandon lifestyles, opportunities, and careers in order to pursue a sexual attraction. Sometimes this is all for the good; sometimes it isn't.

What we realized as we did these interviews is how much of what happens in bed affects what happens in every other aspect of our lives. Where we get into trouble is when we discard realistic thinking and alter our lives to follow a sexual fantasy.

39. *In the beginning of a relationship people don't trust each other enough to talk about sex; by the time they do trust each other, they don't talk for other reasons.*

Everyone agrees that an accepting, trusting environment is a vital requirement for honest sexual communication. Unfortunately, the beginning of a relationship is a fragile time, and understandably, people tend to withhold total trust, and therefore rarely feel free enough to be 100% forthcoming about a variety of sexual concerns including likes, dislikes, needs, fantasies, history, inhibitions, and difficulties. Later on, once intimacy and trust are established, they are afraid to talk for other reasons. They worry that their partners will not understand why they didn't talk in the first place. They fear being accused of dishonesty, deception, or manipulation. They worry about threatening their partner's sense of security, and thus their own. Also, further into the relationship, patterns are established that are hard to break, and there are fewer opportunities for the kind of intense, "soul-searching" exchanges that take place when lovers first meet. Men and women in established relationships tend to feel that "there is never a good time" to introduce conversations about sexual intimacy or preferences, and usually prefer to wait and hope that their partners will break the ice and start talking about sex. Sometimes fifty years later they are still waiting.

40. Poor communication is still the major sexual problem.
Sexual communication means a lot more than just turning to one's partner and saying, "Was it good for you?" If we are to have satisfying sexual relationships, we need to learn how to discuss sex with our partners in great detail, being perfectly clear on the role of emotions, feelings, expectations, and our perception of what sex should be. Do you see sex as primarily romantic? Or do you take a more earthy approach? These feelings and attitudes need to be shared. We should be fully aware, before we make commitments, whether there are insurmountable differences on preferences, frequency, or the role of fantasy.

People who have left marriages because of gross incompatibilities in some of these areas told us that they didn't discuss these issues in anywhere near enough detail before making a commitment, and had no solid sense of how entrenched their partners' attitudes were; they were certain that marriage was going to bring about a change, which, of course, didn't happen.

Talking about sex also means talking about sexual risks such as sexually transmitted diseases or unwanted pregnancy. This is a conversation that should take place before, not after, the first sexual encounter with a new partner.

It's equally important to realize that sexual communication goes beyond you and your partner. It encompasses one's ability to communicate with the rest of the world as well, including friends, parents, and children.

We can't be afraid to talk about our sexually motivated life choices with our friends and family before we act. Scrutinizing our behavior and holding our motivations up to be realistically examined can save a great deal of grief, disappointment, and pain.

And finally, we need to learn how to talk about sex in a nonjudgmental manner. Sharing our honest feelings and concerns, without assigning labels, will enable us to establish a more realistic set of sexual expectations.

Appendix

SEEKING PROFESSIONAL SEXUAL GUIDANCE

Sometimes men and women are realistically unhappy because of sexual difficulties within their relationships. Fortunately, professional help is available for a wide range of sexual concerns ranging from loss of desire to problems with control, orgasm, or impotence, and many people have greatly benefited from counseling and/or treatment.

Unfortunately we cannot personally recommend therapists or counselors across the country because we are unable to visit all of these places and fairly evaluate their services. However, we have compiled a list of recognized clinics and therapists that we hope will be helpful. If none of the following are in your area, and you are concerned with finding a reputable and responsible sex therapist, we suggest you contact the nearest major teaching hospital, one that is affiliated with a university. Ask if they have a human sexuality clinic. If they don't have such a service, ask to be put in touch with the office of the head of the department of psychiatry. Frequently they will be able to refer a suitable doctor or therapist.

Alabama

University of Alabama in
Birmingham
Marital Health Studies
Department of Psychiatry
1700 Seventh Avenue South
Birmingham, AL 35294
(205) 934-2350

Arizona

University of Arizona College of
Medicine
Sexual Problem Evaluation and
Treatment Clinic
1501 North Campbell Avenue
Tucson, AZ 85724
(602) 626-6323

Arkansas

University of Arkansas for
Medical Sciences
Human Sexuality Clinic
4301 West Markham
Little Rock, AR 72205
(501) 686-5900

California

University of California Los
Angeles Center for Health
Sciences
Human Sexuality Program
769 Westwood Plaza
Los Angeles, CA 90024
(213) 825-0243

Bernie Zilbergeld, Ph.D.
573 Wala Vista Avenue
Oakland, CA 94610
(415) 839-5470

Illinois

University of Chicago Hospitals
and Clinics
Sexual Dysfunctions Clinic
5841 South Maryland
Chicago, IL 60637
(312) 702-9703

Loyola University of Chicago
Sexual Dysfunction Clinic
2160 South First Avenue
Maywood, IL 60153
(312) 531-3750

Louisiana

Louisiana State University
Medical Center
Sex and Marital Health Clinic
Department of Urology
1542 Tulane Avenue
New Orleans, LA 70112
(504) 568-4890

Maryland

Johns Hopkins University School
of Medicine
Sexual Behavior
Consultation Unit
600 North Wolfe Street
Baltimore, MD 21205
(301) 955-6318

Massachusetts

Harvard Medical School,
Beth Israel Hospital
Human Sexuality Clinic
330 Brookline Avenue
Boston, MA 02215
(617) 735-2168

New England Male Reproductive
Center of University Hospital
720 Harrison Avenue
Boston, MA 02118
(617) 638-8485

Minnesota

University of Minnesota Medical School
Program in Human Sexuality
2630 University Avenue S.E.
Minneapolis, MN 55414
(612) 627-4360

Missouri

Masters and Johnson Institute
24 South Kings Highway
Saint Louis, MO 63108
(314) 361-2337

New York

Long Island Jewish Hillside Medical Center
Human Sexuality Center
P.O. Box 38
Glen Oaks, NY 11004
(718) 470-2761

Helen Singer Kaplan Institute for the Evaluation and Treatment of Psychosexual Disorders
30 East 76th Street
New York, NY 10021
(212) 249-2914

Cornell University Medical Center
Human Sexuality Program
Payne Whitney Clinic
New York Hospital Cornell Medical Center
525 East 68th Street
New York, NY 10021
(212) 472-6277   472-4819
Referral number for doctors affiliated with N.Y. Hospital:
1-800-822-2694

Pennsylvania

Jefferson Medical College
Department of Psychiatry and Human Behavior
Jefferson Psychiatric Associates
Sexual Function Center
1015 Chestnut Street
Philadelphia, PA 19107
(215) 928-8420

University of Pennsylvania School of Medicine
Division of Family Study
Department of Psychiatry
Marriage Council of Philadelphia
4025 Chestnut Street
Philadelphia, PA 19104
(215) 382-6680

Some experts now believe that a large percentage of men who suffer from chronic impotence do so because of a physiological problem. A wide variety of options are available to these men, including several newly developed methods of medical treatment. For more information, we suggest you write to Bruce and Eileen MacKenzie, authors of *It's Not All in Your Head* (E.P. Dutton, 1988), at Impotents Anonymous, P.O. Box 1257, Maryville, Tenn. 37802.